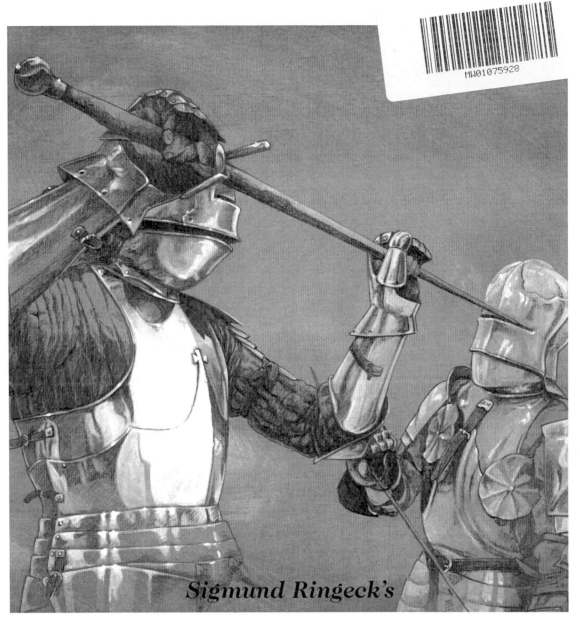

Sigmund Ringeck's

KNIGHTLY ARTS OF COMBAT

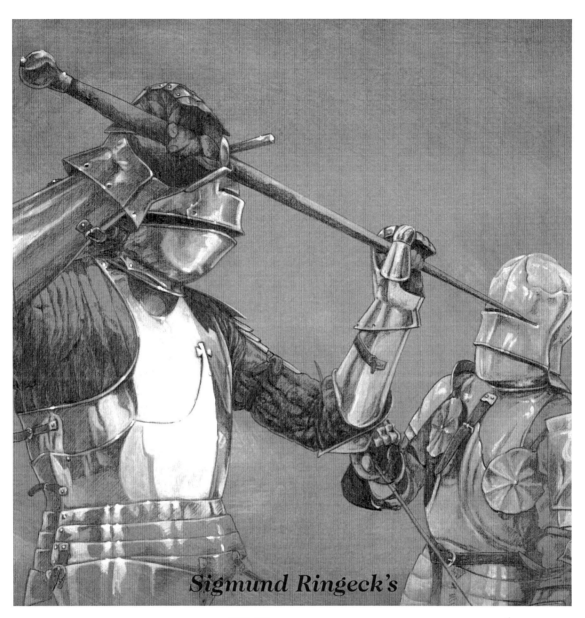

Sigmund Ringeck's

KNIGHTLY ARTS OF COMBAT

David Lindholm
and Peter Svärd

Sword-and-Buckler Fighting, Wrestling, and Fighting in Armor

Paladin Press • Boulder, Colorado

Also by David Lindholm and Peter Svärd
Sigmund Ringeck's Knightly Art of the Longsword

Sigmund Ringeck's Knightly Arts of Combat: Sword-and-Buckler Fighting, Wrestling, and Fighting in Armor
by David Lindholm and Peter Svärd

ISBN 13: 978-1-58160-499-3
Printed in the United States of America

Published by Paladin Press, a division of
Paladin Enterprises, Inc.
Gunbarrel Tech Center
7077 Winchester Circle
Boulder, Colorado 80301, USA
+1.303.443.7250

Direct inquiries and/or orders to the above address.

Visit our Web site at: www.paladin-press.com

Table of Contents

Warning

MANY OF THE techniques depicted in this book are extremely dangerous. It is not the intent of the authors or publisher to encourage readers to attempt any of them without proper professional supervision and training. Attempting to do so can result in severe injury or death. Do not attempt any of these techniques or drills without the supervision of a certified instructor.

THE AUTHORS, PUBLISHER, and distributors of this book disclaim any liability from any damage or injuries of any type that a reader or user of information contained within this book may incur from the use or misuse of said information. *This book is for academic study only.*

Acknowledgments

THIS IS A collective effort by many people, all of whom have contributed in different ways. We would like to thank especially Andreas Ingefjord, Jonas Nilsson, and Henrik Dentz for their patience as models and sparring partners. We would also like to thank Albion Swords and Peter Johnsson for supplying us with their excellent swords for doing the techniques and the illustrations, and Master Armorer Albert Collins of Via Armorari for building superlative suits of 15th-century armor. Next in line for our gratitude are Paladin Press of Boulder, Colorado, and Jon Ford in particular, for giving us this opportunity and having never-ending patience with slow deliveries of the material.

LAST BUT NOT least, we would like to express our love and gratitude to our families, who have shown understanding and support of our odd hobbies and pastimes.

David Lindholm
Peter Svärd

Foreword
by John Clements

As with the first volume of the knightly teachings of the 15th-century fencing master Sigmund Ringeck, this work presents a modern translation and reconstructive interpretation of his martial art in a clear and accessible format that is easy to follow. The approach presented here is straightforward, yet explores the subject seriously and with respect.

This volume of Ringeck's fighting art reveals additional teachings on fundamental areas of the Art of Defense from this time. Included are fencing with the sword and buckler, spear fighting, grappling and wresting, and the longsword in armor.

Sword-and-buckler fencing has gone largely unappreciated but is increasingly gaining the admiration it deserves. As a tradition in Europe the versatile, highly effective sword-and-buckler method was one of the oldest and most continuous combative systems of fencing. Given the range of evidence we have for the sword and buckler, in literature and art and as an established way of fighting in the Middle Ages, there is every reason to believe it was actually more common than fighting with a sword and shield.

The spear was also one of the most common–if not *the* most common–weapon for the battlefield as well as a formidable weapon to face with a sword.

Grappling and wrestling, though often ignored by students of historical combat today, was long integral to fencing practice and was crucial for a fighting man to know. All historical armed combat involved some degree of unarmed techniques and the combat skills of grappling and the art of wrestling have a long legacy in Europe. Whether unarmored or armored, these techniques formed the basis of nearly all personal self-defense.

Fighting in plate armor with a longsword was a regular occurrence for men at arms, and though it has been misunderstood in modern times, this vital skill was given considerable practice. The use of the longsword in armor was also distinct from that used unarmored, even though it derived from and built upon the same core elements.

While popular culture often depicts the medieval armored warrior as a lumbering, over-burdened figure, the notion of the medieval knight as slowly hulking about in heavy armor on foot with a cumbersome bludgeoning sword is the stuff of modern myth. Plate-armor for foot combat was well-balanced, maneuverable, and sometimes even made of tempered steel. It was well suited for fighting in, and was far from the awkward, lumbering cliché presented by Hollywood and Victorian writers.

Whether in close-combat or at a distance, an armored fighting man was far harder to kill than an unarmored one. Plate armor protected a warrior from cuts and thrusts. It gave defense against blunt crushing blows and offered some protection from arrows, crossbow bolts, thrown spears, and hurled rocks. Yet, it did not prevent a fighter from moving with coordination and precision, whether armed or not.

OVER HUNDREDS OF years the skills presented here ranged from knightly arts of war, civilian arts of self-defense, exercises for physical fitness and ritual duel, and eventually to martial sport. Whether for individual personal self-defense or collective action on the battlefield, there was a clear underlying dynamism and flexibility to their approach. It can be surmised that in teaching these skills, historically, material would first be demonstrated and explained by the teacher followed by the student repeating it under the instructor's guidance and assessment. This process continued until the student displayed competency in the lesson components. The lesson might be the proficient application of fighting principles or the execution of techniques or series of techniques. Connected lessons formed a curriculum, which conveyed core concepts of self-defense. A dialectic exchange might also be included in study to develop the student's understanding and reasoning. In the exploration of historical fencing today, competent instruction predisposes that we have coherent lessons of sound interpretations of accurate transcriptions of the historical source teachings. This book will aid such efforts.

THE SPECIALIZED VOCABULARY in which manuals like Master Ringeck's were written changed over time, however, and this makes both translation and interpretation fraught with risks. An inherent problem with modern reconstructive interpretation of what are, ostensibly, mere portions from arguably larger and more involved teachings, is that we invariably come to a point where we must extrapolate. At some instance we must project one possible but logical action out of another or from a combination of others. Even though an action is not a technique specifically outlined in the source, it can often be inferred from the biomechanics of the fighting method. The obvious danger in this implying of new elements is that actions and manners of moving not actually contained within the original teachings can be artificially inserted where they should not. Rather than

suggesting that something was likely done—unless we have contrary evidence otherwise—we instead must offer evidence it reasonably was done. Any hypothesis extrapolating further techniques finds support only from other contemporary texts and combat images combined with sound physical demonstration with historically accurate arms and armor. This should be kept in mind as we study this craft.

WHILE HISTORICAL EUROPEAN martial arts may be studied today for their historical or cultural significance, and even for their personal self-defense value, it is fair to say that most people pursue it for the sheer fun of the craft. Interpretation and application of these long lost teachings obviously rely upon and demand a certain minimal prerequisite physicality. Such interpretation, let alone application, should not begin to proceed without an understanding of the inherent body mechanics of personal armed combat. Reasonably, the more seriously one pursues the physical dimension of study, the more serious will be one's understanding of the subject. Otherwise, it will not be possible to fully realize how these skills and techniques were historically employed in violent personal conflict.

WE CAN ONLY speculate on the differences between the discourses on fencing and the reality of personal combat. But through practice and investigation it is possible to develop skill in these extinct martial arts and a greater appreciation of their source teachings.

THE PURSUIT OF this subject in the manner presented here is refreshing and exciting. The reader will discover a variety of fighting material as well as sound interpretations derived from trustworthy translation. This long-needed work will be an excellent resource. It offers a valuable contribution on the subject to the modern library and the study table of every student of historical fencing studies.

John Clements
Director
ARMA–the Association for
Renaissance Martial Arts
February 2006

Preface

SIGMUND RINGECK, SAID by some to have been the fencing master to Duke Albrecht of Bavaria, was a master in the tradition of the great Johannes Liechtenauer. Master Johannes lived during the middle and second half of the 14th century and became enormously important as the founding father of the major lineage of the German longsword tradition. Whether or not Liechtenauer actually founded the tradition remains an open question; suffice it to say that the later German masters were fond of referring back to him and his teachings when they wanted to emphasize the truth of their own teachings and their true heritage.

LIECHTENAUER LEFT HIS knowledge in the form of verses that are almost incomprehensible and would have remained so had not later masters written explanations and extrapolations on these teachings.[1] In 1389, Hanko Döbringer, who was a priest or clerk, was the first to write a comment on the verses that are today perhaps the finest instruction that we have from the high Middle Ages on the combat arts. Sigmund Ringeck, who composed his work around the middle of the 15th century, followed in the same tradition and wrote clear explanations on what he felt was a complete curriculum on the fighting arts. Our first book, *Sigmund Ringeck's Knightly Art of the Longsword*, dealt with his teachings on the longsword without armor, and in this volume we deal with fighting in armor, wrestling, and using the sword and buckler.

RINGECK IS ONLY one in a long line of combat masters who lived in Germany, Italy, and England—and most likely other countries as well; we just do not know about them yet. Many of these masters decided to encode their teachings in books so that they would not be forgotten when they passed away. The idea that the teacher needs the student is both old and universal; all our knowledge is of little value if it dies with us. In a sense we are carrying on that tradition with this book, but in a very modest way—we present no new teachings, merely the interpretation of the old ones. But it is important to remember that the historical evidence accumulated in our libraries amounts to thousands of books and manuscripts dealing with this lost world of martial arts right here in our homelands, not in some faraway place. The masters left us a legacy, hoping that we would one day look to it and be uplifted by it. What other reason can we imagine to devote so much time in creating and carrying on tradition in the way that went into these books? At least I like to think about it in that way, and when we all one day stand before the Good Lord, I would like to turn to the masters and say that I did my best to honor their intentions, even if I did not become their most skilled student.

AT THE END of this book you will find a short bibliography, but we have deliberately limited it to what can be found in reprints or interpretations of old manuals. The reason is that no matter where you live, these will be books that you can readily get your hands on. We have also recommended a few Internet sites and organizations that might be of value to you if you are new in this field and want to look for likeminded people.

ABOVE ALL, NEVER be afraid!

David Lindholm
Malmö, Sweden, 2005

ENDNOTE

1. These verses can be found in our first book, *Sigmund Ringeck's Knightly Art of the Longsword* (Paladin Press, 2003).

Introduction

THIS IS THE second volume dealing with the *Fechtbuch* (fighting book) of the medieval German master Sigmund Ringeck. We organized this book with the same layout as our first one and have the same intentions, namely to provide a practical book that helps readers understand and play with the fencing and wrestling techniques of the medieval masters. Naturally, no such book will have the final say as far as interpretation–it is up to you to work with this material and come to your own conclusions. All that we can say is that we have tried our best to offer you the most honest interpretation possible and admit that at times we do not have the faintest idea what Ringeck intended. There is nothing wrong in admitting ignorance, and we are all more or less ignorant when it comes to understanding and interpreting the legacy of the European masters of arms. This work is not intended as an academic text dealing with any possible connections or interdependencies between masters and their work; we leave those discussions to other writers with our best wishes. Nor is it an analysis of the manuscript as such; again, we leave that to others. Our interest is the actual techniques and nothing more or less than that.

WE HAVE DECIDED to not include Ringeck's section on mounted combat because we do not know the first thing about riding horses or fighting on horseback. Since work is in progress by people with international recognition for excellent horsemanship, we leave it to them to collect and comment on this material.

THE TEXT

WE HAVE FOLLOWED the order of combat as found in the original manuscript rather than rearranging the material to create a more coherent flow of the techniques. Each technique will have Ringeck's original German text along with our translation of it. This text is important–I wish to stress that since it really is the true original. With each illustration of the techniques you will find our explanation of what is intended. Take these as guidelines, not gospel.

THE ILLUSTRATIONS

WE HAVE FOLLOWED the same idea with the illustrations as in the first book. We have fewer diagrams for the foot movements, perhaps, but we think that the result is clearer. As before, the arrows indicate the path of the sword, the feet, or the direction of the movement of the body. The illustrations explain themselves–at least we hope they do!

HISTORICAL EUROPEAN MARTIAL ARTS IN THE 21ST CENTURY

WHAT WE CALL the European, Western, and/or Renaissance martial arts have experienced an absolutely phenomenal upsurge in the past five years: new groups working with it pop up almost daily. With this has come a staggering output of published material, which is good because this martial tradition is dead and cannot be resurrected. But it can be *reconstructed*, which is something else.

TO DO THIS, we (that is, we who practice) must get access to material and translations that enable us to understand the teachings; we can then try them out and work on our own understanding. But, at the same time it is important to acknowledge that we will probably never actually have to deal with a life-and-death situation while wielding a sword. I would here advance the perhaps radical idea that we will never know what the masters were really talking about unless we actually kill someone with a sword. (And it is our sincere hope that we never do have that experience.) But it does not matter that we will never know, since we are not resurrecting but reconstructing these arts.

RECONSTRUCTING THESE ARTS should be made with care and afterthought. Stressing one point or another—whether it be the martial aspect, historical accuracy, or competitiveness—should not be allowed to become a goal in itself. I believe that we should bother less with these things and just practice, get the stick and do two thousand strikes a day at a pell instead. We should enjoy what we do and let others do the same. In reconstructing these arts, we must remember that since we will never actually know if we are right, we must accept it when others do things differently. If we disagree, we tell them why; if we present a better arguement, we hope they change and if they argue better, then we should change.

THE EUROPEAN MARTIAL heritage is important—I firmly believe that—but I also firmly believe that we must not be lured into thinking "Since I have a better source, fight better, and argue better, I am actually right." It is in the end a question of humility, the primary Chivalric virtue. We are all a part of this reconstruction.

TEACHING AND STUDYING THE EUROPEAN MARTIAL ARTS

THIS IS ALSO a touchy topic. Everybody seems to have an opinion—and I am no exception! Let me point out a few things that I have noticed, especially during the past five years. First, since we are dealing with arts that involve the body, fitness is an issue because a fitter person will fight better or practice longer than one who is unfit. Second, instead of trying to invent our own method of practice, we should look at the proven methods of professional athletes and coaches. I have had much inspiration from the Swedish SISU, an organization that works with professional athletes in Sweden to develop their practice techniques and skills. Experts such as these already know what you should do to become agile and strong without getting slow, and how to train mentally. We should shamelessly steal from these people, since inventing the wheel twice is foolish.

SO, WE STUDY what modern science says and then apply it to our own field of study so that it fits with our tools and becomes useful to us. We are not masters at this game, period. Since we are all beginners more or less, we should all be willing to learn. For instance, if we have 20 minutes a day to practice, how do we train technique for maximum benefit? How do we increase strength, speed, and agility most efficiently? All these things and much more are well researched today by experts, and more is being added every day. Use it.

I'M NOT INCLUDING any suggested readings on these topics, since what is available differs greatly depending on where you live. But an easy way to find good information is to talk to coaches and trainers at your local university, high school, or athletic club. They can usually point you in the right direction.

WHAT TO PRACTICE WITH?

THIS IS A complicated question. All I can say is that we have tried both the techniques and the training tools as thoroughly as we could.

Solo Practice

NOTHING BEATS A high-quality replica, which means a sharp sword either made to copy an existing original or created by a competent swordsmith from measurements gathered from several originals. (Do not buy novelty or fantasy swords—they are not the real things.) Ask people in the organizations that practice historical swordsmanship if you want specific advice.

VISIT ALBION SWORDS (www.albion-swords.com) to see Peter Johnsson's work. His are the finest swords you could possibly buy with regard to handling, quality of workmanship, and historical accuracy. The only thing better would be a truly custom-made sword (which would cost about 10 times as much before there was any significant difference in quality).

Partner Practice

HERE, I AM of two minds. A good steel replica with blunted edges might work, but the fact that the edges are thicker will make the sword unbalanced; there is no good way around this. A sharp sword has a thinner blade and will thus be lighter and have a different balance. But a sharp sword, of course, poses a greater danger. So I recommend wasters—wooden weapons that can be cheaply made by a local woodworker or purchased from one of several companies. With the single-hand sword you can well use a solid stick for practice.

Test Cutting

WE DEALT WITH this issue in our first book so I will not repeat the information here, except to say that at one point or another you ought to equip yourself with a sharp sword and try it out on suitable targets. This will teach you a lot about the actual difference between hitting something and cutting it in half.

Sparring

I USED TO be a great advocate of sparring; nowadays I am not sure that it is always a good idea. The reason is, simply, that the protective gear that you must wear if you are using something that behaves remotely like a sword will, in effect, dress you in armor. That is all well and good for practicing fighting in armor, but for practicing unarmored fighting, it is very bad. Makeshift swords—simulators that are so light or soft that you do not need much gear—have the wrong weight and balance.

BUT WHAT DOES sparring actually teach you? Trying to perfect technique through sparring is misdirected. You should learn the techniques first and then spar—do not try to do them at once. To spar before you have learned the techniques only gives you a double burden, forcing you to unlearn the bad things and learn new ones at the same time. It is also easy to develop bad habits during sparring if it is done too early in the training.

FOR SPARRING, WE use shinais, the bamboo training swords used in kendo. They are light, inexpensive, and readily available, and you can modify them admirably for both longsword and single-hand sword. It is virtually impossible to get hurt. Add a fencing mask (a must!) and a pair of welding gloves and you are good to go.

Bucklers

SINCE THIS MANUAL covers techniques using bucklers, something should be said about those as well. At the mid-15th century, all-steel bucklers were probably available, but wood, with a steel rim and a steel buckle in the middle, would have been more common. Hardened leather bucklers were also popular. Today I would say that a good steel one is best simply because it lasts longer. Just don't get one that is so heavy that you tire quickly.

The Sword-and-Buckler Fight According to Ringeck

SWORD-AND-BUCKLER fighting has a long history in Europe and seems to have been a part of the teachings of several German and Italian masters.

THE BUCKLER, AN eminent tool for defense, was also useful for offense, and the sword was of the common and progressively cheaper single-hand kind. We know of several manuals dating from the Middle Ages that include the sword and buckler; while Ringeck includes only a short section on it, the *I.33* is totally dedicated to it.[1] Hans Talhoffer also devotes a large part of his manuals to the sword-and-buckler fight.[2]

THERE HAS BEEN much debate on interpreting some of the techniques used by the medieval masters, since they diverge from the later and more detailed accounts of, for example, Achilles Marrozzo, an early 16th-century Italian master. While this is interesting, we can clearly see that what Ringeck offers are just some combinations of the sword-and-buckler play. Ringeck presents complementary comments and suggestions rather than a complete system in itself, and he presupposes a working knowledge of the single-hand sword and buckler from his readers.

SWORD-AND-BUCKLER fighting is, in a sense, more complex than that with the longsword, demanding a greater degree of mobility and alertness for the changing strategic situations of combat. It is also generally faster than the longsword fight, with more situations that might go wrong, since both combatants were wielding two implements instead of one. It is indicative of the status of the intended reader that sword-and-buckler techniques receive so little space as opposed to fighting in full armor. The sword and buckler method was used by people from all walks of life for sure, but was more common among the nongentle classes of society.

AFTER EXAMINING THE following pages, you will see that the sequences of Ringeck's sword and buckler consist of basic strikes, thrusts, and guards, which can be combined into many more combinations than the six the master gave us. Pick the sequences apart and rearrange the pieces into new and interesting patterns and they will reward you well for the time and effort.

ENDNOTES

1. The *I.33* (also known as *MS I.33*, or the Tower Fechtbuch) deals exclusively with the use of the single-hand sword and the buckler and is commonly dated to the end of the 13th century, which makes it the oldest known manual. For an in-depth analysis of this material, see *Medieval Sword and Shield: The Combat System of Royal Armouries MS I.33* by Paul Wagner and Stephen Hand, and also the facsimile translated by Dr. Jeffrey Forgeng, both from Chivalry Bookshelf.

2. Hans Talhoffer was a famous German master of defense who lived circa 1420–1490. He authored, or had made, no fewer than six different manuals of the art of defense. The most renowned, published in 1467, contained longsword, dagger, wrestling, mounted combat, pole ax, messer, sword and buckler, judicial combat, and other forms of combat of the era.

Herein is described the techniques with the buckler.

The first technique with the buckler is from the oberhaw. When you strike an oberhaw to the man, place the pommel of your sword inside of your buckler at your thumb. Then thrust at him from below at his face and wind against his sword and snap around. This works on both sides.

Hernach stond geschriben die stuck mitt dem buckler

Das erst stuck mitt dem buckler uss dem oberhaw wen du den den oberhaw trybst zu dem manne So setz mitt dem knoppfe din schwert inwendig uff dinen buckler zu dinen daumen Und stich im von unden auff zu sinem gesichte und wind gegen sinem schwert und lauss uberschnappen. Das gät zu von bayden sytten

Both opponents hold their swords in an upper guard. Relax the shoulder of the sword arm so your shoulders don't bunch up. Keep the buckler advanced a little bit and angled slightly to the outside.

[Ringeck says that we should adjust the grip on the sword by our thumb–this is probably after the oberhaw has been displaced. This is a continuation, not an admonition to do the strike with the buckler by the thumb of the sword hand.]

Step forward with the right foot and strike an oberhaw on the near side of the buckler. This does not mean that you must follow with the buckler exactly in front of your hand; doing that slows you down a lot. Instead, follow with the buckler slightly above and behind–that way you are covered just as well and you can move both arms independently. The opponent catches the strike on the buckler and supports with his sword as well, in effect a double block.

Thrust up from below and, as you do so, wind the sword inside your buckler. This way, if he deflects with his sword, you are already going into the next attack by winding, as shown in the illustration. This is done in an instant without moving the feet.

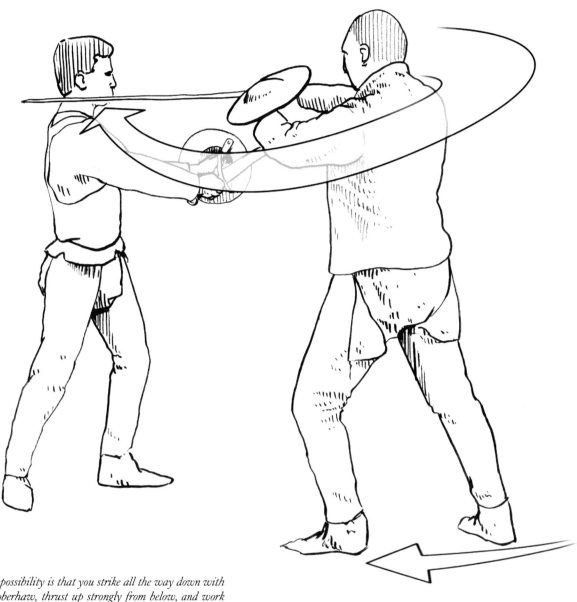

A second possibility is that you strike all the way down with the first oberhaw, thrust up strongly from below, and work on from the deflection or bind of that attack.

Snap the sword around and step out to the side with the left foot as you strike at his neck. Cover the sword hand with the buckler as you attack.

THE SECOND TECHNIQUE

Note that from the unterhaw when he strikes at you from above from his right shoulder, then wind against him on your left side against your shield so that you come into "two shields." Then wind to your right side opening and grab him by the face. If he counters this and holds his shield up to defend, then go for the left leg. This works on both sides.

DASS ANDER STUCK

Item uss dem underhaw wenn er dir oben eyn hawt von siner rechten achseln so wind gegen im uff din lincken sytten gegen dinen schilt so stest du in zwayen schilten So wind dann uff din rechte sytten blöss und gryff im nach dem maul Wert er dir das und helt den schilt uff so nym dass linck bayn. Dass gät zu bayden sytten zu

You stand in a tail guard, for instance, and the opponent strikes from above with an oberhaw.

Move the buckler up and support it with the sword. In effect, you do a winden on the inside of the buckler to get the sword into position and give added support to your block. You can step forward as you do this or remain in position; going forward gives you a stronger block.

Wind again but this time to your right outside, still keeping his sword on your buckler. Your sword deprives him of the opportunity to slide over the edge of the buckler. Aim the point at his face and thrust.

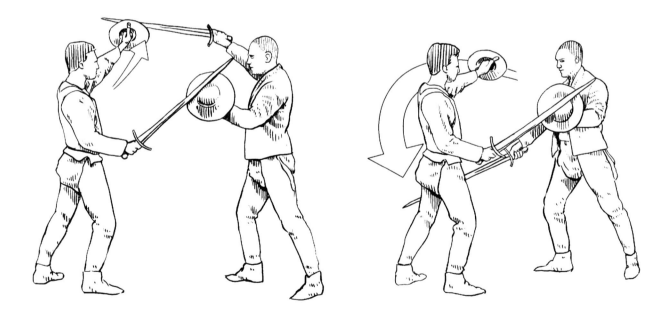

If the opponent deflects your thrust with his buckler to your right side (left), then strike down at his forward leg at once, aiming just above the knee. At the same time, slap his sword to the side with your buckler to get his attention.

THE THIRD TECHNIQUE

Note with the buckler, from the wechselhaw, strike from the left side from the buckler above him at his sword and then strike at him from the left side at his head and wind to the opening to thrust him in the face. If he defends with sword and buckler then strike with the long edge at his right leg. *[Author's note: "Long edge" means the forward edge, or the one on the same side as your knuckles on the sword hand.]* This works on both sides.

DASS DRITT STUCK

Item uss dem buckler Uss dem wechselhaw streych von der lincken sytten uss dem buckler fast ubersich in sin schwert und haw im dann von der lincken sytten zu dem haupt unnd wind blöss und stoss im nach dem maul Hept er mitt schilt und schwert unnd wert dass so haw mitt der langen schniden unnd nach dem rechten bain Das gät och zu baiden sytten

This is one possible starting position.

This a second starting position, in which you cover your hand with the buckler. (In my opinion, the first option is faster and safer.)

You strike upward using the false edge into a high guard. (You also can use the true edge as well, just by turning your hand.) If you hit the opponent, that's great, but if you miss him just continue without stopping.

Strike down again on his left side, aiming at his head. The opponent defends with both buckler and sword. (It is possible for him to wrap the buckler around and under his sword so that the front of it meets the strike, but this works better in real fighting.)

Wind the sword up so that you can aim your point into his face. It is possible to do this while pressing forward with the sword, thus winding and thrusting in one motion. If you want, follow up with the buckler to cover the angle into the hand, or let it stay down.

The opponent defends using his sword to deflect your point. Strike his leg as you go downward. (Where you hit depends on where your point is when you start.) Where does not matter; just hit him.

The fourth technique

Note that from the mittelhaw strike the zwerch to both sides and the schaittler with the long edge and thrust below in the groin.

Dass vierd stuck

Item uss dem mittelhaw mach die zwerch zu baiden sytten und den schaittler mitt der langen schniden und stich im unden zu sinen gemächt

The zwerchhaw is usually done with the back edge, turning around the sword so that the crossguard is in front of the head. The mittelhaw is simply a horizontal strike, usually at shoulder height; schaittler is a vertical strike going from high to low.

From a ready position. Other positions work as well; these are suggestions.

Step forward and strike a zwerch to the right side. In the illustration we do it as a normal horizontal strike since trying to do it with the false edge makes the attack very weak. The buckler covers the weapon hand without hindering the movement. The opponent defends by doing a double defense with both buckler and sword. Doing the strike as a proper zwerchaw is possible. The first strike will be somewhat weak, but the second one will be stronger.

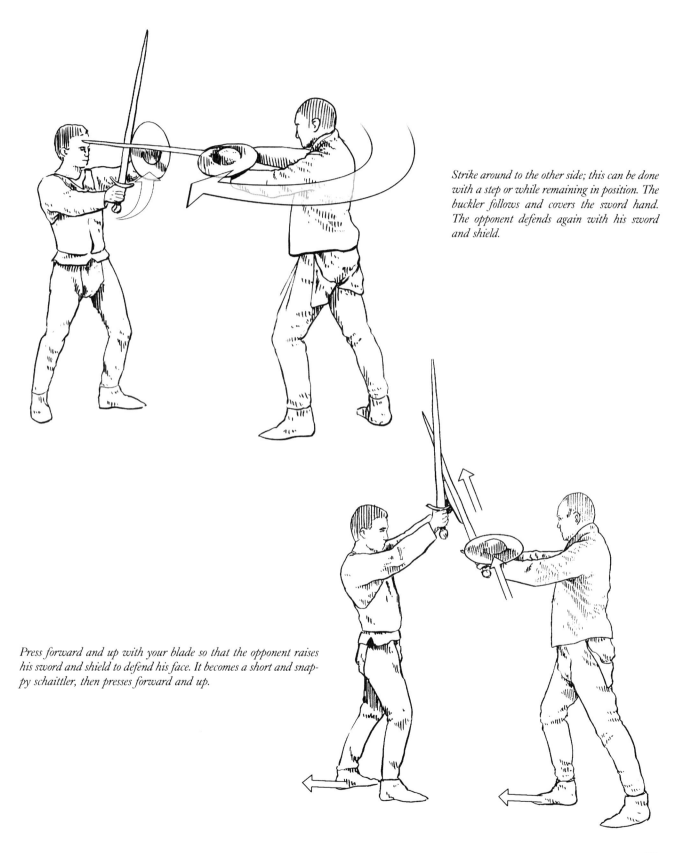

Strike around to the other side; this can be done with a step or while remaining in position. The buckler follows and covers the sword hand. The opponent defends again with his sword and shield.

Press forward and up with your blade so that the opponent raises his sword and shield to defend his face. It becomes a short and snappy schaittler, then presses forward and up.

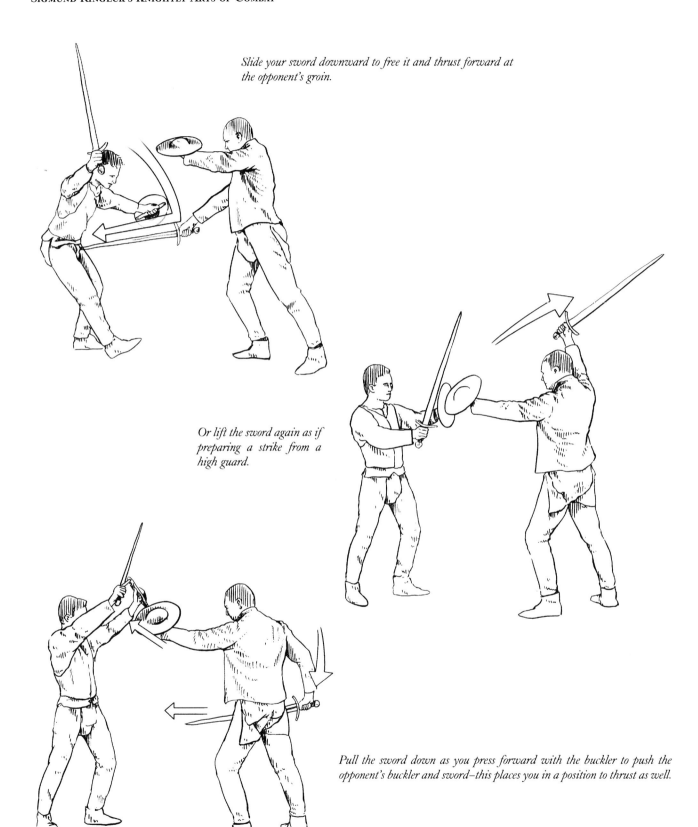

Slide your sword downward to free it and thrust forward at the opponent's groin.

Or lift the sword again as if preparing a strike from a high guard.

Pull the sword down as you press forward with the buckler to push the opponent's buckler and sword—this places you in a position to thrust as well.

THE FIFTH TECHNIQUE

Note: from the sturtzhaw (plunging strike) do as if you were to thrust at his left side over his shield, and then go below and through with the point and thrust at him on the inside of his shield into the body. And then wind at once to your left side; if he defends against this then get his right leg with the true edge.

DASS FUNFT STUCK

Item uss dem sturtzhaw thu alss so du im zu der lincken sytten uber sinen schilt wöllest strechen und far mitt dem ort unden durch und stich im inwendig sines schilts zu dem lybe Unnd indes wind uff din lincke sytten wert er dir das so nym sin recht bayn mitt der langen schnyden

From a ready stance, relax the sword arm while advancing the buckler slightly. Get ready to defend against an incoming attack. This is a position that I like a lot.

This is after a sturtzhaw, which I take to be something between a strike and a thrust aimed with the false edge at the opposite side of the opponent's head (i.e., left if you are on the right). Remember to move the buckler a bit closer to the sword hand to cover it. The opponent defends using both his buckler and sword. The actual position he takes will differ depending on his intentions.

Angle your sword down and in so that you slip the point in behind the opponent's buckler while raising your own buckler slightly to cover your arm and face.

If he defends, then wind in a smooth movement to your left side while covering with the buckler and aiming your point in his face. The opponent defends against this as well.

Go out and down (you may have to raise the sword slightly to get clear of his blade), and strike the opponent in the legs.

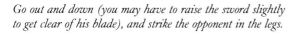

THE SIXTH TECHNIQUE

Note: take your blade and the buckler in your left hand and wind against him with the half-sword. If he strikes or thrusts at you above at the face or below to the leg, then let your right hand go and displace him with the shield and the sword. Then grab hold of his shield rim from below with your right hand and pull it to the right—then you have taken his shield from him.

DASS SECHST STUCK

Item nym din clingen zu dem buckler in din lincke hand und wind gegen im alss mitt dem halben schwert hawet er oder sticht er dir oben zu der gesicht oder unden zu dem bayn So lauss din rechte hand faren von dem pinde und versetz im das mitt schilt wol undersich und dree in uff din rechte sytten So hastu im den schilt genomen

This is a new on-guard position where you assume a position similar to one of the half-sword guards with the longsword when in armor.

As the opponent strikes at your head, turn the pommel of your sword up to vertical and block with both your buckler and sword.

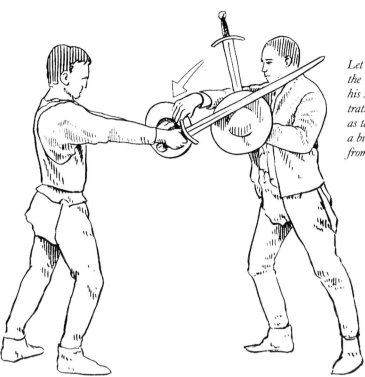

Let go of the pommel and quickly reach out to grab the rim of the opponent's buckler. (This technique only works if he covers his sword hand with the buckler, thus indicating that the illustrations in, for example, I.33 are correct in showing the buckler as tagging along with the sword hand.) Push your own buckler a bit to the outside as you take hold. This will guard your hand from his sword.

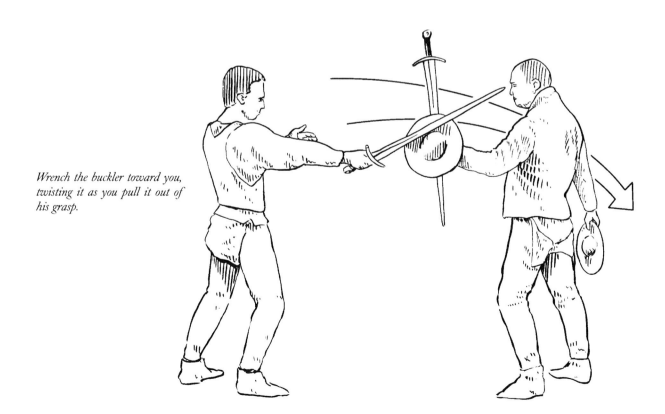

Wrench the buckler toward you, twisting it as you pull it out of his grasp.

You can also grab his buckler from underneath, which gives you nice leverage as you pull back.

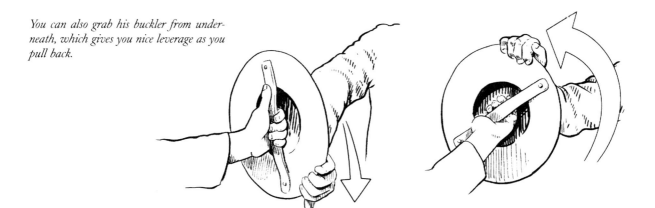

Or you can take hold on the top. Either way works, but your position will make one easier than the other. Remember that you should try not to take a step as you grab his buckler; you must be in a position where you can reach it without stepping for the technique to succeed.

Beginning on-guard position from the front.

Wrestling

WRESTLING (RINGEN) WAS an integrated part of the masters' teachings in medieval and Renaissance Europe. In fact, wrestling techniques make up about half of the content of the surviving manuals from the 14th, 15th, and early 16th centuries, which says something of its importance.

THE REASONS FOR its importance to the masters are easy to understand: close combat was always a possibility, regardless of other circumstances of a fight such as armor being worn, location of the fight, or weapons used by the combatants. The techniques appear very similar to many that we see in Asian martial arts, and for good reason: the principles work, and people are constructed in the same way no matter where you go.

IN RINGECK'S TECHNIQUES we find throws, joint locks, trips, and strikes to vulnerable areas. What is conspicuously absent in the manuals is instruction in a developed system of punching and kicking, perhaps because it was considered common knowledge.

THE TECHNIQUES IN the manuals are difficult to interpret and, therefore, we have made only a suggestive interpretation that is not conclusive in any way. One reason for this is that not all techniques are described precisely, and the manuals often do not supply an entering technique or move, just the central technique. This makes it hard to resurrect the technique, since the entering move is by far the most critical and difficult part of all close combat. Another problem with interpreting these wrestling techniques is that Ringeck does not offer any on-guard positions or principles of footwork.

ALSO, THE CONTEXT of the wrestling moves is problematic. While wrestling was used in combat, it was also used in sporting competitions, at fairs as a show and pastime, and at banquets as entertainment performed by traveling troupes. So some wrestling moves that have survived in the manuals do perhaps reflect play rather than mortal combat.

MANY OF THE wrestling moves used with weapons were probably not conceived for that specific case; rather it was a carryover from unarmed sport wrestling (that could turn ugly as well), something we can see by the presence of similar techniques. But vital information is missing in all the works dealing with wrestling in the 15th century, again, because it may have been so common that nobody bothered to write it down. Therefore, we have applied the entering move as we have seen fit. These are *possible* solutions but not the *only* solutions.

WE HAVE TRIED to interpret the techniques in a way that we feel is not only consistent with the text but also likely from a martial perspective. In this wrestling chapter there are sections dealing with "murder" strikes, arm breaks, ground techniques, and more. These show that this was intended as a more or less complete system of wrestling. (Some of the starting positions resemble bare-knuckle boxing because we participate in that and were inspired by it.)

HERE BEGINS THE good wrestling and other good techniques.

Let the opponent take a hold even if you can prevent it. If he takes hold of you under the arms and tries to lift you, let yourself drop down and take hold of him under the knee. Resist him and press his head back over his back with both hands. Thus you throw a stronger as well as a weaker man to the ground.

HIE HEBEN SICH an gutte ringen und ander gutt brich

Gib im zu fessen also dass du das kundest brechen jo Wenn er dich nun gefasst hat under den armen an der statt, druckt er dich an in darnach stät och sin syn dass er dich will uff heben mitt den armen soltu nider schweben in under dass kny zefassen in sinem trucken ste wol mitt hassen jm das haupt uber den ruck mitt bayden armen du nitt zuck Also wirfest du den starcken man mitt diner schwachait uff die ban

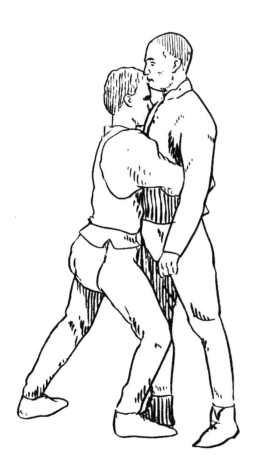

Let him take hold. Make sure that you have a firm center of balance.

Sink down. As you do so you will also press him down since you are applying your weight on top of his arms. Drop down with a sharp movement rather than a slow sinking, which would give him time to adapt to the situation. As you reach as far down as you wish to go, take hold behind his knee.

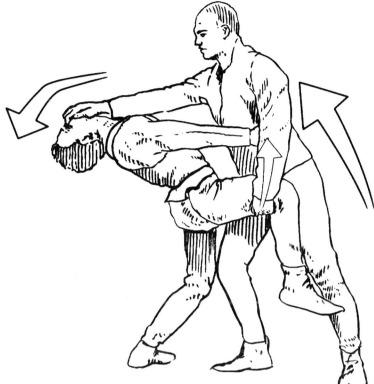

Apply pressure to his chin with the other hand and lift the knee at the same time. To throw him, strike the chin instead of pushing it and heave the knee up. Make sure that his knee does not go between your legs or he will kick you in the balls; his knee should go on the outside. Here only one hand is used to press the head back, which works just as well.

This works well on the other side, too.

ANOTHER TECHNIQUE

If you want to grab hold of him and take him with force and speed, when he tries to use an arm lever, let go of his arm quickly and take hold of his hair, pull your hand back to your shoulder and then run him head first into a wall. Thus is he defeated.

AIN ANDER STUCK

Wenn du dich mitt ainem wilt fassen und nymst in mitt zorn und mitt hassen wenn er dir tut den schwuch so lauss den arm farn schnell ruck in by den harnn Darzu ruck heb uff mitt bant uff die achsel all zu handt mitt sinem haupt lauu an die wand do er ist denn also versto

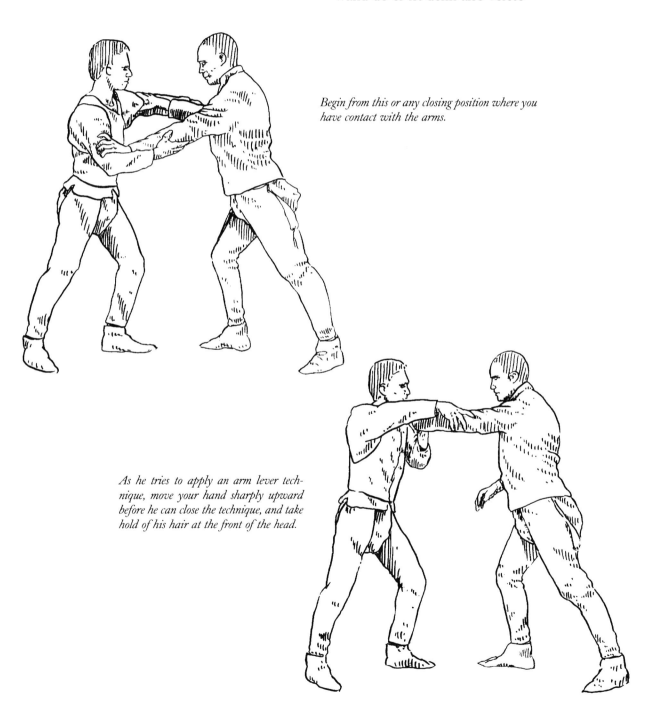

Begin from this or any closing position where you have contact with the arms.

As he tries to apply an arm lever technique, move your hand sharply upward before he can close the technique, and take hold of his hair at the front of the head.

Pull him toward you sharply. Then as he relaxes as it ends, pull toward yourself again. If possible, take hold with the other hand as well and pull toward your chest.

Run him face first into the nearest hard surface you can find. If it is a sharp angle such as a corner, all the better.

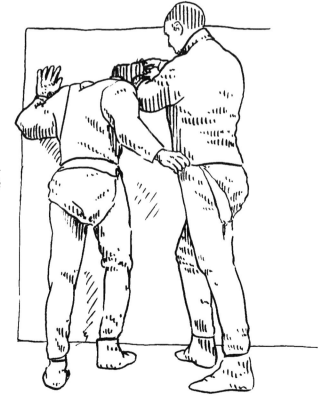

ANOTHER TECHNIQUE

First note that when you close with someone and he pulls his arms back, then step in with your left side forward and let the left arm slide quickly around his neck while your right hand goes between his legs, then throw him over his head to daze him.

AIN ANDER STUCK

Zu dem ersten mal mörck nun Wenn du mitt ainem luffest zu und er och die baide arm zucket mitt gantzem lyb und zucket so lauff an in mitt der lincken sytten den lincken arm lass chnell gleyten die zwer unb sinen halss zu hand die rechte zwischen sin bain bekant und sturtz in uber dass haupt damit wird er bedaupt

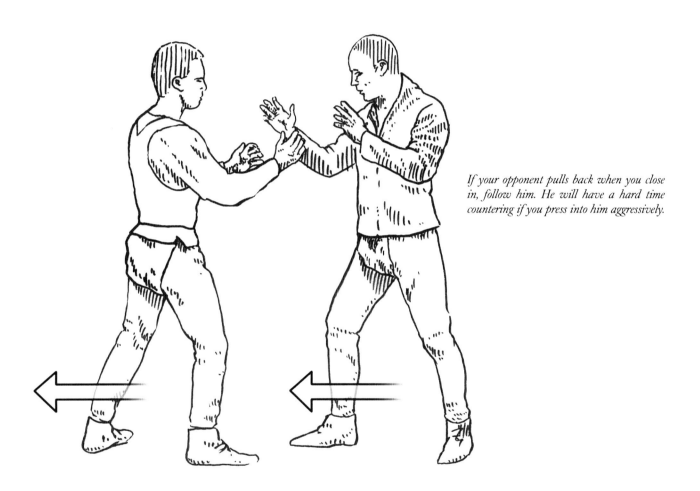

If your opponent pulls back when you close in, follow him. He will have a hard time countering if you press into him aggressively.

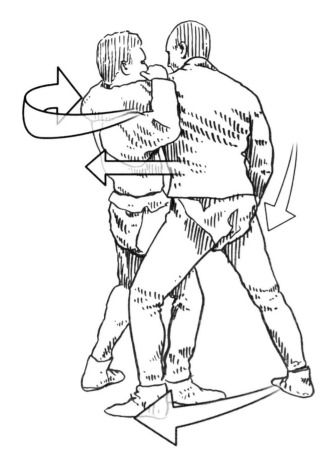

As you close with him, wrap your left arm around his neck and, as you do so, pull your hand sharply toward you so that you also apply pressure on his neck. The right hand goes down and grabs his genitals. Grab, twist, and pull, but retain a solid hold.

To throw him, jerk with force upward with your right hand and, at the same time, pull his head back with your left hand. If you want to be truly wicked, drop him but retain your hold on his genitals as he drops.

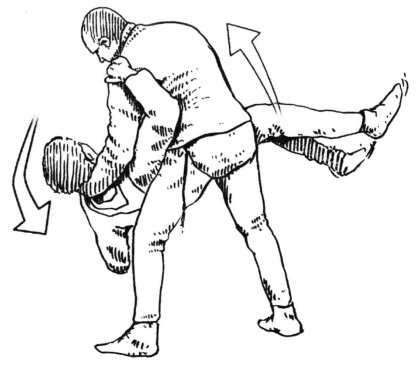

You can also apply the grip around his neck from the front. This variant also works very well and is in many ways easier to apply in a live situation since you can strike your arm across his throat (larynx) rather than wrapping it around the neck from behind.

This is the same move as shown at the bottom of the previous page. Throw and be happy!

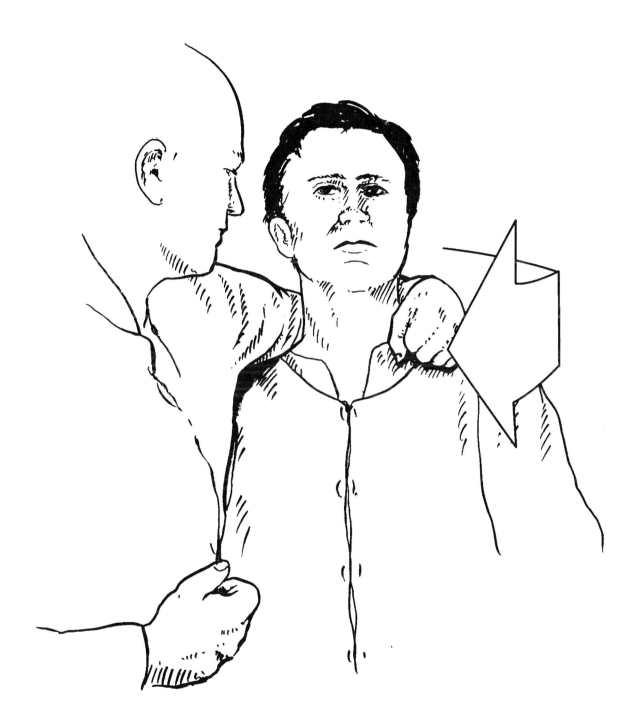

The neck wrap seen from the front.

ANOTHER TECHNIQUE

When you close with someone of equal strength, do not hesitate in following through with your grappling; if you grab him in a full run, he will not be able to counter it. Seize him from below using your hands and throw him down. (Be sure that he does not do the same to you.) *[Author's note: This technique was crossed out in the original text.]*

AIN ANDER STUCK

Wenn du zu lauffest mitt ainem glychen diner störck solt du nitt wychen in follem lauff zu dem fassen er mag es warlich nitt gebussen Und fach in unden mitt den henden und sturtz in uff die lenden (Doch lug dass es dir nitt geshiech noch)

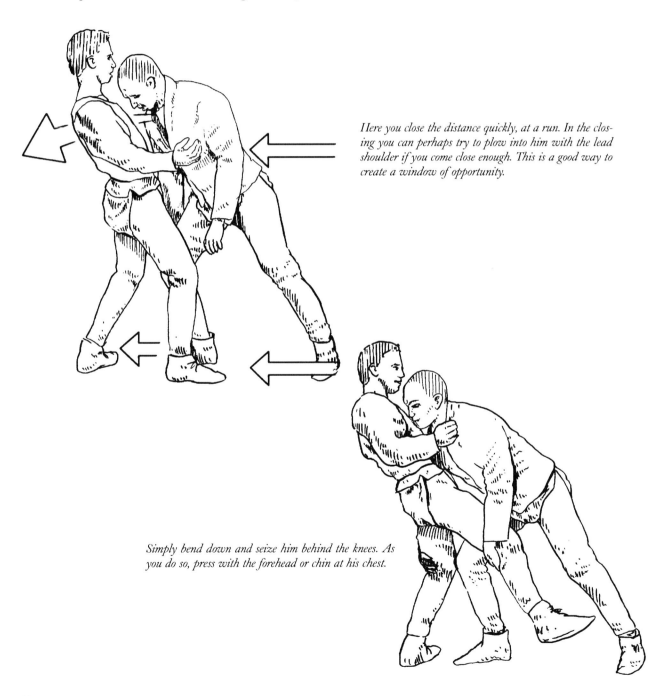

Here you close the distance quickly, at a run. In the closing you can perhaps try to plow into him with the lead shoulder if you come close enough. This is a good way to create a window of opportunity.

Simply bend down and seize him behind the knees. As you do so, press with the forehead or chin at his chest.

To throw him, pull your hands first toward you and then upward as you straighten your legs and then your body.

Closing in seen from the rear.

ANOTHER TECHNIQUE

From a full run, grab his right hand with your left and step through quickly under his arm. With the quick stepping through make a throw by quickly and nimbly taking hold of his leg. Then throw him on his head.

AIN ANDER STUCK

Mitt follem lauff gryff im sin rechte hand mitt diner lincken Tuck lauff zu im begant durch sinen arm gar schnelle Mitt behenden lauff mach dir ain gefelle Nym in by dem schenkel faste doch sin hand halt veste Und setz in uff dass haupte sin nach allem willen din

(Ich globss nitt)

From any starting position, grab his right hand with your left hand. Keep the other hand up to protect your face. Make sure that you have a firm hold on his arm.

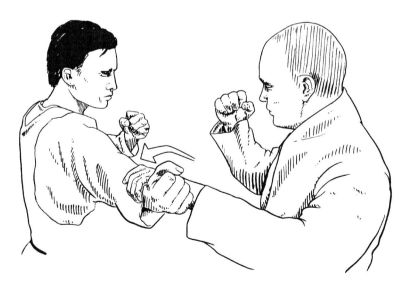

As you step through, make sure that you pull his arm well out as you step to take his point of balance. If you don't you won't be able to throw him. (In this illustration, the opponent has withdrawn his front leg. However, it does not matter whether his leg is to the fore or the rear.)

Take another step toward him with your rear foot to get in a good position to take hold of his leg. If you keep pressure on his arm, he will be unable to counter you.

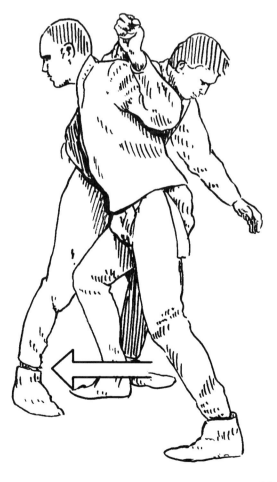

Slip your arm between his legs and straighten your legs. Don't push up with your upper body—use the legs.

Detail of how the arm is held across the back. Remember to pull it out and hold it firmly to apply pressure to the joint.

ANOTHER TECHNIQUE

When you close with someone, quickly take hold of his left arm with your left and take hold of his leg with your right so that he is forced to turn his back to you. You can then strike him in the head or push him down. But if he bends over quickly and slips through your arm, then he has avoided your technique.

AIN ANDER STUCK

Wenn du mittainem lauffest zu sinen lincken arm fach du nur gar schnell uss der ebichen hand (left hand) mitt der rechten syn bain sy dir bekant und mitt dem selben zucken muss er dir kören den rucken So magst du uff sin haupt ain gefell oder stoss in gar schnell kain besser buss ist dowider dann er buck sich schnell nyder und schlyff durch den arm din so hat er gewonnen die buss din

Entering position.

Slip your left arm across and between you and take hold of his right arm, behind the hand if possible.

Pull him down and out on your left side to expose his left side. This is a good position for kidney punches to soften him up.

As you pull and push him toward your left using his arm and leg, strike him in the back of the head with your elbow, or push him down on the ground.

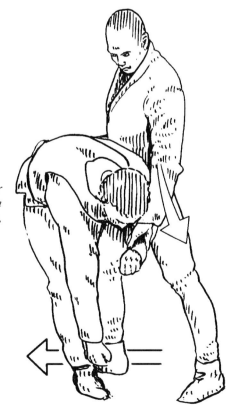

ANOTHER TECHNIQUE

The first technique; place your lower arm over his upper arm before the neck and the other behind his knee. This works on both sides.

AIN ANDER STUCK

Das erst ringen nym din undern arm uber sin obern arm vor dem halss alss ferr du magst unnd den andern arm in knycklen dass gat zu von bayden sytten

As you step in close, strike one arm across his throat. No need to be gentle here.

With the other hand, take hold behind his knee from the inside. Then push back with the arm across his throat and lift with the other in order to throw him.

THE TECHNIQUE/COUNTER

The arm that is topmost is for the change: grab the front of his neck with the other hand on his leg. Note that when you do not come to the first wrestling, then change both hands with the under-most hand above and the upper hand below. One hand at the neck and the other at the leg: this works on both sides. This complete wrestling move is called "leg break with the arm."

DER BRUCH

Der arm der oben ist den wechsel und gryff im fornen an den halss mitt der anderen hand aber an dass bain

Item wann du zu dem ersten ringen nicht komen kanst so wechsel die underen handt oben und die obern unden also dass die ain hand sy an dem halss und die andern an dem bain dass tryb von baiden sytten Der vil ringen gert unnd haisset der bainbrusch an dem arm

This is the basic position with a mutual hold.

Push forward with a short, sharp jerk. This will take away his focus and balance and set you up for the technique.

Place one hand on his neck/throat and with your other hand lift his leg behind the knee from the outside. It does not matter which side you do this on. But remember to lift his leg on the outside of your leg; otherwise you will get his foot in the balls. Unpleasant.

A TECHNIQUE

In this third wrestling, whichever arm is under, strike it over his arm and take hold with the other hand to help. Then move the same foot on the same side as his leg and step back to throw him on his face. This works on both sides.

AIN STUCK

Dass dritt ringen welchen arm du unden häst den schlach uber sin arm und gryff mitt der anderen hand der zu hilff und versetz den fuss derselben sytten von sinem bain woll hin dan Und wirff in fur dich uff dass antlitz das get uff bayden sytten zu

From the entering position.

You have hold of his arm with your right hand. With the same hand, strike him over the elbow joint and begin to press him down. The left hand locks his hand/forearm.

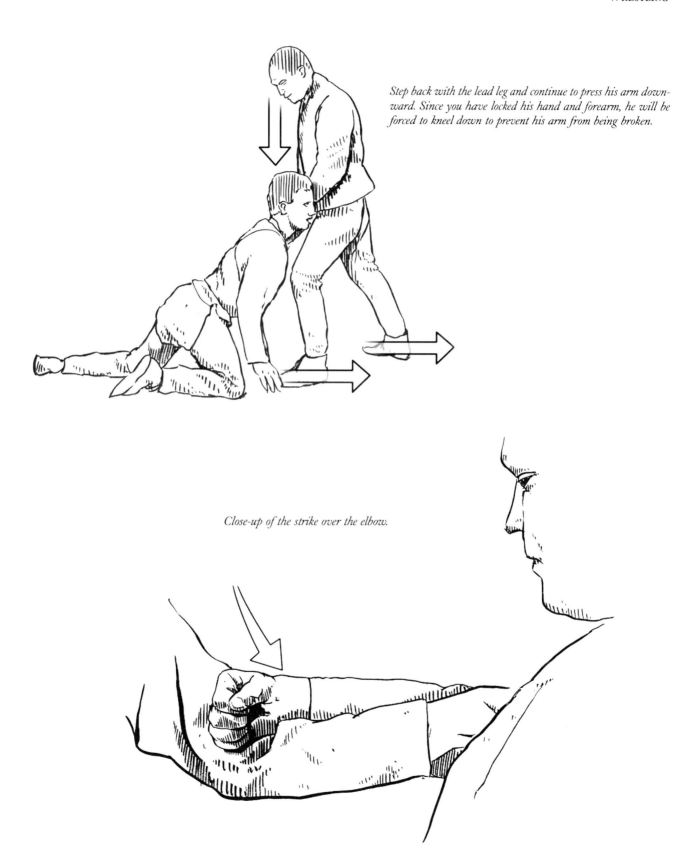

Step back with the lead leg and continue to press his arm downward. Since you have locked his hand and forearm, he will be forced to kneel down to prevent his arm from being broken.

Close-up of the strike over the elbow.

NOTE THAT YOU press with the lower and the upper hand and push him down by the neck and step behind him with the foot.

These are the three wrestling techniques; you can do them while closing in on either side and also as counters.

ITEM SCHLUSS DIE untersten hand die obresten und zeuch in by dem halss niden und tritt in mitt den fussen hinder dich.

Dass sind die dreuy ringen Die mag man triben und zulauffents uff baiden sytten unnd och die bruch die da wider syenn

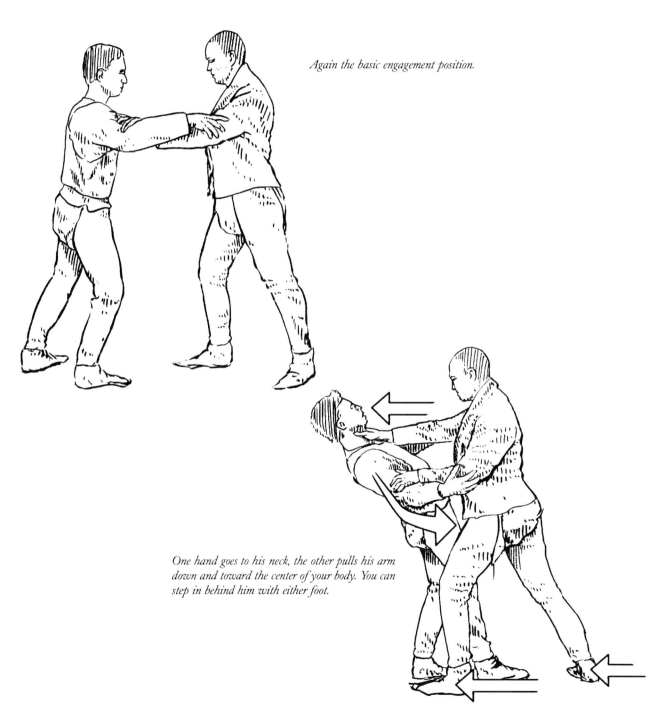

Again the basic engagement position.

One hand goes to his neck, the other pulls his arm down and toward the center of your body. You can step in behind him with either foot.

ANOTHER TECHNIQUE

If he has seized you under the arms and holds you with force or if he tries to throw you.

THE COUNTER

Go with both arms to his throat and push.

ANOTHER COUNTER

Turn his head around using both hands, one at the chin, the other at the back of the head.

COUNTER

Place both your thumbs on his throat and fingers in his eyes.

COUNTER

Press with the thumbs at his temples.

AIN ANDER STUCK

Ob ain man baide arm under gaffen hätt und welt dich weg tragen oder werffen mitt störck

DER BRUCH

Fall im mitt baiden armen an sin kel und truck in

AIN ANDER BRUCH

Wennd im den kopff umb baiden henden die ain hand an dass kun die ander hinden an das haupt

BRUCH

Baid daumen unden an die kell un die andern finger an die ogen

BRUCH

Druck in mitt den daumen an den schlauff

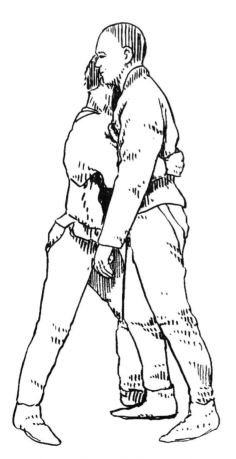

Your opponent has seized you under the arms and prepares to throw or trip you.

Grab his head with both hands and turn it away from you. If he has hair that you can grab, pull with that hand and push with the other.

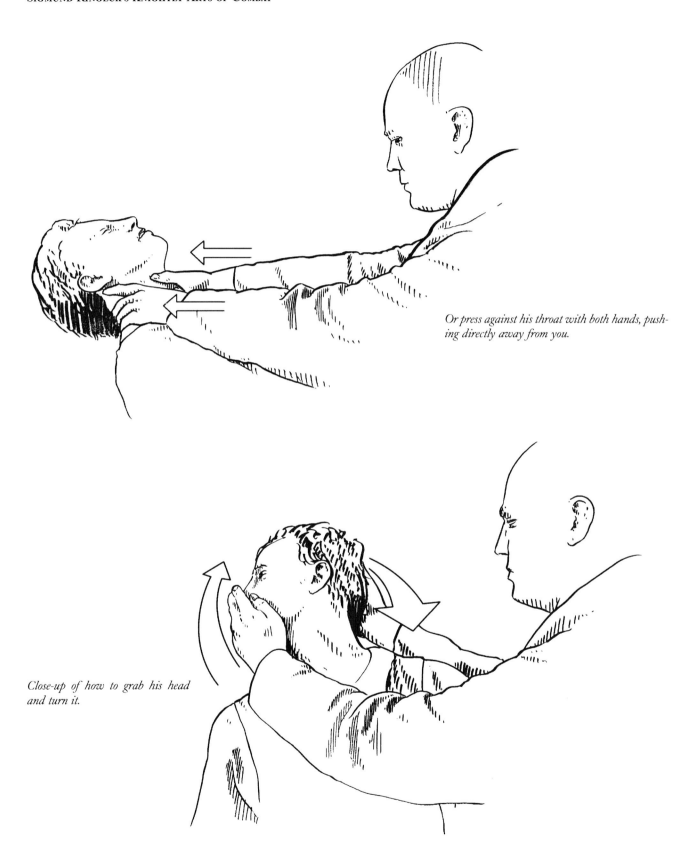

Or press against his throat with both hands, pushing directly away from you.

Close-up of how to grab his head and turn it.

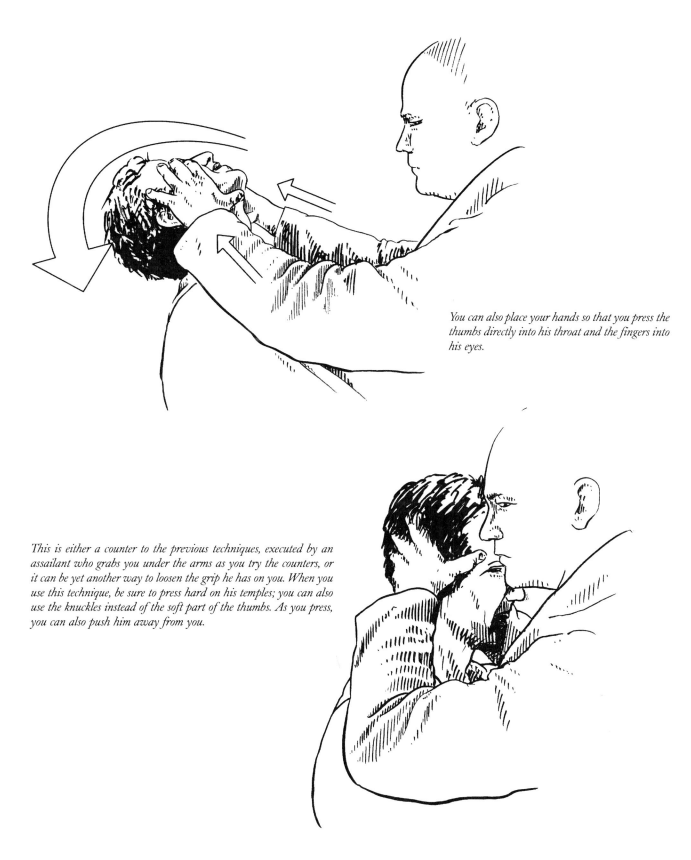

You can also place your hands so that you press the thumbs directly into his throat and the fingers into his eyes.

This is either a counter to the previous techniques, executed by an assailant who grabs you under the arms as you try the counters, or it can be yet another way to loosen the grip he has on you. When you use this technique, be sure to press hard on his temples; you can also use the knuckles instead of the soft part of the thumbs. As you press, you can also push him away from you.

Another technique

If you wish to close in, then place both your arms before your chest and thrust forward at his throat. Then bend down and, using both your hands, grab hold of his leg below the calf and throw him over you.

Ain ander stuck

Wilt du mitt ainem ringen zu lauffen so schluss bayd arm uber din brust un stos in fur den halss damitt buck dich und griff in by dem bain under den waden mitt baiden henden und wurf in uberdich

It is easier to press him back if you cross your hands as you push, but it works without crossing them as well.

When you have created some space between you and your opponent, bend down quickly and grab his front foot above the ankle. Be very observant so that you don't get a knee in the face. You will need both hands to lift your opponent's leg.

Lift it sharply upward and keep his leg close to your body, which will make it easier to lift the weight and counter any resistance.

Lift the leg all the way up and, as you do so, push it away from you. That way you will press your opponent down and backward, a combination that makes it impossible for him to remain standing

IF HE GRABS you from behind at the middle, then take hold of his fingers, the index finger of his uppermost hand, and turn yourself around and step in behind him and from here you can wrestle as you see fit.

OB DICH HINDER in begrifft in der mitt so nym sines fingers war das zaigers an der obersten hand unnd wend dich umb und volg hinder den man Damitt tryb ain ringen dar nach din bestes ist Also thu oben umb och mitt dem finger dass haiset ain lern bruch

Your opponent seizes you around the body under your arms (the technique works even if he has seized you over the arms). With either hand, take hold of the index finger of his upper hand and pull it sharply out and up.

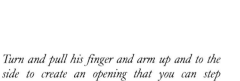

Turn and pull his finger and arm up and to the side to create an opening that you can step through and end up to his rear.

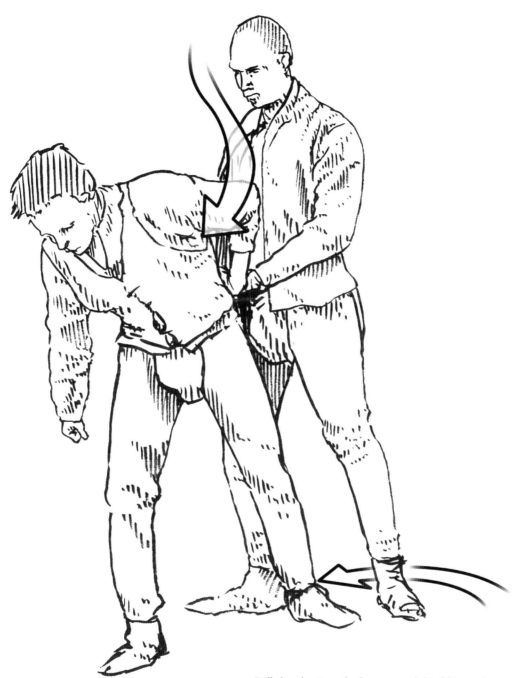

Pull sharply upward when you are behind him and use your other arm to get a good hold.

THE OTHER COUNTER

Turn yourself around a bit and step with your feet close to his feet on either side, and grab the closest leg above the knee using both your hands. If he does not let you go, then throw him onto his head.

DEN ANDERN BRUCH

Wenn dich ein wendig umb und tritt mitt baiden fussen nahent sinen füssen uff welche sztten du wilt Und begriffe im daß nechste bain ober dem kny mitt baiden henden Last er dich nitt so wirff in uff das haupt

When your opponent has seized you from behind, turn around a bit by stepping forward with one foot and slipping the other foot a bit back and in between his legs.

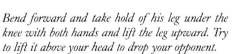

Bend forward and take hold of his leg under the knee with both hands and lift the leg upward. Try to lift it above your head to drop your opponent.

THE THIRD COUNTER
Grab behind yourself with both hands and push.

DEN DRITTEN BRUCH
Griff hinder dich ainem zwischen die händen und truck in do mitt

Again your opponent has seized you from behind.

Lift both your arms, place your thumbs into his eyes, and press. You can also take hold of his head and press the thumbs into his eyes in a gouging motion.

53

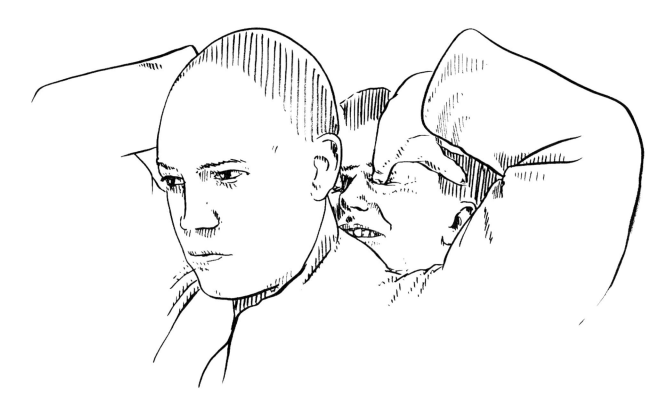

Close-up of the placement of the fingers.
This technique can also be interpreted to mean that you grab his hair and twist or pull backward and to the side, but if he does not have any hair, you may have to do something else.

ANOTHER TECHNIQUE

Grab one of his hands with yours and take hold of two of his fingers with each hand and pull them apart.

This is a closing. Strike with your other hand below his neck and wrestle.

AIN ANDER STUCK

Begrzff ainen man mitt baiden henden in ainer hand in yegelich hand zwen finger die by ain ander steen Und zuck die finger von ain ander

Dass ist zuloffents stoss in mitt der anderen hand under den halss und domitt ring

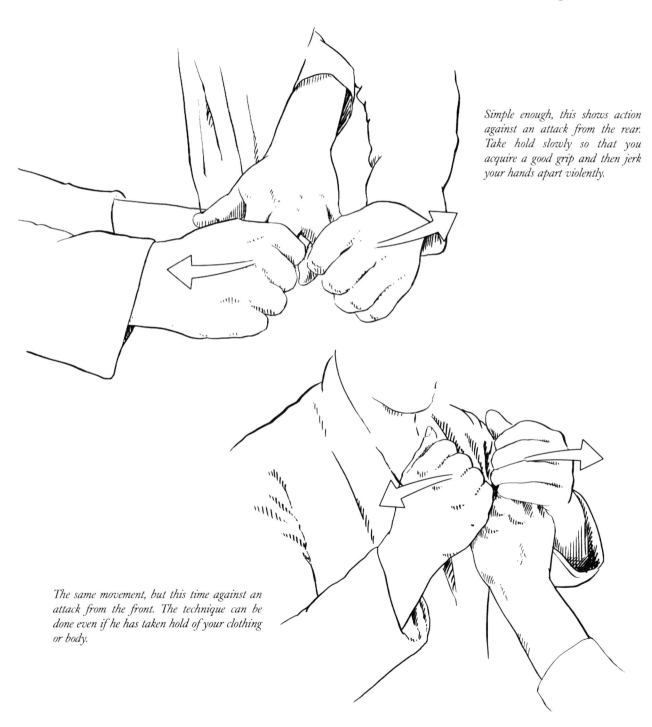

Simple enough, this shows action against an attack from the rear. Take hold slowly so that you acquire a good grip and then jerk your hands apart violently.

The same movement, but this time against an attack from the front. The technique can be done even if he has taken hold of your clothing or body.

55

THE FIRST PINNING-DOWN TECHNIQUE

Grab hold behind his right hand with your right hand while wrestling, and grab his elbow with your left hand. Put his arm on against yours and step behind him and hold him well. If this is not good, take hold of his right leg below the calf with your turned hand and throw him on his nose. You can hold him with both hands or just with one; you can also use either hand on him.

DASS ERST UNTERHALTEN

Gryff in dem ringen mitt diner rechten hand an sinen rechten arm hinder sinen rechten hand und gryff mitt diner lincken hand an sinen elnbogen unnd leg sin arm in din arm und tritt hinder in und halt in föstHaust du in nicht gefölt so begriff im syn rechten fuss under den waden mit diner gerechten hand und wirff in uff die nasen Und halt in mitt baiden henden oder mitt ainer wie du wilt oder magst och zu der anderen hand thun Sonder wechsel din hand an sinen arm

We start from a general wrestling position.

Grab hold behind his right hand with your right; this is easier if you turn your body a bit to the side you are grabbing. At the same time take hold of his elbow. If you seize his hand first, give it a sharp, hard tug. This will create a window so you can take hold of the elbow.

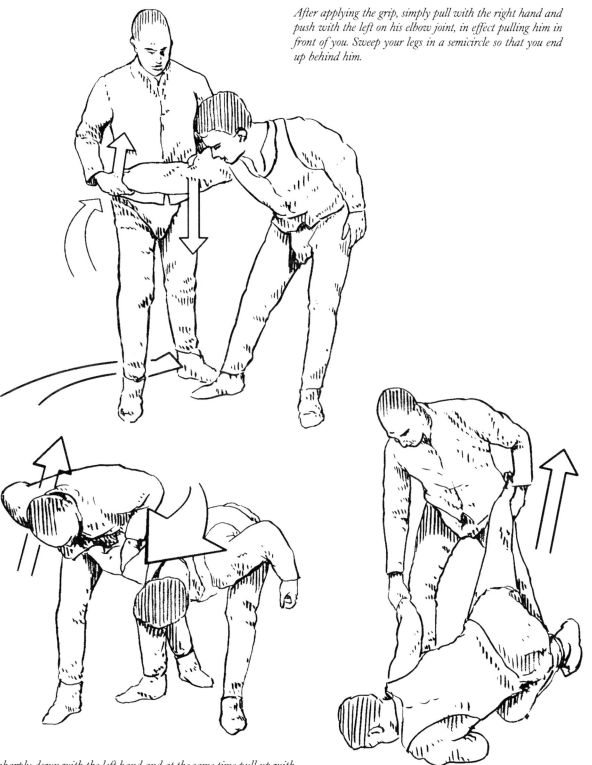

After applying the grip, simply pull with the right hand and push with the left on his elbow joint, in effect pulling him in front of you. Sweep your legs in a semicircle so that you end up behind him.

Press sharply down with the left hand and at the same time pull up with the right hand. Make sure that you are pressing on his elbow joint and keeping his arm taut. If you don't, he can turn the elbow inward and straighten himself up.

When you have a good position, take hold of his foot and pull it sharply back and up to throw him on his face.

57

THE SECOND PINNING-DOWN TECHNIQUE

If you throw someone on his back, then fall with your left knee on his left arm in the middle at the joint and place the left arm at his neck and press hard. Grab hold of his left hand using your right and then take hold of it with your left hand so that you can strike him at will with your right. This can also be done from the left side.

DASS ANDER UNTERHALTEN

Wirffest du ain uff den ruck som fall im mitt dem lincken kny uff den rechten arm mitten in dem glencke und fall im mitt dem lincken arm in sin hals und druck in hart Und begryff im sin lincke hand mitt diner rechten und bring im sin lincke in din rechte hand und fasss in den mitt diner lincken hand so magstu im thon mitt der rechten wass du wilt Dass magst du och thon zu der lincken sytten.

Here you have him down and have pinned him on three points: elbow, head, and wrist. It is important that you get your knee on his elbow joint; otherwise he may move his arm. Press down with all your weight.

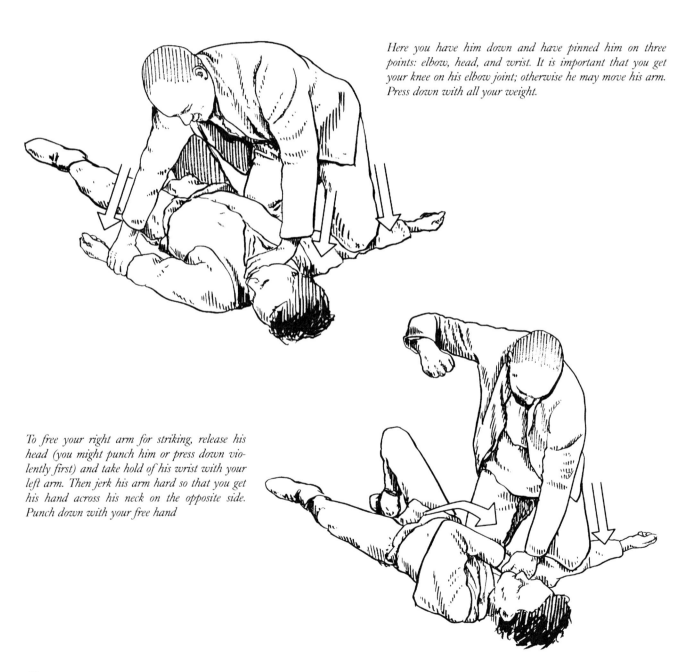

To free your right arm for striking, release his head (you might punch him or press down violently first) and take hold of his wrist with your left arm. Then jerk his arm hard so that you get his hand across his neck on the opposite side. Punch down with your free hand

THE THIRD PINNING-DOWN TECHNIQUE

If you have thrown someone on his back, then grab hold of his legs at the knees as he falls and then lift them as high as you can and fall down with your knees in his groin. Then hold his legs so that you can hold them with one hand alone and use the other as you wish.

DASS DRITT UNTERHALTEN

So du ain magst werffen uff den ruck in dem selben begryff im baide bain under dem kny mitt baiden henden und heb im die bain uff so du höchst känst und fall mitt baiden knyen zwischen sine bain uff sine hoden und ug dass du mitt ainer hand sine bayde bayn gehalten magst so erwerst du mitt der anderen hand nach dinem willen

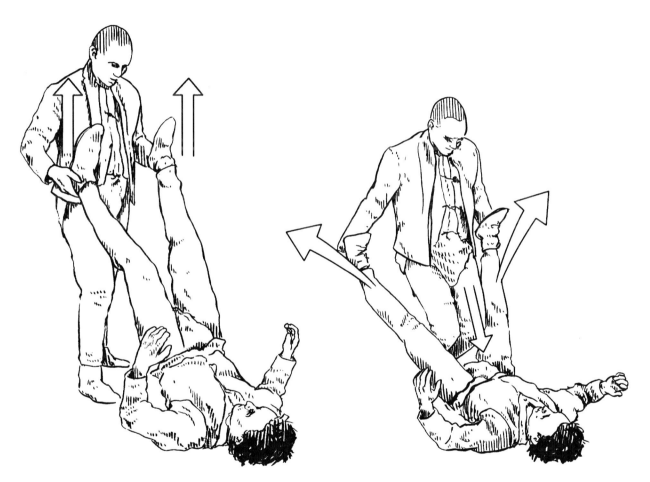

This technique presupposes that you have taken hold of the opponent's legs and thrown him down while retaining your grip.

This is simple enough–just drop down with your knees in his crotch. Remember to hold his legs wide apart for solid impact.

After the impact he will curl up in a little heap. Sit down on his legs to pin him and pummel him with your hands.

THE FIRST GROUND-FIGHTING TECHNIQUE

If you wish to do the first ground-wrestling technique [eventually this should be a pinning-down technique], then allow yourself to fall down willingly. And lift the knee as high as you can and hold him by the back. Pull him violently toward your knee and stretch one knee (either one) so that he falls off. Follow him with both hands and feet and pin him down with one of the techniques that you already know.

DIE ERST UFF STON

Wilst du dass erst uff ston brechen in dem ringen so fall selbert nider mitt guttem willen Und heb die kny uff so höchst du magst und halt in by dem ruck Zuch dem man hart nach dir uff die kny dar nach streck ain kny welches du wilt so glet er ab So folg im nach mitt baiden henden und fussen und halt in under dir mitt aim underhalten alss du wol waist.

From a standing position, drop down by lowering your butt and pulling the opponent with you.

Drop all the way down in a fluid motion and, as you do, lift your knee up so that the opponent gets it in his gut. By pushing him up and over you as you pull with your arms, you send him over your head.

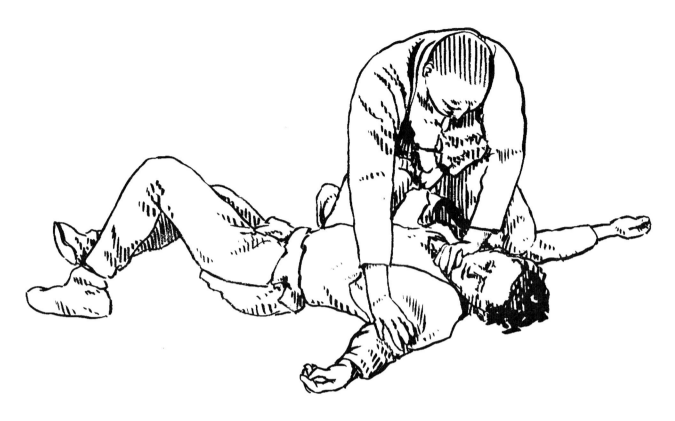

Continue with the rolling motion so that you end up on top of him, and punch him in the face or pin him down by pressing his head to the side and locking his arm with your knee. (This is a fairly complicated technique that you should practice on a suitable mat.)

THE SECOND GROUND-FIGHTING TECHNIQUE

Note that when your opponent applies a hold from above, then bend his head in under his chest and tear him toward yourself and fall down on your back and bend your knees as high as you can and grab hold between his legs with either hand and throw him over yourself. Be quick to get off him and apply a pinning technique, either if you are above or whatever else.

DAS ANDER UFF STON

Item bewyss dein man ain obern griff damitt so buck dass haupt im under die brust und zuch in nach dir und fall nider uff den ruck und beug dine kny so du höchst magst unn´d gryff im die griff zwischen den bain mitt welcher hand du magst unnd wurff in uberdich Und biss schnell uff in und thu ain underhalden welches dir eben ist oder werden mag

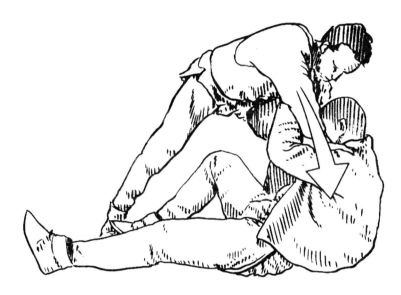

When the opponent applies a hold from above, push your closest knee up into his gut as you pull him down by his arms or clothing.

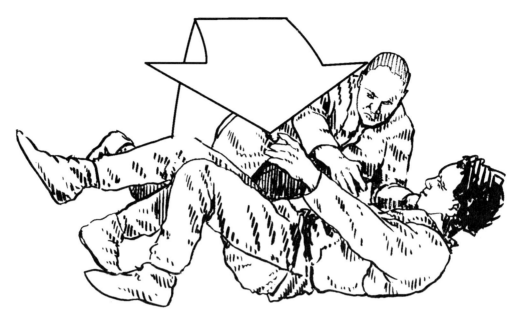

Turn over to the other side from the side with the raised knee. As you do so, pull sharply down with your hand on the same side. Turn the whole body and you will push the opponent off and down beside you.

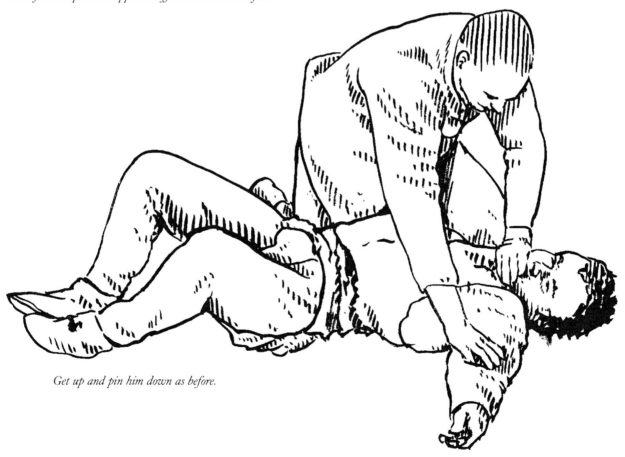

Get up and pin him down as before.

THE THIRD GROUND-FIGHTING TECHNIQUE

When a man has you under him, grab whichever of his hands is uppermost on the side where you can do an arm break, which is often used in wrestling. Take hold with arms and legs using all your strength so that you roll the opponent underneath you, then hold him pinned down as described before.

DAS DRITT UFF STON

Ob dich ain man gar under im hätt so nym war weche hand er oben hat die selben griff nach der sytten an dem arm dass haisst ain bainbruch unnd gat in vil ringen In dem griff vol mitt henden und mitt bainen und mitt gantzem lyb byss du den man under dich bringst So thu der under halder ains alss vor geschriben stat

The opponent has you pinned on the ground and is straddling you.

Take hold of one of the opponent's arms to force it inward against the joint. As you do this, wrap your outer leg around him on the same side and roll him over.

65

THE FIRST MURDER STRIKE

Grab him with the left hand above the belt where you please and strike with your right fist with force to his heart, then grab hold to wrestle as good as you can and continue with techniques and counters. You can use the same techniques and counters in all situations, on horseback or on foot, armed or unarmed, standing or on the ground.

VON MORD STOSSEN DER ERST

Greyff den man mitt der lincken hand ober der gurtel wo du wilt do mitt stoss in mitt diner gerechten zugeschlossen (Fist) mitt kröften an sin hertz do mitt greyff ain ringen so es dir beste werden mag unnd folg dem ringen mitt bruchen und wider bruchen Die selben bruch und wider bruch thu in allen ringen Zu ross/zu fussen/gewäpnet oder bloss/zu lauffens/ligend oder uffstendig

Here you strike your left arm in across his right to prevent any counters to your attack. Step in at this point if you need to close the distance.

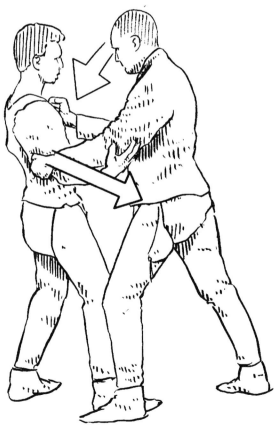

Take hold of his right arm with your left hand and pull him slightly outward and strike with your fist at his heart as hard as you can. To effectively hit the heart, strike in a downward motion, not straight at it but from above and inward. And strike with the knuckles, not the flat bottom of the hand. (NOTE: PRACTICE THIS VERY CAREFULLY!)

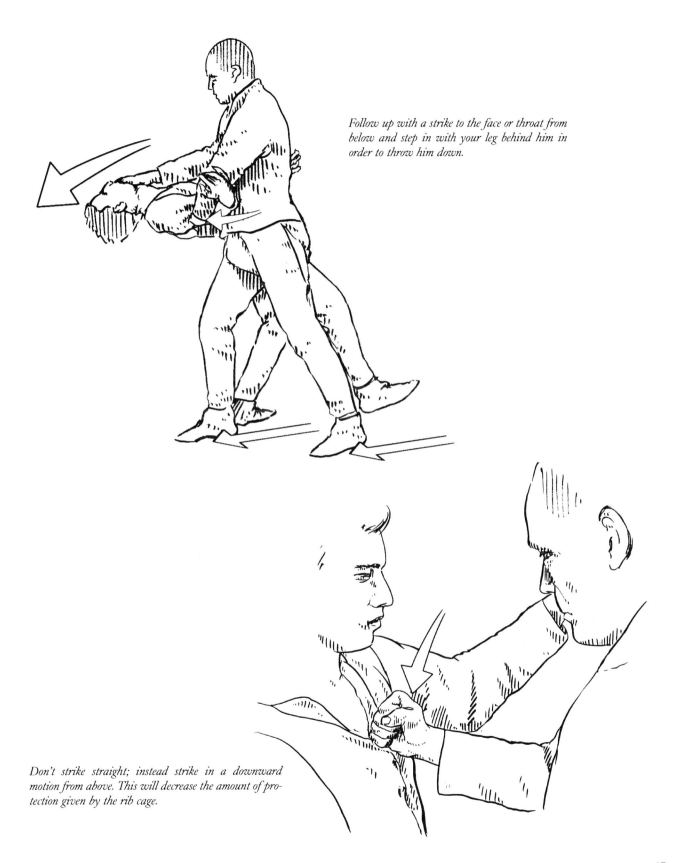

Follow up with a strike to the face or throat from below and step in with your leg behind him in order to throw him down.

Don't strike straight; instead strike in a downward motion from above. This will decrease the amount of protection given by the rib cage.

ANOTHER MURDER STRIKE

Grab hold of him with the left hand above the belt and strike with either knee into his groin from below and follow with strong wrestling techniques.

Note that in all wrestling, use the ground pins when needed and the holds as well, and afterward use murder strikes and leg breaks (throws).

DER ANDER MORT STOSS

Greyff den man an mitt der lincken hand ob der gurtel und stoss im mitt ainem kny mitt welchen du wilt von unden uff an sin hoden und do mitt ain starcks ringen

Item in allen ringen die du tust so nym war underhalden ober gepurt und och uff ston Darnach nym war ob es dir nott tut mort stöss und bain bruch.

From a starting position, deflect his left hand with your right as you step in and grab his right arm from above using your left hand. It does not matter where you take hold above the opponent's belt, just as long as you can pull him toward you and your incoming knee.

Pull him sharply toward you and bring your knee up at the same time. A good follow-up is to throw him backward with a strike to the chin from below as you step behind him. As you knee him, step in with the body–don't just lift the knee, use the whole body in the attack and you can lift him clean of the ground.

The third murder strike

Grab the man above the belt with your left hand and strike with your right hand at his temple as hard as you can. Start at once with your best and strongest wrestling techniques.

Der dritt mort stoss

Greuff den man an mitt der lincken hand ob der gurtel und schlach in mitt gerechten hand zu geschlossen an den schlauff so du hertest magst und domitt ain starck ringen uff din bestes.

From a starting position, grab hold of his left arm to create an opening as you step in with your rear foot. Cock your right hand.

Strike him in the left temple with your fist. Again, strike in a descending motion rather than straight at it.

THE FIRST BONE BREAK

These are common wrestling moves using the arms that are called leg breaks/bone breaks and are done with force. If you take hold of his right arm then step with the right foot behind him and the left foot in front of his leg and thrust him forward over the hip.

VON BAIN BRUCHEN/DER ERST BAIN BRUCH

Das ist das gemain ringen an armen dass do haist ain bain bruch das tryb mitt kröfften Und begryffest du im den gerechten arm so tritt in mitt dem rechten fuss hindersich und versetz im mitt dem lincken fuss fur sin bain und stoss in fur sich uber die huff damit volg

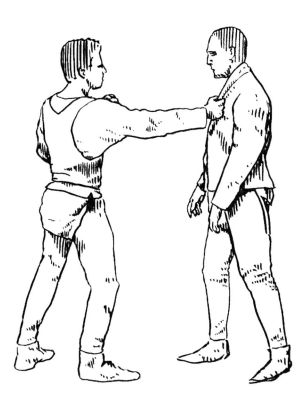

From a basic starting position, the opponent grabs your jacket.

Take hold of his hand with either hand (in this case, the right) to lock it close to your body.

Step in with the left leg in front of his, pivoting as you step to end up with your side/back toward him. As you step, make sure that the opponent's arm/hand is pulled and held close to your body. Then it is a simple thing to throw him over your lead leg, snapping the elbow joint as you go.

A SECOND BONE BREAK

Regardless of which hand he grabs you with, seize his hand using both of your own behind his hand and turn around with your back to his stomach. At the turning lift the arm to your next shoulder and press down so that you break the arm. If he tries a counter, turn around and wrestle.

AIN ANDER BAIN BRUCH

Mitt welcher hand ain man dich an grifft der hand nym war und begryff den arm mitt bayden henden hinder siner hand und wend umb din ruck fur sein bauch An dem umbwenden so heb sin arm uff din nächste achsel und druck do mitt nider so brichst du im do mitt den arm Ob dir der bruch volgt wend dich unb und ring.

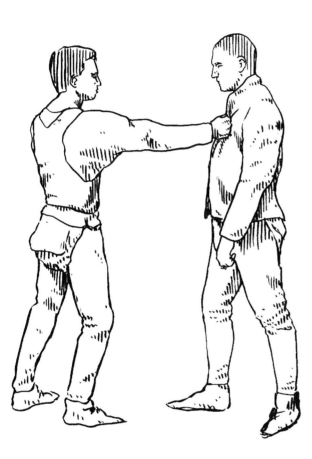

From the same starting position as before, thrust up with your hands from below and take hold of his hand. As you do this, continue to press upward to create space for you to step around.

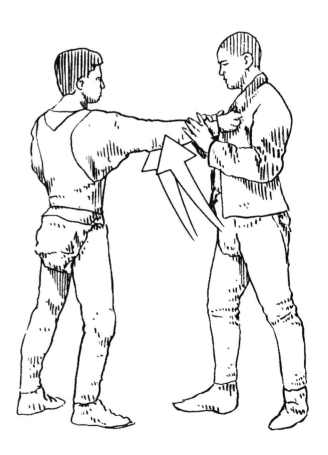

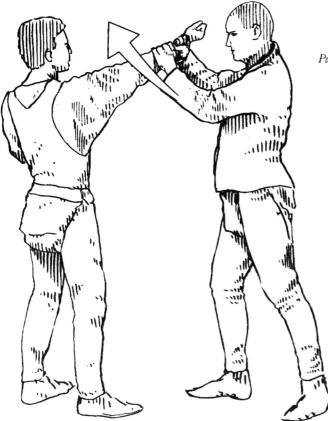

Push upward.

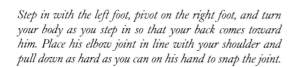

Step in with the left foot, pivot on the right foot, and turn your body as you step in so that your back comes toward him. Place his elbow joint in line with your shoulder and pull down as hard as you can on his hand to snap the joint.

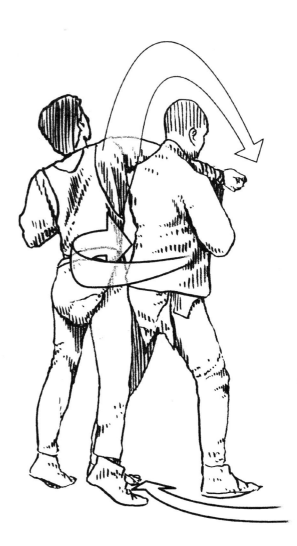

THE THIRD BONE BREAK

When he extends a hand toward you to grab you with either strikes, thrusts, or wrestling, take hold of his hand. Seize it from below with the left hand and take hold with the right through and under his shoulder, and take hold of his arm by the left hand. Step and place your right foot behind his right leg and push backward over your thigh and hold him in the grip.

DER DRITT BAIN BRUCH

Wie dir ainer die hand zaygt und will dich gryffen mitt schlengenn oder mitt stossen oder mitt ringen der hand nym war und begryff sy von unden uff mitt der lincken hand Und gryff mitt der rechten hand durch sin uchsen an dem selben arm by derlincken hand Zu lauff und versetz din rechten fuss hiinder sin rechts bain und truck in hindersich uber die lende Do mitt thu ain griff und halt in föst

Again the opponent reaches out to take hold of you (of course, this can happen in myriad ways). In response, you take hold of his hand.

Step forward as you take hold and begin to twist his shoulder and elbow joint.

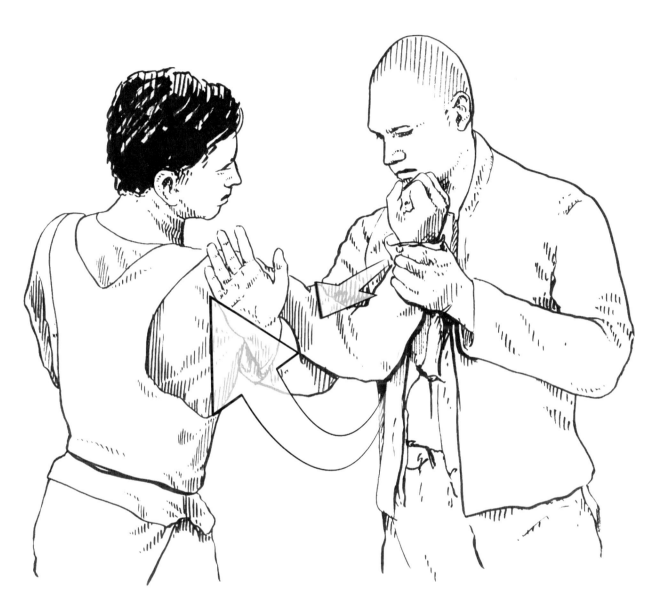

Let your free arm and hand strike from below to create an angle in his elbow joint as you press your other hand back and down.

THE FOURTH BONE BREAK

Take hold of whatever hand he extends to grip as in the previous technique, and move through with your head under the same arm and pull hard on his arm, then pull up his nearest leg, and then he will fall.

DER VIERD BAINBRUCH

Mitt wölcher hand dich ainer angrifft der selben hand nym war und begryff im die hand alss du tust in dem andern bain bruchen und wisch im mitt dem haupt und lyb durch den selben arm und truck im dann syn arm hart Und ruck im denn sin nechsten fuss so fölt er

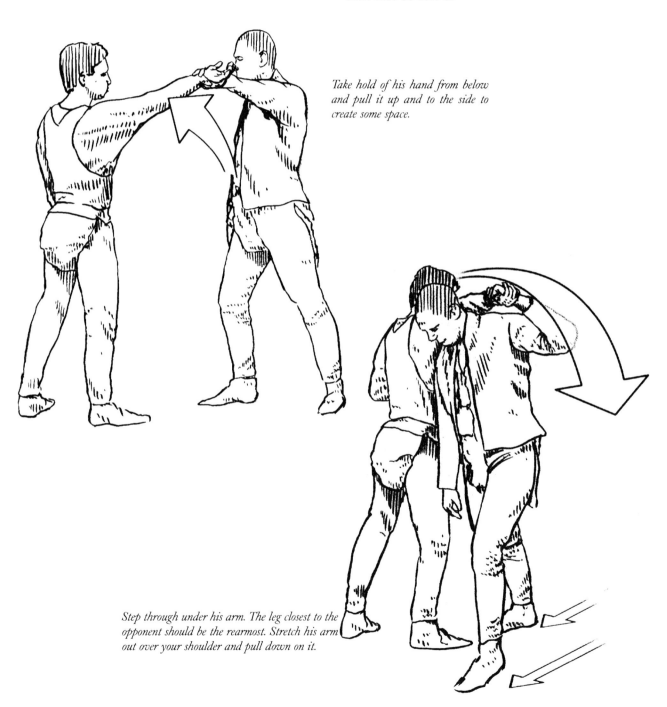

Take hold of his hand from below and pull it up and to the side to create some space.

Step through under his arm. The leg closest to the opponent should be the rearmost. Stretch his arm out over your shoulder and pull down on it.

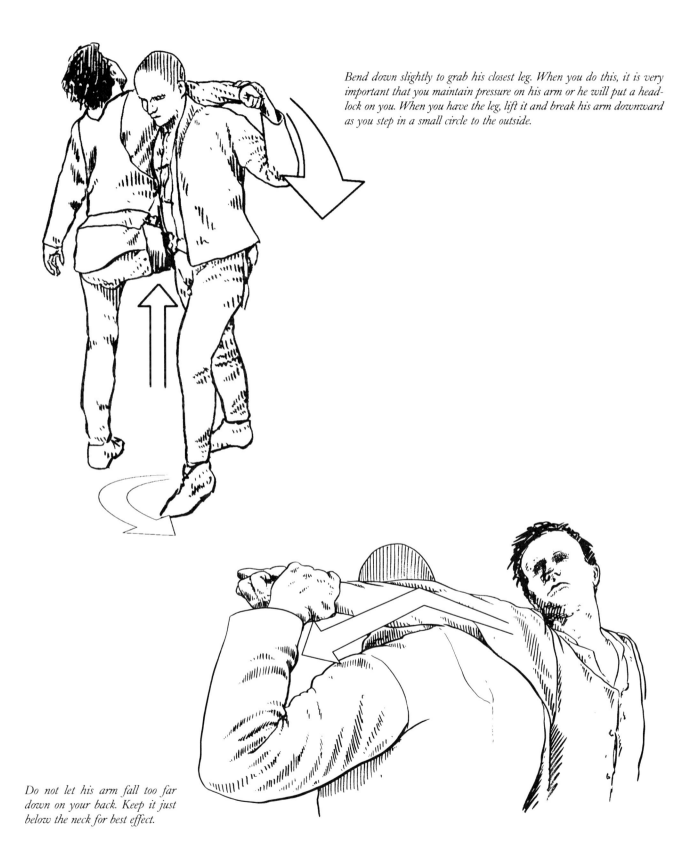

Bend down slightly to grab his closest leg. When you do this, it is very important that you maintain pressure on his arm or he will put a head-lock on you. When you have the leg, lift it and break his arm downward as you step in a small circle to the outside.

Do not let his arm fall too far down on your back. Keep it just below the neck for best effect.

At the leg there are two counters
The first
Take hold of his leg with both hands over the ankle and the other at the knee, and from here you can break the leg.

In dem bain sind zwen brich
Der erst
Begryff im sin bain mitt baiden henden an mitt der ainen hand ober dem enckel mitt der andern an das kny Das gät dar alss der erst bainbruch

Here we did not really know what to make of the text. We interpreted it to mean that you have already seized a leg at the ankle, since it does not make much sense to bend down to look for one.

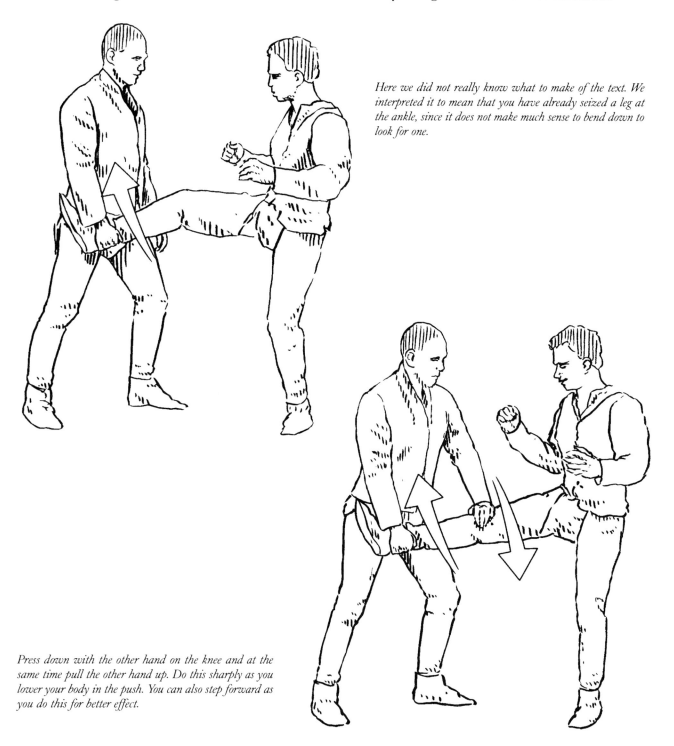

Press down with the other hand on the knee and at the same time pull the other hand up. Do this sharply as you lower your body in the push. You can also step forward as you do this for better effect.

THE OTHER COUNTER

Take hold of a leg and yank it over your shoulder: thus you break the leg.

DER ANDER BRUCH

Begreyff im ain bain ober dem anckel mitt baiden henden und ruck im das uber die achsel so bruchst du im das bain

Take hold of the leg and raise it as high as possible and at the same time push it toward your opponent.

A MURDER STRIKE

Thrust with both fists as hard as you can at the throat, then wrestle.

AIN MORT STOSS

Stoss in mitt baiden fernnsten henden zu geschlossen so du hartest magst an den halss Darnach ring

A strike to the throat using both hands must come from the sides. Try to hit inward and down with clenched fists. (An option is to thrust from the front, but this will push him back.)

A close-up of the neck strike.

A possible follow-up: take hold of his head (your hands are already there) and give him a solid head butt. Aim for the nose and mouth area using your forehead. This is one of my absolute favorites. [On this page are the authors' own variations.]

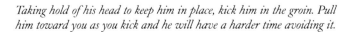

Taking hold of his head to keep him in place, kick him in the groin. Pull him toward you as you kick and he will have a harder time avoiding it.

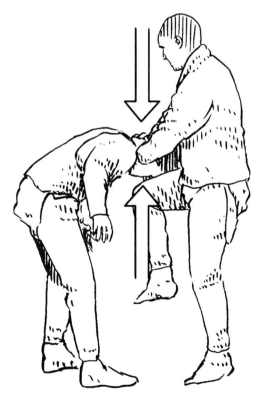

Taking hold of his head, push it sharply down and at the same time thrust your knee up as hard as you can.

A MURDER STRIKE

Put both thumbs in his cheeks and the other fingers over his head and strike/push as hard as you can with the right hand.

AIN MORT STOSS

Tu im bayde daumen in bayde bachen und die andern finger oben an dass haupt und stoss in mitt der rechten hand mitt gantzer macht

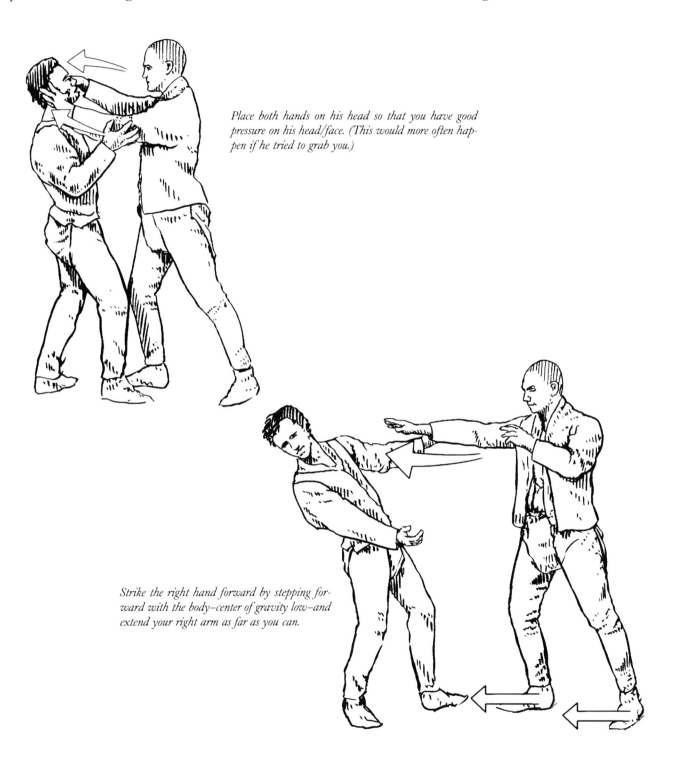

Place both hands on his head so that you have good pressure on his head/face. (This would more often happen if he tried to grab you.)

Strike the right hand forward by stepping forward with the body—center of gravity low—and extend your right arm as far as you can.

A MURDER STRIKE

Strike as hard as you can at his navel with your right hand. Note, use your left arm to take hold of his right arm biceps and with your right hand grab him around his left side and hold him with force behind by the jacket or hoses and move your arse in front of his hip so that your right leg gets in front of his right and then throw him over your hip.

AIN MORT STOSS

Stoss in mitt der rechten hand an den nabel so du hertest magst Item nym din lincken arm und gryff im uff sin rechten arm uff die mauss (Biceps) und mitt dine rechten hand fall im umb syn lincke sytten und halt in föst hinden by der juppen oder hosen und wirf im denn dinen arss in sin schoss also das din recht bain vor sinem rechten stee und in dem selbigen wirff in uber die huff

Strike as hard as you can at his lower abdomen to soften him up. Step forward as you strike, keeping your mass low and using the hips in the strike.

Step behind him with your right foot and take hold of his right biceps with your left hand. Grab him around the waist with the right arm and throw him with a turning motion from right to left.

85

A COUNTER

Note that when he wants to throw you over his hip when you are behind him, take your left arm and strike it around his [arm] or over his throat and push backward toward your left side, thus you will throw him.

AIN BRUCH

Item wann dich ainer uber die huff will werfen so du hinder im stäst so nym din lincken arm und schlach i umb syn halss und druck in hindersich gegen diner lincken sytten so wirffest du in

The opponent has stepped in and is preparing to throw you over his hip. This is bad.

Thrust your left arm in front of or around the opponent's neck.

Press backward to your left side, using your right hand for help at the neck or around the opponent's waist.

NOTE THAT WHEN someone is behind you and you want to counter the first technique [above], then bend backward just as if you were falling to the rear, grab his left leg with your left hand and pull it upward–then you will throw him.

ITEM WANN AINER hinder dich stät und will dir das erst stuck brechen so buck dich hindersich sam du hindersich wöllest fallen begriff im mitt der lincken hand sin linck bain und rucks im ubersich so wirffst du in

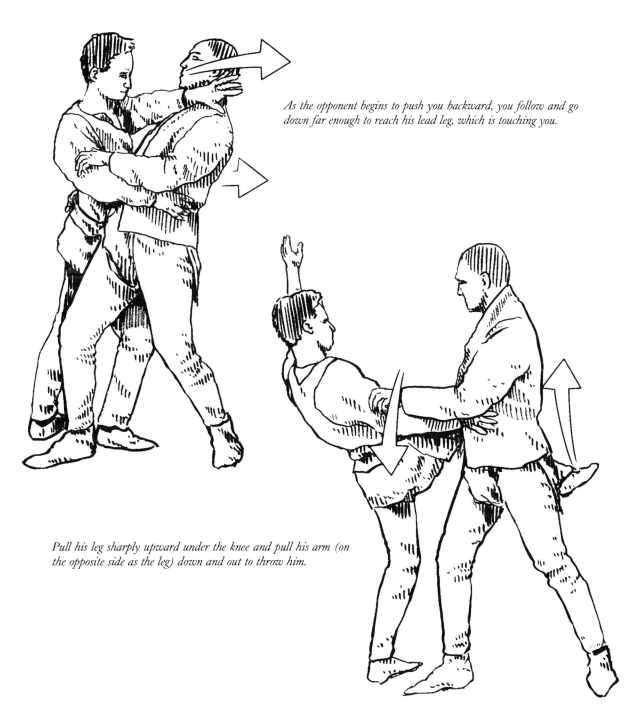

As the opponent begins to push you backward, you follow and go down far enough to reach his lead leg, which is touching you.

Pull his leg sharply upward under the knee and pull his arm (on the opposite side as the leg) down and out to throw him.

NOTE, FALL WITH your left hand on his right arm, grab his biceps and hold him. With your right arm around his left side, place your right leg on the inside close to his right leg. And at the same time go down to your right side and take hold of his right leg with your left hand below by the arse and then throw him.

ITEM FALL IM mitt diner lincken hand uff sin rechten uff die mauss und fall im och mitt dinem rechten arm umb syn lincken sytten und setz im din recht bain inwendig wol hin an zu sinem rechten bain Und in dem selbigen dree dich umb gegen diner rechten sytten und begryff im mitt diner lincken hand sin recht bain oben by dem arssbacken so wirfest du in

Grab his left arm as you step in to throw.

Step in again with the rear leg and, as you do so, take hold around his waist with the right hand.

Drop your center of gravity by bending at the knees so that you can reach behind his right knee. It is important that you bend with the knees and not with the back.

Pull his right leg sharply up and back and, at the same time, straighten your legs and push your weight forward to take his balance. Your legs should not, however, become straight, as this will knock you off balance. You can also take a small step forward as you straighten up.

HERE ARE OTHER good wrestling and counter techniques

Note that when someone has hold of you by the arms and you have placed the left foot forward and he has his right foot close by your left on the outside and tries to pull you over using his arms, then pull your foot backward quickly. And at the same time take hold of his right foot and thrust him in the chest and he will fall.

HIE HEBEN SICH an andere gutte ringen und bruch

Item wann dich ainer gefasst hät in den armen und du in wider und redtlich den lincken fuss furgesetzt hat und er also gesteyd dass er dir mitt sinem rechten fuss schreyt usswendig wider dinen lincken und will dich by den armen daruber rucken so ruck dinen fuss frisch hindersich uff zu ruck Und fass im damitt sinen rechten fuss und stoss in oben fur die brust so fölt er

The opponent is preparing a throw or pull you over his lead leg, supposedly after closing in to place the hold.

Bend at the knees to take hold behind his knee; quickly step back with your lead foot as you do this. Then straighten up and thrust him in the chest or punch him in the face as you pull his leg back and up.

ANOTHER WRESTLING TECHNIQUE

As he grabs you around the shoulders from behind, push your arm up by the opponent's elbow on the side with his leading foot. With the other hand, help push out on the side outward on the opposite side. Hold his arm with your hand and with the other hand take hold of him by the throat. With the foot, step down on the side of his knee of his forward leg that has the heel toward you.

ABER AIN RINGEN

Item ob dich ainer ferr hinden begrifft uber den achseln far uber mitt dinem arm in die waich sins elbogens an der sytten do er fuss vor stät und mitt der andern hand hilff zu dir trucken uff die sytten usswendig genubenn Und halt im den arm mitt der ainen hand und mitt der anderen hand gryff im in die dross (*drossel, Kehle*) und mitt dem fuss tritt in die knybugen sines usgesetzen fuss zu dir gespert mitt der fersen

A grab from behind.

The freeing action is accomplished by pushing up with one elbow and outward with the other. You unbalance the opponent and make it difficult for him to retain his hold. Do this with a strong movement as you lower your center of gravity slightly by bending the knees.

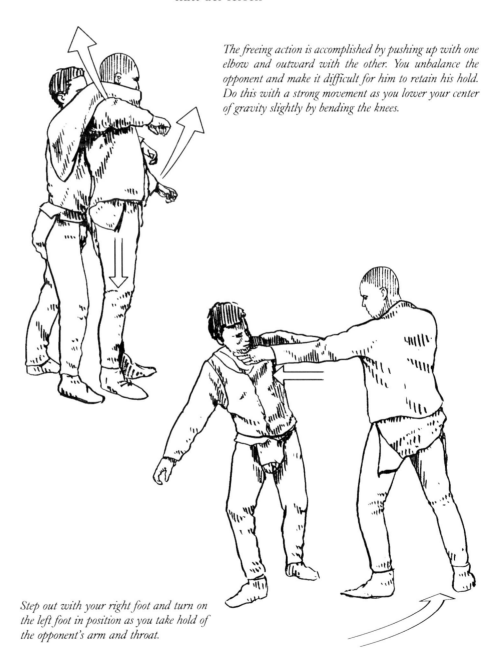

Step out with your right foot and turn on the left foot in position as you take hold of the opponent's arm and throat.

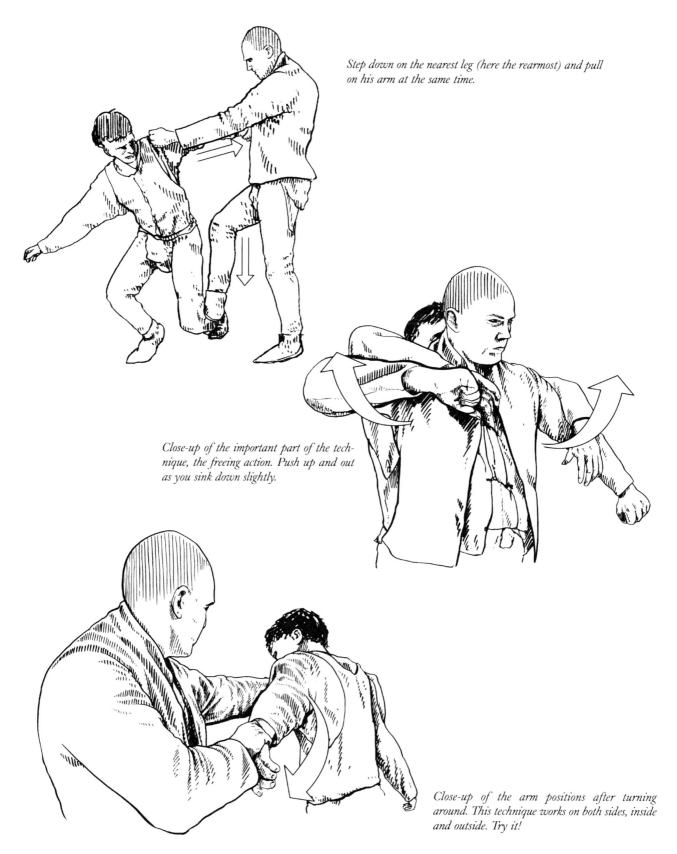

Step down on the nearest leg (here the rearmost) and pull on his arm at the same time.

Close-up of the important part of the technique, the freeing action. Push up and out as you sink down slightly.

Close-up of the arm positions after turning around. This technique works on both sides, inside and outside. Try it!

ANOTHER WRESTLING TECHNIQUE

Note, strike him with your right hand and grab his finger on his right hand. And with the left hand strike his right arm that you seized, upward over him and throw him over your left leg.

ABER AIN RINGEN

Item schlach uss mitt diner rechten hand und begryff im die finger siner rechten hand Und mitt der lincken hand siner rechten arm ubersich geschlagen vornen gefasst und zu ruck geworfen uber din lincks bayn

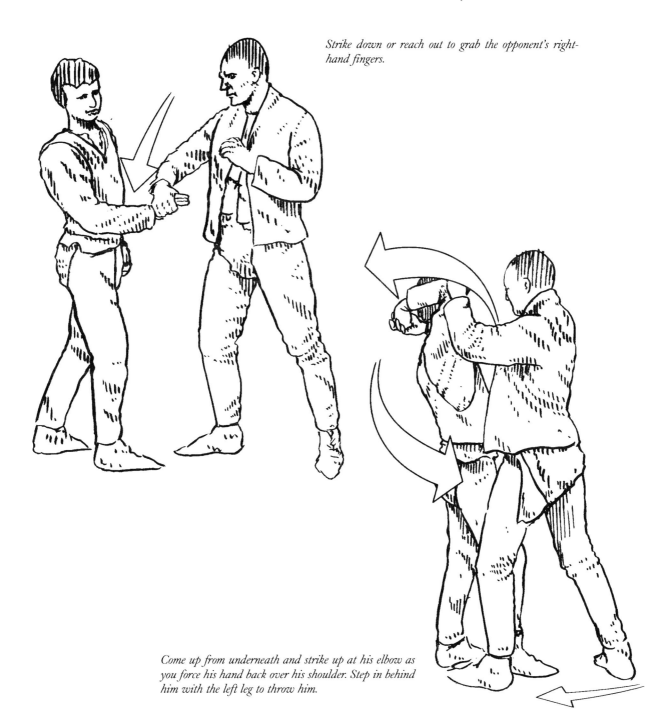

Strike down or reach out to grab the opponent's right-hand fingers.

Come up from underneath and strike up at his elbow as you force his hand back over his shoulder. Step in behind him with the left leg to throw him.

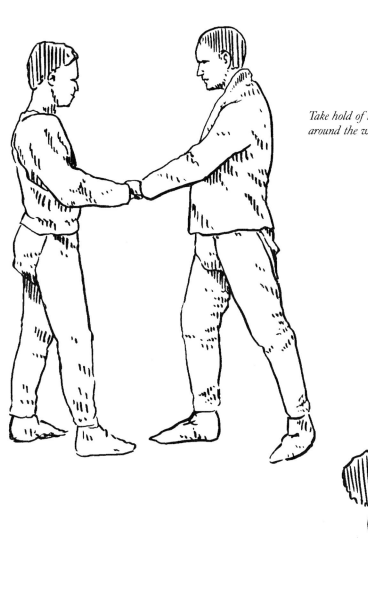

Take hold of the opponent's right hand with your right hand, then grab around the wrist from above, your thumb on the outside of his wrist.

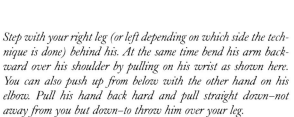

Step with your right leg (or left depending on which side the technique is done) behind his. At the same time bend his arm backward over his shoulder by pulling on his wrist as shown here. You can also push up from below with the other hand on his elbow. Pull his hand back hard and pull straight down—not away from you but down—to throw him over your leg.

ANOTHER WRESTLING TECHNIQUE

Note, strike out his left hand with your right hand. Go between his legs with your hand and take hold of him by the body or the elbow. Lift him and strike him away from you with the left hand so that he falls backward on his head.

ABER AIN RINGEN

Item schlag uss mitt diner rechten hand sin lincke Und im mitt (der) hand zwischen der bain durchfarn und fass in hinden by dem wames oder by dem elnbogen und heb in uff und stoss in eben von dir mitt der lincken hand so feldt er hindersich uff den kopff

Strike his right hand out to the side to create an opening, allowing you space to close in.

Take a quick, strong step in close and take solid hold between his legs. Then, strike him in the throat with the left elbow to push him away from you.

95

A counter against the wrestler who takes hold of you between the legs.

Note, break it when someone has a grip with his right hand between your legs and hold you fast by the body. Then bend over with your head against him and go downward with your hands to his right arm with both arms and pull upward–then he can't throw you. (Pulling upward against the elbow joint.)

AIN BRUCH WIDER dass ringen so dir ainer mitt der rechten hand durch din bain fört

Item also brich dass Wann dir ainer mitt siner rechten hand zwischen dine bain durch fört und fast dich hinden by dem wammes so buck dich mitt dinem haupt gegen im und far von ussen unden durch sin rechten arm mitt den baiden armen und heb da mitt ubersich so mag er dich nicht werffen

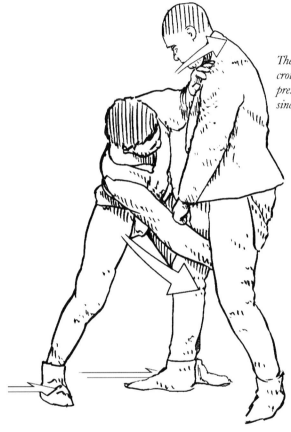

The opponent has a hold of both your body and crotch. This is very bad. But dropping and pressing his arm down will prevent a throw since he is weaker than you in this position.

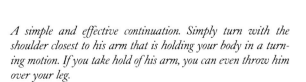

A simple and effective continuation. Simply turn with the shoulder closest to his arm that is holding your body in a turning motion. If you take hold of his arm, you can even throw him over your leg.

ANOTHER WRESTLING TECHNIQUE

Note that when someone grabs holds of you by the hand with both of his and pulls down and has you by the left hand and wants to pull you to his right side, then let your right hand go over and through his left arm to his right side and take hold of his breast with the right hand and go with the left grab him behind the knee.

ABER AIN RINGEN

Item ob dich ainer by ainer hand begryfft und dich neben sich ruckt mitt sinen baiden henden und hatt dich gefasst by der lincken hand und wolt dich rucken uff sin rechte sytten so lauss din rechte hand oben durch sin lincken arm in sin rechte sytten und fass in in der brust mitt der rechten und mitt der tencken fall im in ain knybug

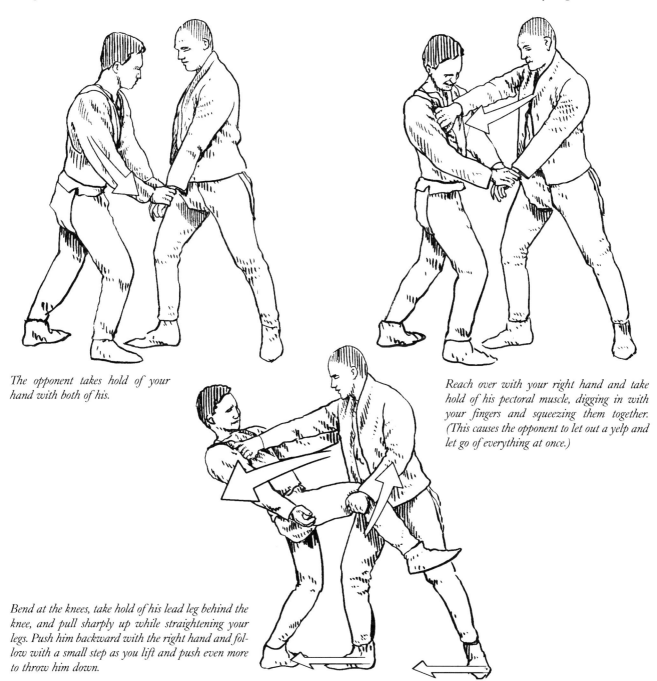

The opponent takes hold of your hand with both of his.

Reach over with your right hand and take hold of his pectoral muscle, digging in with your fingers and squeezing them together. (This causes the opponent to let out a yelp and let go of everything at once.)

Bend at the knees, take hold of his lead leg behind the knee, and pull sharply up while straightening your legs. Push him backward with the right hand and follow with a small step as you lift and push even more to throw him down.

97

ANOTHER WRESTLING TECHNIQUE

If someone takes hold of your chest with both hands, go between and above with the right over his left hand. With the left hand go to his elbow and trip him with the right foot.

ABER AIN RINGEN

Item fasst dich ainer fornen by der brust mitt bayden henden so far oben durch mitt der rechten uber sin lincke hand unnd awing im die und mitt der lincken hand (far) an sin elnbogen und schrenck (*daruber zu werfen*) mitt dem rechten fuss

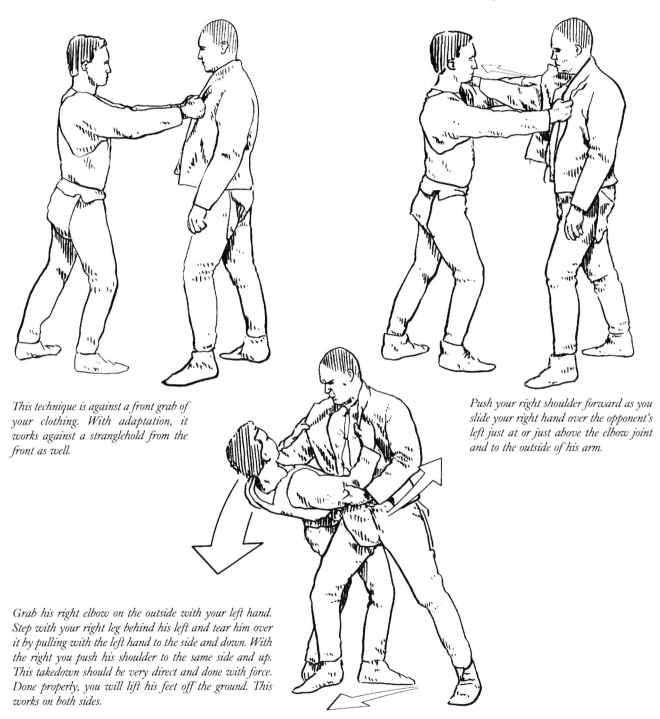

This technique is against a front grab of your clothing. With adaptation, it works against a stranglehold from the front as well.

Push your right shoulder forward as you slide your right hand over the opponent's left just at or just above the elbow joint and to the outside of his arm.

Grab his right elbow on the outside with your left hand. Step with your right leg behind his left and tear him over it by pulling with the left hand to the side and down. With the right you push his shoulder to the same side and up. This takedown should be very direct and done with force. Done properly, you will lift his feet off the ground. This works on both sides.

ANOTHER WRESTLING TECHNIQUE

Note, if he does an arm lever technique to your arm, then with your right hand make a lever against him with the left.

ABER AIN RINGEN

Item wider schrenck in armen ain bruch wann dir ainer schrencken will mitt der rechten hand so schrenck im mitt der lincken

The opponent has placed a figure-four lock on your right arm. (Other arm locks done from the front or side usually work as well, and you may need to adapt the technique a bit.)

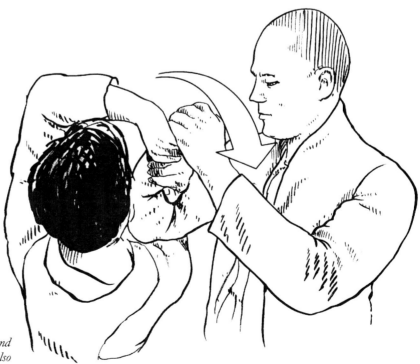

Simply place your free hand on your other hand and pull sharply to the side and down. It is also nice to step in behind him as you do this

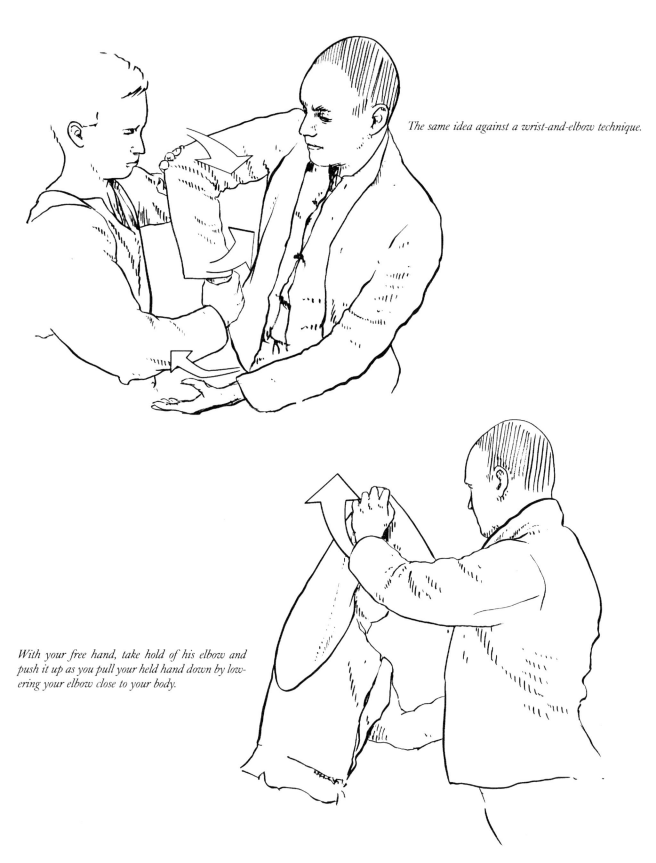

The same idea against a wrist-and-elbow technique.

With your free hand, take hold of his elbow and push it up as you pull your held hand down by lowering your elbow close to your body.

ANOTHER WRESTLING TECHNIQUE

Note, strike away with both hands and fall with the hands behind his knees, and pull toward you and at the same time strike him in the chest with your head and throw him on his back.

ABER AIN RINGEN

Item schlach uss mitt bayden henden und fall mitt bayden henden in baid knybug und zuch zu dir und stoss in mitt dem knopff oben fur die brust und wirff in zu ruck

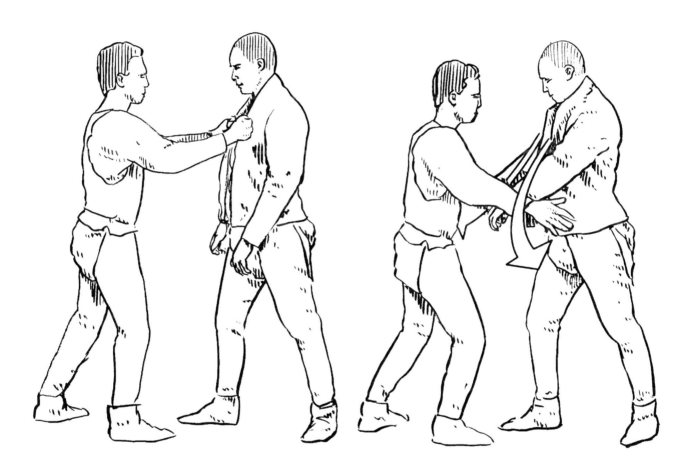

If your opponent has taken hold of you in front, or if he holds his hands out in front of him, bring your hands up and inside his arms and strike down and outward just behind his hands.

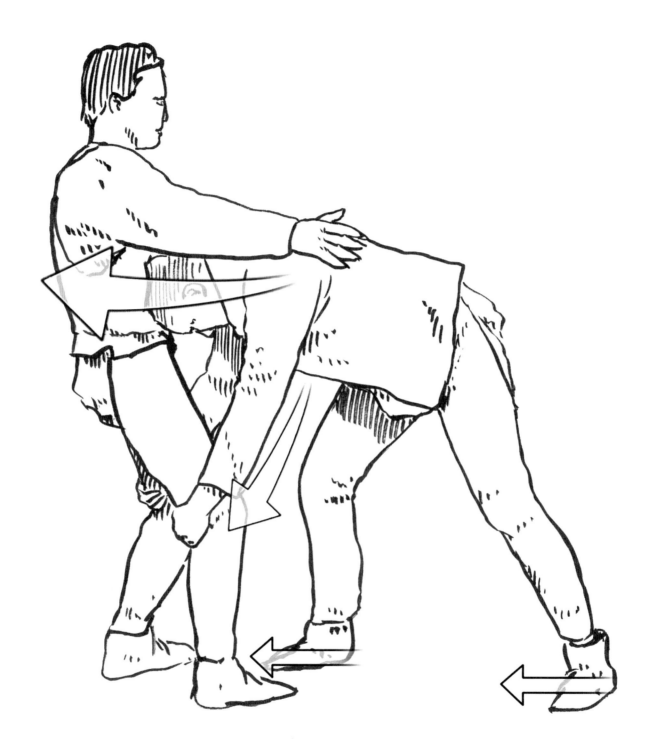

Bend down and take hold behind his knees and, as you do so, place your head in his chest. When you have a hold, push with the head and pull with the hands and you will see something funny! It is important to pull upward sharply with the hands, as if you were trying to reach your armpits.

A COUNTER TO THE WRESTLING TECHNIQUE (ABOVE)

Take hold of him from above through his armpits and hold him fast. Step back so that he cannot seize your legs, and then press him to the ground.

AIN BRUCH WIDER DASS RINGEN

Item, also brich dass fass in oben by dem halss under den yechsen (Shoulder/armpit) und leg dich fast oben uff in Und tritt wol zu ruck mitt den fussen das er dir kainen begryffen mug so truckst du in zu der erden

When the opponent tries that on you, bend down, take hold around his chest, and take two steps back starting with your leading foot. Lower your center of gravity to prevent him from throwing you.

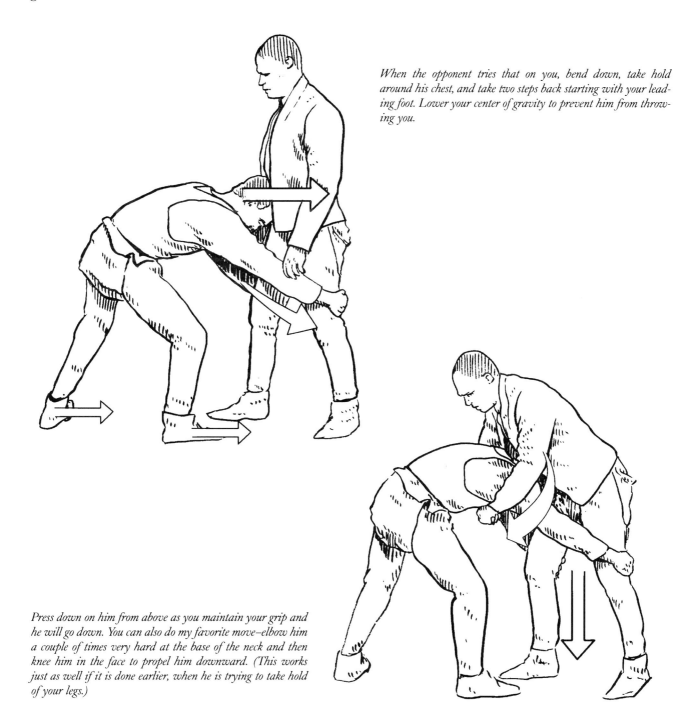

Press down on him from above as you maintain your grip and he will go down. You can also do my favorite move–elbow him a couple of times very hard at the base of the neck and then knee him in the face to propel him downward. (This works just as well if it is done earlier, when he is trying to take hold of your legs.)

ANOTHER WRESTLING TECHNIQUE

Note, if he leads with his right foot, then go in with the left hand and pull his right arm and strike him at the ankle/joint of his right foot and push him over. Or go with the right hand to his throat and push him backward (over his back).

ABER AIN RINGEN

Item, ob er den rechten fuss fursetzt so zuch in mitt der lincken hand by syner rechten hand Und schlag in an den enckel sines rechten fuss und truck in nider Oder fall im mitt der rechten hand in die kel und truck in uber ruck

This is somewhat unclear instruction since Ringeck is literally asking us to hit the opponent's foot with our fist—not the best idea. So we have done an alternate entering move. Try going for the ankle and tossing him over your back—it works also, and is a bit less dangerous than bending down to strike his foot.

Grab the wrist and pull out to the side.

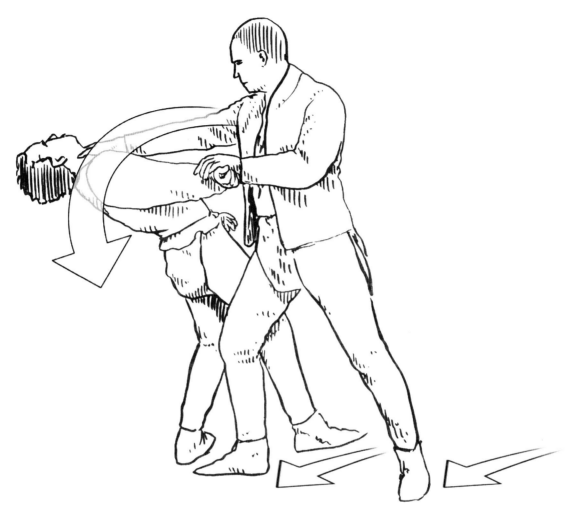

Step in behind his lead leg and strike his throat to throw him backward.

ANOTHER WRESTLING TECHNIQUE

If he holds you by the arms only then with your left hand take hold of his right and hold him tight and strike with your right. Go through under his right arm and take hold around his chest and with the left at the knee.

ABER AIN RINGEN

Item, halt dich ainer bloss by dinen armen so griff mitt der lincken hand nach siner rechten und begriff in by sinem umgernn und halt in vast und schlag uff mitt diner rechten und far im durch under sinem rechten arm und fach in in der brust Mitt der lincken *fall* in ain knybug

The opponent holds your arms. (You can try other holds as well, and they usually work.)

Grab hold of his right hand and pull it close to you. Bring your right arm up and over his left, making him lose his grip.

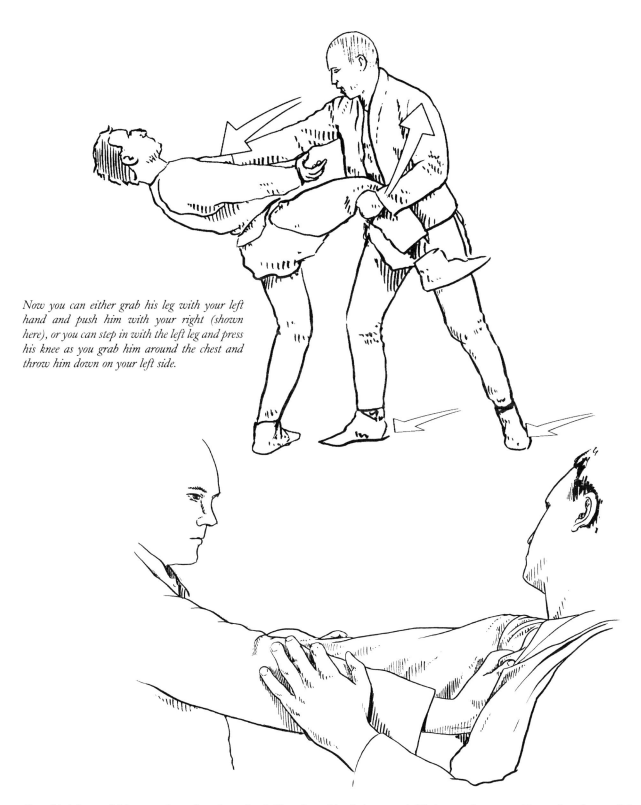

Now you can either grab his leg with your left hand and push him with your right (shown here), or you can step in with the left leg and press his knee as you grab him around the chest and throw him down on your left side.

For added fun, grab his pectoral muscle and use that hold to throw him. It is very painful since you hang on to his muscle as he goes flying. Dig your fingers in and twist the grip a bit–it works wonders to convince him to go where you want him to go.

ANOTHER WRESTLING TECHNIQUE

Note, if he take should of you by the belt from [behind] then push your self down [*sink down*] If he tries to pull you up then turn around against him and throw him over a barrier [*a leg perhaps?*].

ABER AIN RINGEN

Item, fast dich ainer hinden by der gurtel so truck dich nider Und wan er dich erhöpt so wend umb under im und wirf in uber schrancken

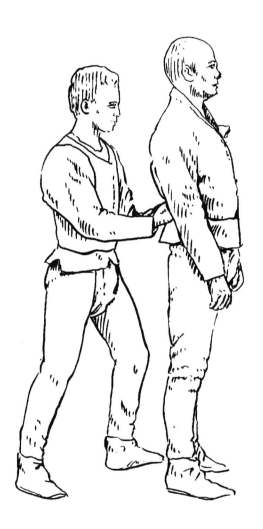 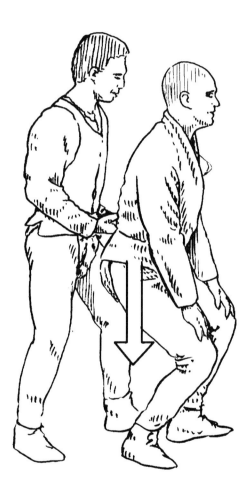

Here is a possible interpretation that works well. If he seizes you from behind, let yourself sink down. Lowering your center of gravity will make you more difficult to lift, preventing him from throwing you.

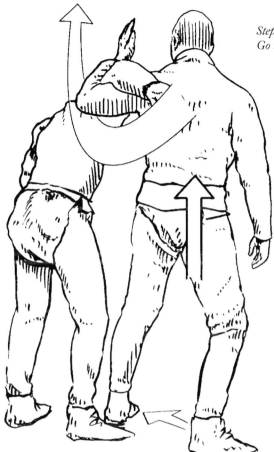

Step slightly to the outside with either leg and slip the opposite arm to the rear. Go up with it behind his elbow, which will turn his arm.

Throw him over your leg by moving your arm, which is wrapped around his, forward and down.

ANOTHER WRESTLING TECHNIQUE

Note, go through with your right hand and grab hold of his waist on the side. Go with the left hand over and through his right shoulder and seize his right hand at the wrist and hold it tightly, then pull him up and with your right arm lift his left knee and throw him before you.

ABER AIN RINGEN

Item, gee mitt der rechten hannd durch und fach in oberhalb der huff in der waiche Und far mitt der lincken hand oben durch sin rechten uchsen und fach den sin rechte hand im glenck und halt die föst und heb in uff Und mitt dinem rechten arm erheb im sin lincke kny und wirff in fur dich

---

ANOTHER WRESTLING TECHNIQUE

Note, seize his left hand with both your hands and pull it to your right side. Step in with your right foot behind his right and go with your right arm to his left side and throw him over your right foot.

ABER AIN RINGEN

Item, begryff im sin lincke hand mitt baiden henden und zeuch in uff din rechte sytten Und schryt mitt dinem rechten fuss hinder sin rechten und far im mitt dem rechten arm in sin lincke sytten Und wurff in uber dein rechten fuss

From a starting position, take hold of his hands without stepping.

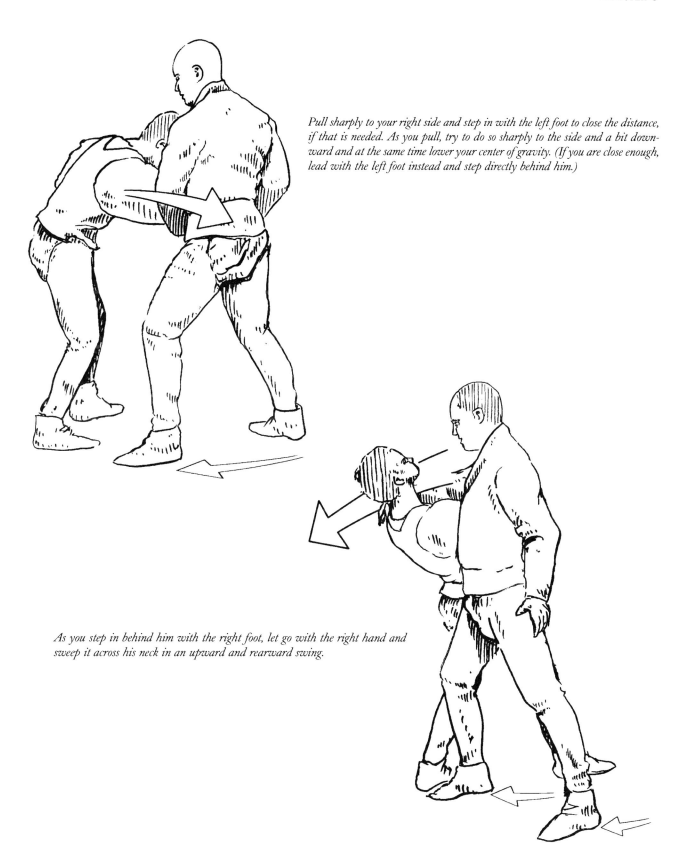

Pull sharply to your right side and step in with the left foot to close the distance, if that is needed. As you pull, try to do so sharply to the side and a bit downward and at the same time lower your center of gravity. (If you are close enough, lead with the left foot instead and step directly behind him.)

As you step in behind him with the right foot, let go with the right hand and sweep it across his neck in an upward and rearward swing.

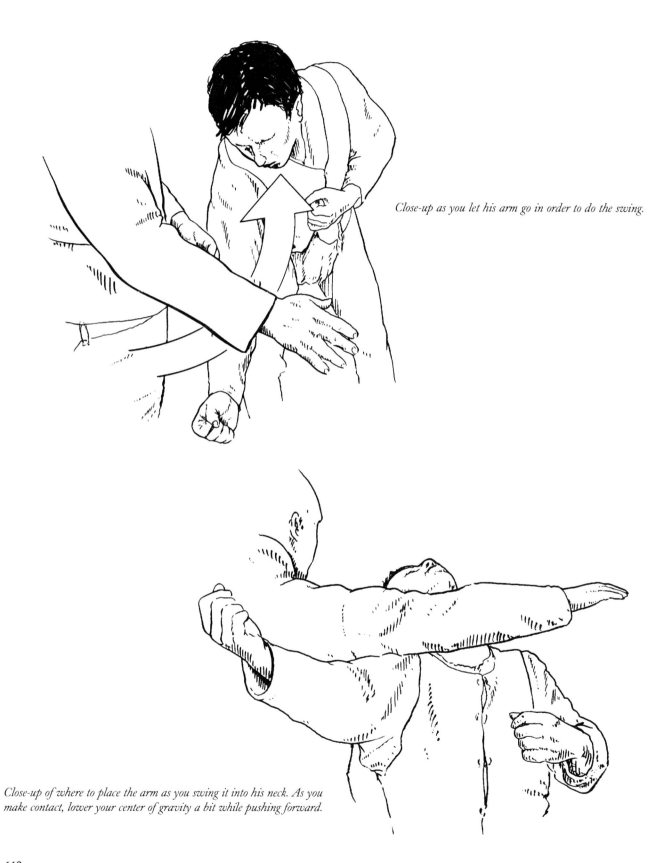

Close-up as you let his arm go in order to do the swing.

Close-up of where to place the arm as you swing it into his neck. As you make contact, lower your center of gravity a bit while pushing forward.

ANOTHER WRESTLING TECHNIQUE

Note that when he wants to seize you with both arms under your shoulders, then bring both your hands down from above on the outside and under his elbows. Close your arms together and throw upward with force to break his arms.

Note that you can also grab him by the throat and push him back.

ABER AIN RINGEN

Item, wann dir aber ainer mitt baiden armen will under faren under dine baid arm so far von oben nider mitt dinen baiden armen ussen under sin elnbogen und schluss diin arm zesamen under sin elnbogen und heb mitt störcke ubersich und brich im die arm

Item, so magstu im in die kel fallen und in zu ruck trucken

From a starting position, your opponent slips his arms under yours and clasps his hand on your back.

As he does so, sweep your arms outside of his and down, then lift your hands up on the inside. As you do this, you will straighten and lock his elbow joints and apply pressure on them from below.

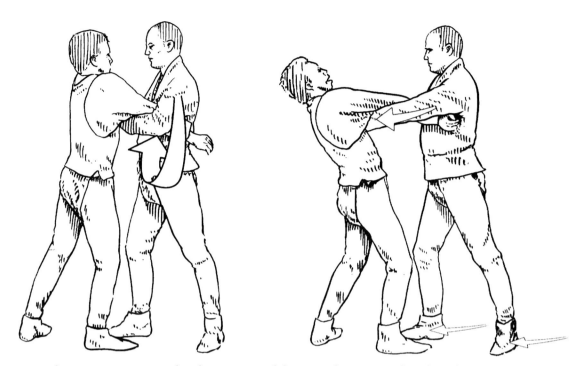

You can then press up even more and at the same time push him away from you in order to break his grip.

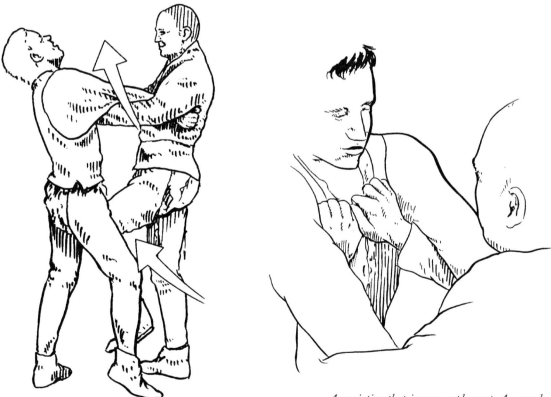

When you have this solid grip, don't forget that since he can't move any-where, you can knee him in the groin.

A variation that is very unpleasant. As your hands come up, grip his breast muscles firmly and twist and pull up as hard as you can.

NOTE, ANOTHER WRESTLING TECHNIQUE

Note, when you are above with your arms you can seize him by the throat or by the jaw and break his neck over his back. Or you must move your arms under his arms.

ITEM ABER AIN RINGEN

Item, wann du (*oben*) bist mitt dinen armen so magst du in oben fassen by der kelen oder by dem knybacken und im den halss wol uber den rucken brechen Oder du must wol mitt dinen armen durch sin arm faren

If you are in close with your opponent, you can always seize his throat. This is done most easily when your hands are on top.

When you have a grip, press your opponent back to counter his attack or counter.

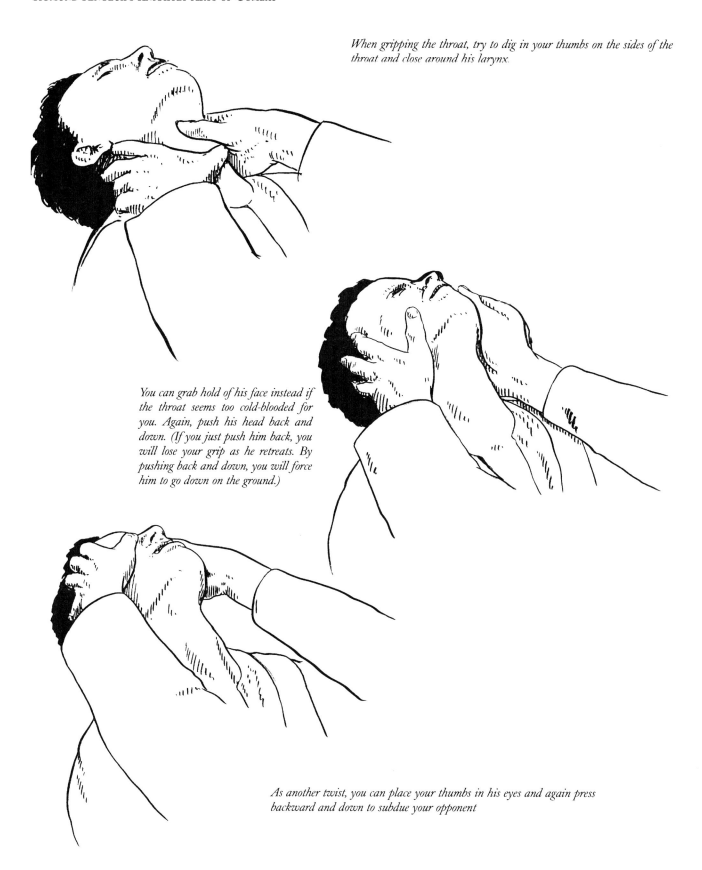

When gripping the throat, try to dig in your thumbs on the sides of the throat and close around his larynx.

You can grab hold of his face instead if the throat seems too cold-blooded for you. Again, push his head back and down. (If you just push him back, you will lose your grip as he retreats. By pushing back and down, you will force him to go down on the ground.)

As another twist, you can place your thumbs in his eyes and again press backward and down to subdue your opponent

ANOTHER WRESTLING TECHNIQUE

If your left hand is low, then go with your right hand to his throat and step with the left foot behind him and push him over it by pushing on his throat. Note that you can throw him to both sides over your foot.

ABER AIN RINGEN

Item, bist du mitt dem lincken arm under so fall im mitt dem rechten in die kel und schrytt mitt dem lincken fuss hindersich und truck in dar uber by dem halss Item, wirff in uff den fuss zuo baiden sytten

---

ANOTHER WRESTLING TECHNIQUE

If you push both your arms through and under his arms, then if he is of your size or smaller seize him around the waist, close your hands fast on his back and lift him on your left side. If you can, push him downward to the ground with his back over your knee.

ABER AIN RINGEN

Item, wann du ainem mitt baiden armen durch sin arm gefaren bist und ist er also gering alss du bist oder ringer so fass in in der mitte und schluss dine hend fast zu samen uff sinem rucken und heb in uff die lincke sytten Unnd wenn du dich aines umb getrawest so stoss in nider uff die kny und brich im der ruck zu dir

As you close in you can lead with either leg. Put your face close to his shoulder, which will make it harder for him to strike you or give you a head butt. Lock your hands on his back.

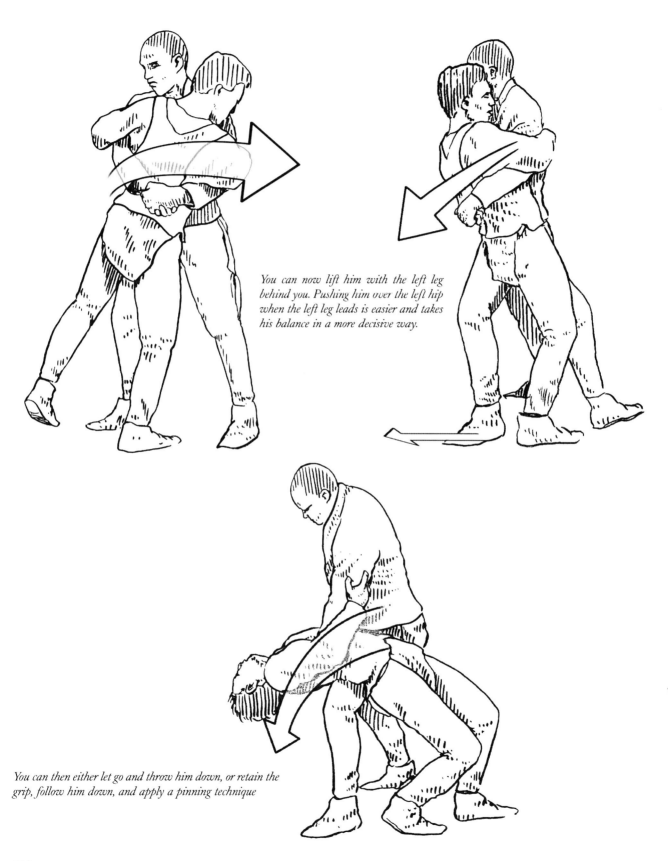

You can now lift him with the left leg behind you. Pushing him over the left hip when the left leg leads is easier and takes his balance in a more decisive way.

You can then either let go and throw him down, or retain the grip, follow him down, and apply a pinning technique

A WRESTLING TECHNIQUE

If he pulls you toward him (an around-the-chest hold from the front), then place your elbow at his throat or in his chest and push him away from you with force. At the same time step back with the left foot.

Item, also brich das Wann dich ainer zu im truckt so setz die elnbogen in kel oder in die brust und truck in von dir zubehent unnd dass din lincker fuss zu ruck stee

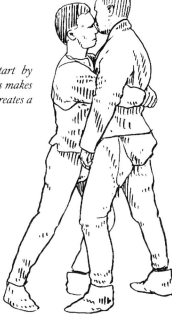

When he seizes you, always start by dropping your center slightly. This makes it harder for him to lift you and creates a small opening for you to counter.

Since your arms are on the outside, it is easy to place an elbow at his throat. Place it over his Adam's apple.

As you straighten your arm, step back (with the left foot in this case). The technique works equally well on the other side.

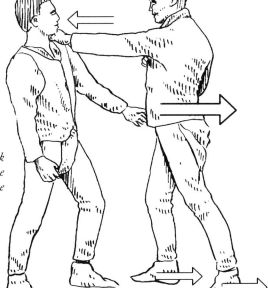

119

ANOTHER WRESTLING TECHNIQUE

If he tries to step through under your arm to throw you over his right shoulder, then seize him with your arm around his neck and press down on him with your chest to push him down.

ABER AIN RINGEN

Item, wan dir ainer mitt dem haupt durch din arm faren will und will dich uber sin recht achseln werffen fach in mitt dinem arm by dem halss und truck in fast zu dir und leg dich mitt der brust oben uff in und schwer dich nider

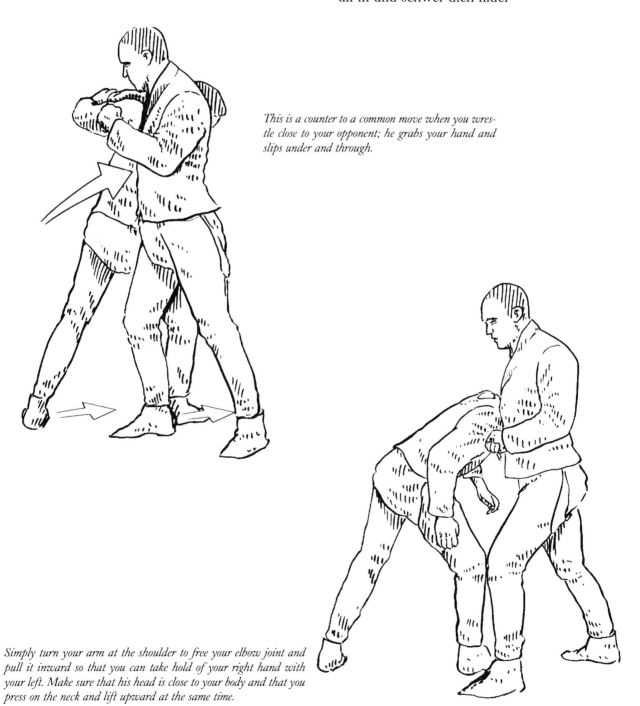

This is a counter to a common move when you wrestle close to your opponent; he grabs your hand and slips under and through.

Simply turn your arm at the shoulder to free your elbow joint and pull it inward so that you can take hold of your right hand with your left. Make sure that his head is close to your body and that you press on the neck and lift upward at the same time.

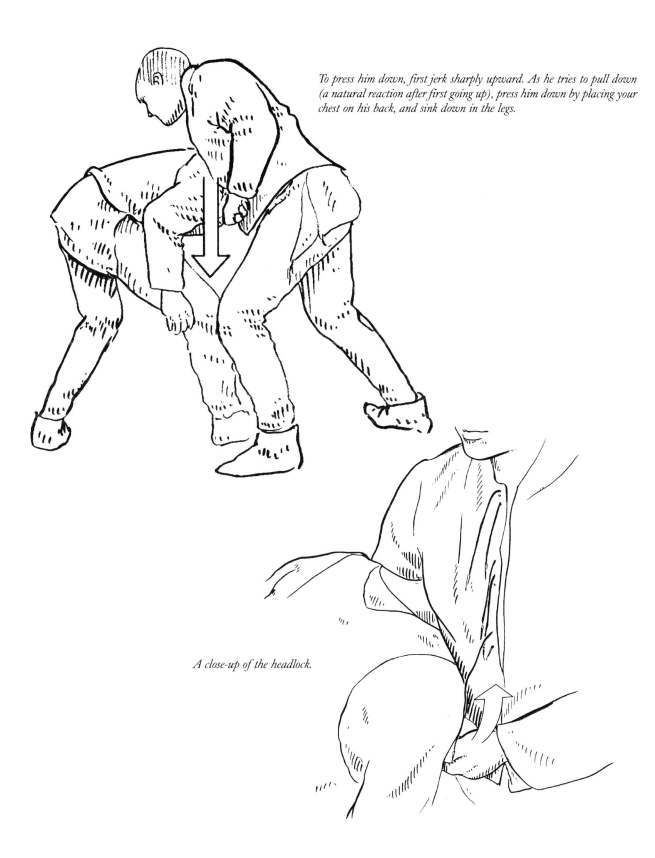

To press him down, first jerk sharply upward. As he tries to pull down (a natural reaction after first going up), press him down by placing your chest on his back, and sink down in the legs.

A close-up of the headlock.

ANOTHER WRESTLING TECHNIQUE

If someone takes hold around you, turn your back to him and quickly raise your arms, and then bend forward to throw him over you. Or take hold of a leg with your hand.

ABER AIN RINGEN

Item, ob dich ainer begrifft wann du im den rucken zu haust keret oder gewendt und hept dich fast iin sin arm so brauch dich behend furdich und wirff in uber dass haupt Oder fach in unden by ainer hand niden by ainem bain

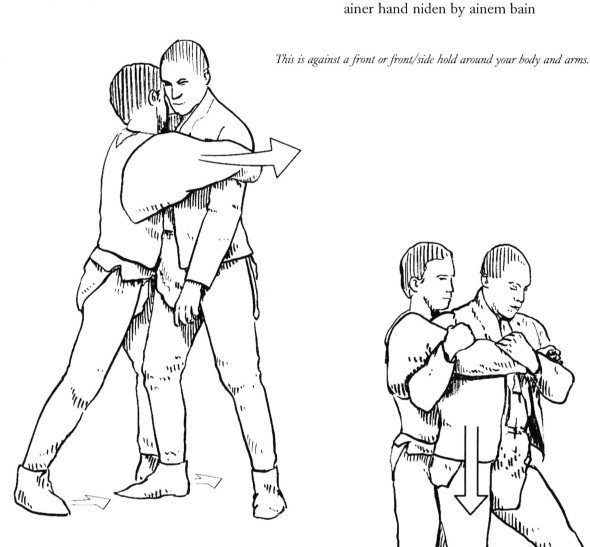

This is against a front or front/side hold around your body and arms.

Turn around so that your back is facing him (either side works well) and take hold of one of his arms as you do so.

Bend forward and, making sure that you hold his arm close to you, throw him over your shoulder.

Retain your grip on his arm if you can; that way you can control him when he hits the ground and easily follow up.

ANOTHER WRESTLING TECHNIQUE

If he has grabbed you from behind and has both his arms under yours, then if his hands are not closed grab one of his fingers, and then he must let you go.

ABER AIN RINGEN

Item, hat er dich hinden gefasst und hat sinen arm under dinem arm und hatt er die hendoffen so begriff im ain finger so muss er dich laussen

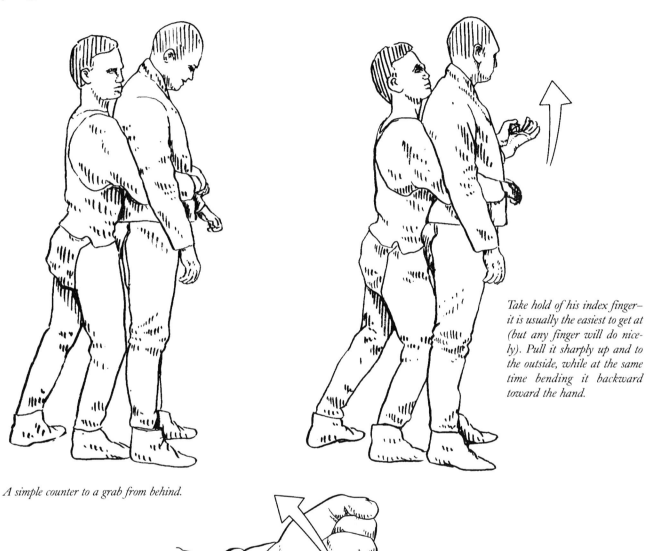

Take hold of his index finger—it is usually the easiest to get at (but any finger will do nicely). Pull it sharply up and to the outside, while at the same time bending it backward toward the hand.

A simple counter to a grab from behind.

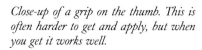

Close-up of a grip on the thumb. This is often harder to get and apply, but when you get it works well.

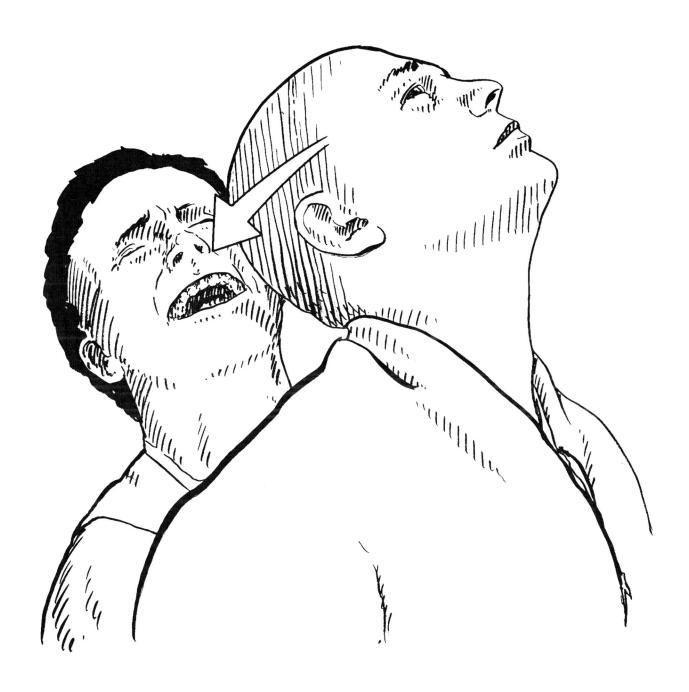

If his hands are clenched tight, you need to create an opening. Head butting him in the face will give you an opening to seize one of his fingers. Drop your head slightly forward and then slam it back as hard as you can.

ANOTHER WRESTLING TECHNIQUE

If he takes hold of your neck with one hand from behind and holds you fast, then turn back through his arm with your head and he will let you go. Or you can take hold of him also at the same time. If someone grabs hold of your collar from behind, then turn through with your head and you will free yourself.

ABER AIN RINGEN

Item, ob dich ainer by dem goller (collar) fasst mitt ainer hand und helt dich fast so wend dich hinden durch sinen arm mitt dem haupt so lausst er dich Oder magst du in den da ungefär begryffen dass ist auch gut

Item, fasst dich ainer hinden by dem goller wend dich mitt dem haupt unden durch sin arm so wirst du ledig

This rear hold is also common and good to know how to counter.

First take hold of his arm with either hand and pull down so that you release the pressure on your throat. (If you want to you can give him an elbow with your other arm at the same time. This will also make him relax a bit in preparation for your turning around.)

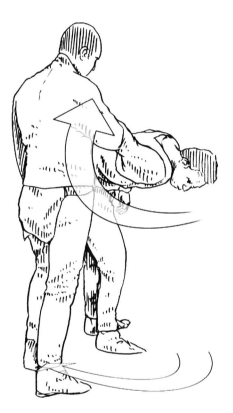

As you turn, duck in under his arm. By retaining the grip on his arm, you will create an arm lock. As you turn and step, pull on his arm so that you can get some space to step away from him a bit in order to make it less likely that you become tangled together.

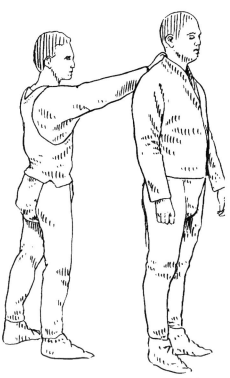

If he grabs your collar instead (this grip is less likely to occur, but it's fun to practice), drop down slightly as you turn and duck under his arm.

Complete the turn and straighten up and his grip will fail.

ANOTHER WRESTLING TECHNIQUE

When he holds you with both hands on the chest, then strike his right elbow away, push through and seize him around the waist.

[For this technique we did two interpretations, one with a single-hand grip, since the idea works on that as well. We begin with one hand and then show the classic two-hand hold.]

ABER AIN RINGEN

Item, ob dich ainer fasst mitt baiden henden vor der brust so stoss im den rechten elnbogen uff und truck dich durch und fass in in der waiche

Your opponent takes hold with one hand on your collar and prepares to strike you with the other hand. (Of course, this position is, in a way, rather inane. It never happens like this, but it is a useful way to start working on the technique.)

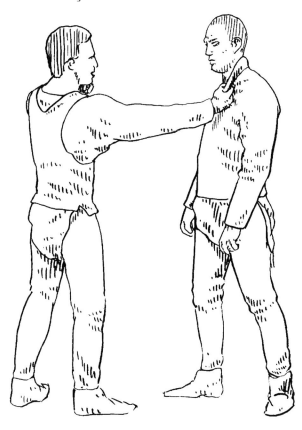

Block his strike with your right hand by straightening it forward and up. Tuck your chin inside close to it. At the same time take hold of the hand gripping your collar, placing your fingers in the inside of his hand and your thumb on the back of his hand.

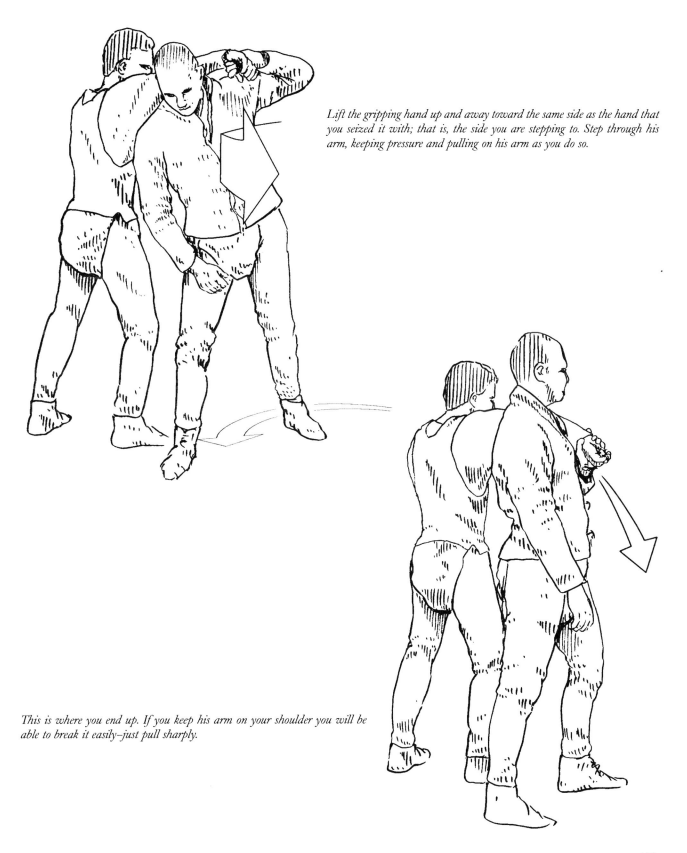

Lift the gripping hand up and away toward the same side as the hand that you seized it with; that is, the side you are stepping to. Step through his arm, keeping pressure and pulling on his arm as you do so.

This is where you end up. If you keep his arm on your shoulder you will be able to break it easily–just pull sharply.

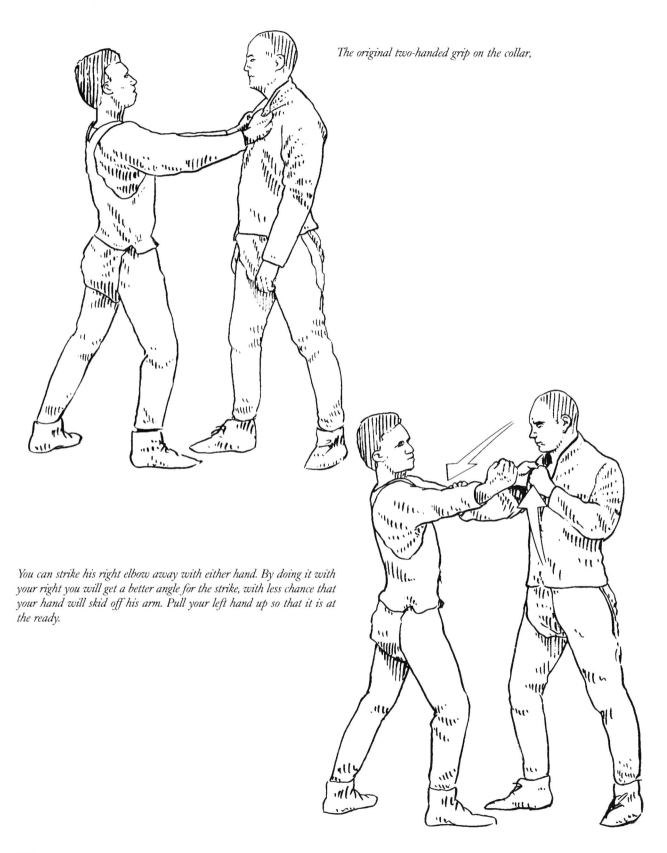

The original two-handed grip on the collar,

You can strike his right elbow away with either hand. By doing it with your right you will get a better angle for the strike, with less chance that your hand will skid off his arm. Pull your left hand up so that it is at the ready.

After striking his arm away, move your right arm back over his left. You can also step in the gap created by pushing his right hand away and begin wrestling at once.

As your right arm goes over and pins his left, wrap your left arm under his right arm and put your cheek close to his face or neck on the side opposite from the free hand. This makes it harder for him to strike you with his right hand.

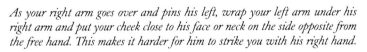

131

Another wrestling technique

Note, if you have taken hold of him by his right arm biceps using your left hand and push him backward, if he then goes over with the right arm on your left hand and presses his hand firmly to your chest, then go with the same elbow at his right side and lower yourself down. Step with your left foot behind his right foot and grab behind his right knee and throw him away from you.

Aber ain ringen

Item, wenn du ainen gefasst hast mitt diner lincken hand in der mauss sines rechten armss und truckest in domitt zu ruck und wenn er dann uberfölt mitt dem rechten arm von ussen uber din tencke hand und truckt sin hand fast an sin brust so far im mitt dem selben elnbogen in sin rechte sytten und senck dich nider und spring mitt dinem lincken fuss hinder sinen rechten fuss unnd gryff im mitt der rechten hand in sin knybug und wirff in von dir

Push the opponent's right arm by the biceps out to the side.

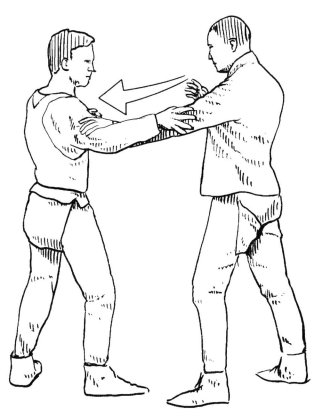

The opponent counters this by going over your right arm and beginning to press on your chest.

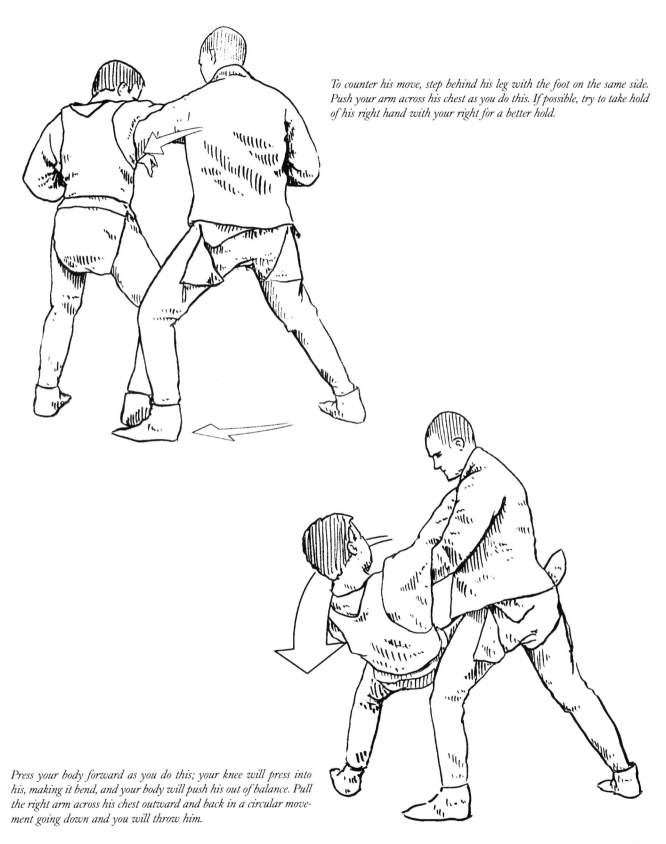

To counter his move, step behind his leg with the foot on the same side. Push your arm across his chest as you do this. If possible, try to take hold of his right hand with your right for a better hold.

Press your body forward as you do this; your knee will press into his, making it bend, and your body will push his out of balance. Pull the right arm across his chest outward and back in a circular movement going down and you will throw him.

133

HERE BEGINS THE CLOSING IN TECHNIQUES

THE FIRST CLOSING TECHNIQUE
Grab his right arm and his left, then let the left go and strike your right arm around his left and throw him on his head.

[This is a suggestion on how to do this. Again, there are several possibilities.]

HEI HEBENT SICH AN DIE ZULAUFFENDEN RINGEN

DASS ERST ZULAUFFEND RINGEN
Item, so fass sinen rechten arm und syn lincken und lauss den lincken farn Und schlach dinen rechten arm umb sinen lincken und wirff in uber den kopff

You have both taken hold of each other's arms by the elbows.

Let the opponent's left arm go and instead begin to push. At the same time, start to pull on his right arm.

Step in behind his leading leg and continue to push and pull. Make sure to pull the arm you are holding close to you and down.

THE SECOND CLOSING TECHNIQUE

When he has hold of you with both hands under your arms, thrust your right arm under his left and place your hand on his chest and push him away from you.

DASS ANDER ANLAUFFEND RINGEN

Item, wann er dich hatt gefasst under baid arm so schlach im din rechten arm under sin lincken und setz im die hand an sin brust und dann schweng in von dir

This is a counter against a frontal hold, common in wrestling.

Lift your right arm and insert your hand inside of his left arm. Press it down and out so that you apply pressure at his elbow joint. Do this in a forceful and snappy movement–if you do it slow and try to press, he will be able to adapt to the situation.

After you have created some space, you can place either hand on his chest and, as you do so, drop down slightly; this will give the push additional force. It is also possible to do this technique by inserting your hand up from below rather than down from above to get inside his arms.

THE THIRD CLOSING TECHNIQUE

Strike your left arm around his neck and grab his left leg to throw him on your right side.

DASS DRITT ANLAUFFENT RINGEN

Item, schlag im den lincken arm umb sin halss und nym in by dem lincken bain uff und ruck in uff die recht sytten

This starting position is at a distance, but you might just as well start from a close distance.

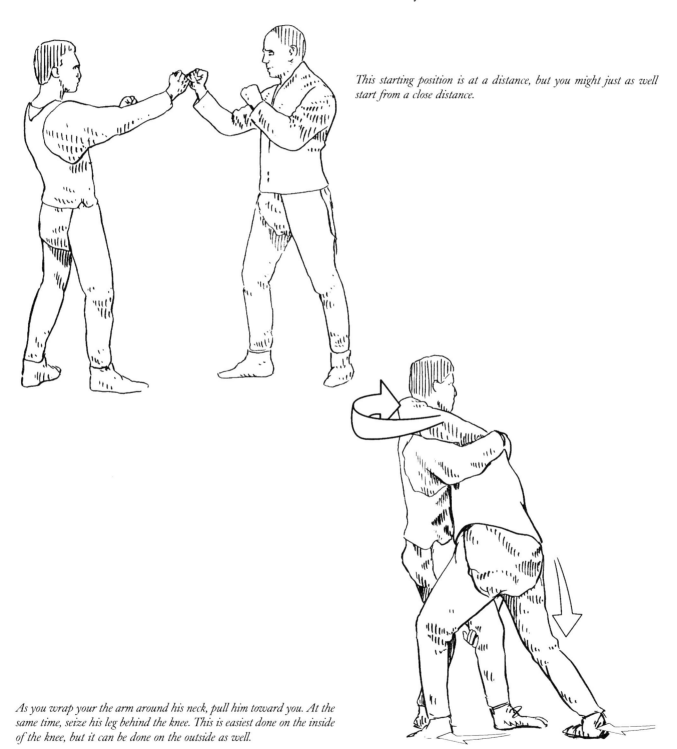

As you wrap your the arm around his neck, pull him toward you. At the same time, seize his leg behind the knee. This is easiest done on the inside of the knee, but it can be done on the outside as well.

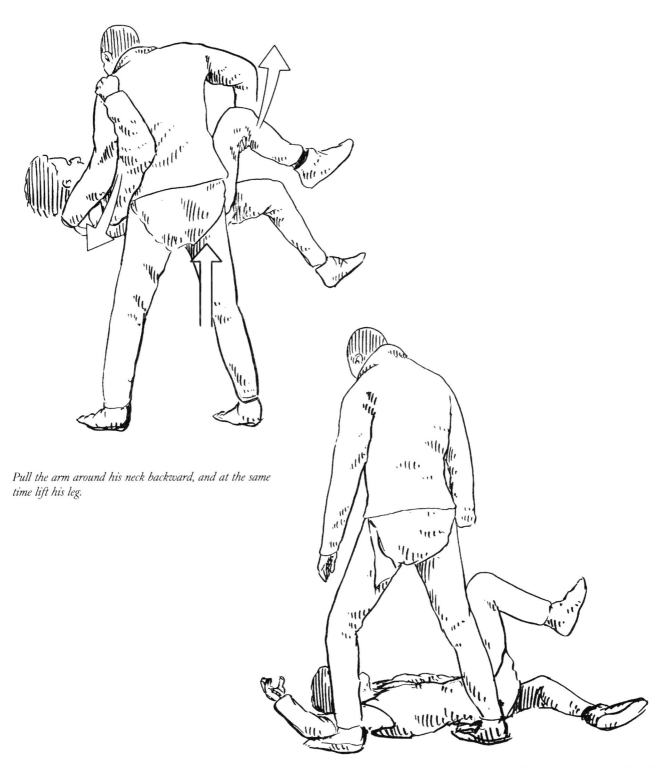

Pull the arm around his neck backward, and at the same time lift his leg.

Lift him up if you are strong enough and then drop him straight down, preferably on something hard.

THE FOURTH CLOSING TECHNIQUE

Grab his right hand using your left and step through his arm. Grab his right leg with your right hand and throw him over you.

DASS VIERD ANLAUFFENT RINGEN

Item, nym sin rechte hand mitt diner lincken und durch lauff im sin arm und nym in mitt der rechten hand by sinem rechten bain und wirff in uber dich

From a starting position (this can also be at close distance), seize his right hand with your left and prepare to step through at once. Lift his arm up and out at about 45 degrees to take his balance as you step in.

Pull your opponent close to your shoulder/upper back and again make sure that his arm is taut.

Bend down and seize his right leg and, as you do so, make sure that you have him over your upper back, not your neck. (It is impossible to make the throw if he is over your neck.)

Straighten your legs. (Do not try to rise from the back—straighten your legs first, then straighten your upper body.) Maintain the pull on his arm. You can then either let go of the arm, which will dump him on his head if you maintain the hold on the leg a fraction of a second, or just throw him down. This throw does not work well if the opponent is significantly larger than you. Although a technical maneuver, it requires some strength to do well.

THE FIFTH CLOSING TECHNIQUE

Grab him by his right hand with both your hands and step through his arm and throw him over yourself.

DASS FUNFT ANLAUFFENT RINGEN

Item, nym in by siner rechten hand mitt dinen baiden henden und durchlauff im sin arm unnd wirff in uberdich

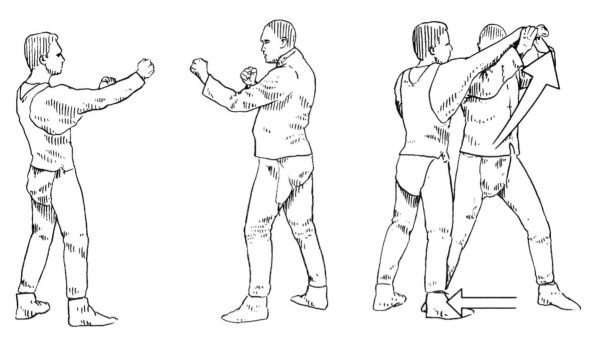

From an opening position (it works from a close distance as well), grab his right hand with both your hands just above his wrist and at once apply pressure immediately. Pull on his arm to straighten it and at the same time lift it up to create space to step through.

Pull him close and throw him over you as shown in the illustration, or throw him the same way as in the previous technique, but without the leg hold.

THE SIXTH CLOSING TECHNIQUE

When you close with him, then bend over and grab him by one of his legs. Pull it upward and strike him with your left hand so that he falls.

DAS VJ. ANLAUFFENT RINGEN

Item, wann du zu im lauffst so buck dich und nym in by ainem bain und zuck im das redlich uff und schlag im mitt dine dencken (lincken) so fölt er

If he has his hands up, strike the right one to the side with your left hand as you close in.

Take hold of his leg and lift it up. Try to end the lift at your waist. His leg is heavy when lifting like this, so you want to keep your hand close to your body for increased strength.

Strike him in the face or throat to drop him backward, lifting the leg higher as he goes back.

The seventh closing technique

When you close with him, take hold of his arms and strike his chest using your head so that he falls to the ground

Das vij. Anlauffent ringen

Wann du zu im lauffcst so begryff im sine baid arm und stoss in mitt dem häupt an die brust so fölt er an den rucken

I have some misgivings about the actual functionality of this technique, no matter how it is done. However, as you close in, control his arms by pressing them down with yours.

Strike him with your head. You can also step in as you do this to create force. A small step with the lead foot will give the best control. Also, drop your center slightly as you strike.

From the previous position, a good variation is to head-butt him from below. This will give him something to think about. How you can make him fall by head-butting him in the chest is beyond me, but it is a good position for a follow-up technique.

THE EIGHTH CLOSING TECHNIQUE

When he grabs your shoulders with force, then strike downward with your hands at his arms and push them aside. Then wrestle with him using whatever technique you want.

DAS VIIJ. ZULAUFFENT RINGEN

Item, wann er dich hertenclich fast by den achseln so schlach im din hand unden uff und truck im die arm en zway (auseinander) und fach mer an zu ringen mitt wölchem stuck du wilt

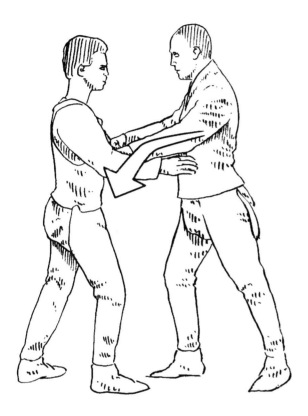 

As he tries to grab your shoulders or upper arms, strike down and out with your hands. Aim for the inside of his elbow joint.

A possible continuation is to thrust up and strike his jaw, then take hold with the left hand, pulling him in a twisting motion to the left side.

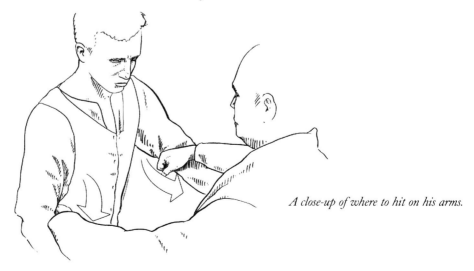

A close-up of where to hit on his arms.

THE NINTH CLOSING TECHNIQUE

You grab him with both hands from below and set both elbows into both his arms. Thrust him in the chest with your head, and grab both his legs.

DASS VIIIJ. ZULAUFFENT RINGEN

Ist dass du in mitt baiden henden fassest von unden uff und setz die baid elnbogen in sin baid arm und stoss in mitt dinem haupt an die brust und begryff in mitt baiden bainen

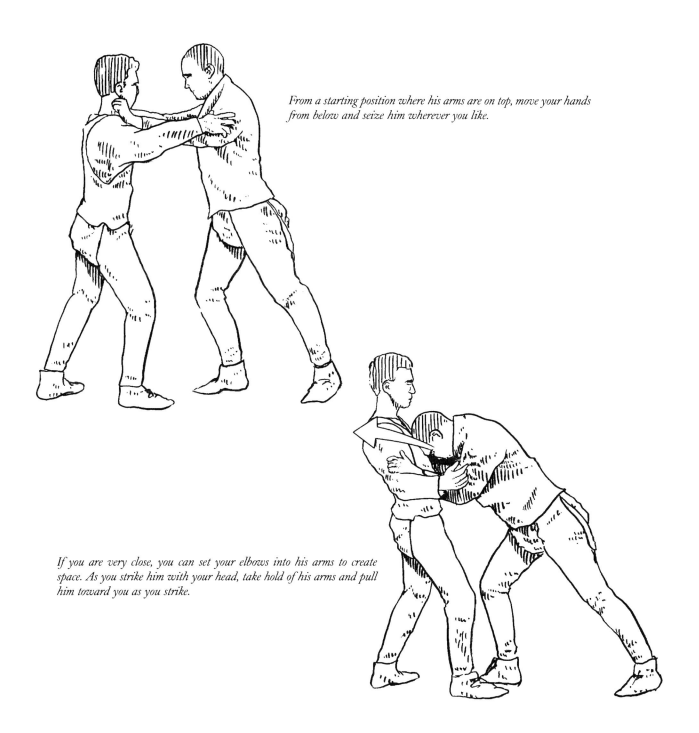

From a starting position where his arms are on top, move your hands from below and seize him wherever you like.

If you are very close, you can set your elbows into his arms to create space. As you strike him with your head, take hold of his arms and pull him toward you as you strike.

Immediately reach down and take hold of his legs behind the knees.

Pull your hands toward you and then up, lifting as high as you can. If you try to lift him without pulling him toward you first, he will be able to resist. You need to pull his feet from under him first.

Instead of striking him in the chest, you can do the old favorite instead–head-butt him in the face.

THE TENTH CLOSING TECHNIQUE

Take hold of both his hands and throw him on his back.

DAS X. ZULAUFFENT RINGEN

Item, dass du in by baiden henden nympst und wirff in uff den rucken

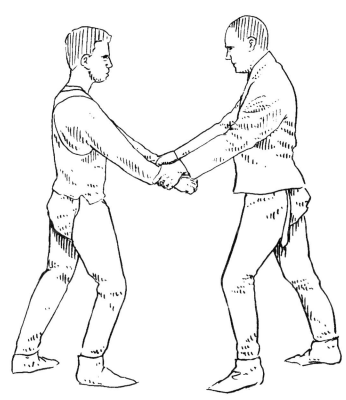

It is impossible to know the original intent of this technique, since there are many ways of doing it. Here is our suggestion. As you take hold of his arms behind the hands, turn in front of him so that his left arm comes under his right. As you do this, step in a semicircle with your rear foot. (If you do it on the other side, then the right arm will be under.) Continue pulling on both his arms and do the entire sequence quickly and as one movement.

149

Turn in so that his left arm rests in between his right arm and your shoulder.

Bend forward and throw him over your shoulder. This will also fracture the lower arm.

THE ELEVENTH CLOSING TECHNIQUE

Watch how you close with him and take hold of his right arm using both your hands, then step through and break it.

DAS XI. ZULAUFFENT RINGEN

Item, brieffe am lauffen wa du zu im lauffest so nym sinen rechten arm mitt din baiden henden und durchlauff im den und brich im den enzway

A very useful technique that can also be done from a close distance.

Take hold of his hand and turn in toward him on the same side–that is the shortest way to turn if you want to place his arm on your shoulder. (You can strike him in the ribs with your nearest elbow as you turn.)

Pull down sharply on his hand and the elbow joint will snap.

THE TWELFTH CLOSING TECHNIQUE

When you close with him and take hold around his chest and he does the same, then strike the arm away and thrust with your left hand behind his left arm. Grab one of his legs with your right hand and throw him.

DAS XIJ. ZULAUFFENT RINGEN

Item, wen du in anlauffest und an die brust gefasst und er dich och also so schlag im den arm ab und stos in mitt diner lincken hand hinden sinen lincken arm Begryff in by ainem bain mitt der rechten hand und uberwurff in

From a starting position at close distance, you step in.

Step in with your left leg and seize his left shoulder.

Using your left arm, press the opponent backward to take his balance as you reach down to take hold of his leg. As you reach down, bend with your knees rather than your back.

Straighten your legs and pull the hand holding his leg as high as possible, keeping it close to your body. At the same time, press down strongly on his left shoulder.

Close-up of the left side of the opponent. Press on his throat with your forearm rather than with the hand alone

THE THIRTEENTH CLOSING TECHNIQUE

When he has a hold on your arm and you grab him also, then release his right arm and with your left arm take hold between his legs and lift him on your shoulder. Then throw him where you want.

DAS XIIJ. ZULAUFFENT RINGEN

Item, wann er dich fasst by dem arm und du in och also so lass den rechten arm gen und begryff in by sinem lincken arm zwischen siner bain und heb in uff die achsel und wirff in wie du wilt

From a starting position at a close distance, drop his left arm and pull it up and out. At the same time, step in close and slide your left hand between his legs. (This can be done in a more or less unpleasant way.)

With a snappy movement, straighten your legs and throw him.

A WRESTLING TECHNIQUE

When he takes hold of you under your shoulder, thrust your right hand at his arm and then wrestle.

AIN BRUCH IN DEM RINGEN

Item, ain bruch wann er dich under die achsel begryfft so stoss von dir den arm mitt der rechten hand und fall in dan mer an zu ringen

When he has a hold under your arms, press down hard on the inside of his left elbow joint with your right hand.

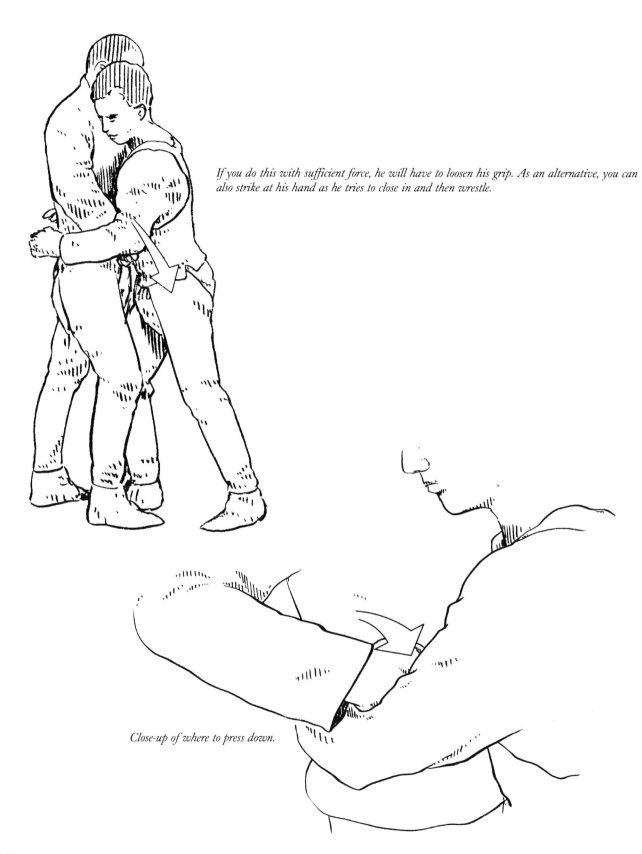

If you do this with sufficient force, he will have to loosen his grip. As an alternative, you can also strike at his hand as he tries to close in and then wrestle.

Close-up of where to press down.

The Spear

It's hard to imagine a time when fighting with the spear was not an integral part of the martial world. First seen as a simple staff or sturdy stick, the spear is probably the most common weapon found in European Bronze and Iron Age burials, and in German and Scandinavian sagas the spear holds the place of pride even before the sword. (It is the weapon of choice of Odin, the Teutonic god of war and death.)

The spear (and, later, polearms) was always seen as a weapon for war or judicial dueling, as is attested by the laws of personal combat in the Frankish kingdoms and in Viking-age Scandinavia, for instance.

When discussing the spear, we may wonder at the brevity of this section. But as opposed to the complex art of sword fighting, spear fighting is wonderfully simple, as are all pole-arms techniques. Especially when fighting in full armor, without the encumbrance of a shield, fighting with the spear more than anything resembles fighting with the staff.

This connection with the staff is important, I believe, since later German masters such as Joachim Meyer state that the staff is the foundation of all polearms, and we can see that the guards with the spear are very similar to those used with the staff. I would therefore believe that they are virtually one and the same and coexisted side-by-side up to the 16th century, when the spear disappears and the staff remains as the reminder of lost glory.

In Ringeck's manual we find thrusting rather than striking (which is not surprising, since a wooden shaft against a steel plate is not very effective), but from the movements it would be easy to land some strikes against an unarmored opponent. But when fighting against an armored opponent, the possible targets are far fewer and consist of the armpits, sides of the neck, groin, inside of the hands, inside of the elbows and upper arms, and the back of the legs. Of these, the armpits and the groin are the targets most easily and most often hit. (For more information on fighting with the staff, see *Fighting with the European Quarterstaff* by David Lindholm, Chivalry Bookshelf, 2006.)

IN THE NAME of St. George here begins the art
Here is the fighting in earnest mounted and on foot as written down in concealed words by the master Johannes Lichtenauer.

IN SANT JORGEN namen höpt an die kunst
Hie höpt sich an der ernstlich kampff zu ross und fuss Alhie hept sich ann Maister Johannsen Liechtennawers vechten im harnasch zu kampff dass er laussen schriben mitt verborgen worten Das stet hie nach in disem biechlin glosiert unnd ussgeleget das ain yeder fechter vernemmen mag die kunst der anderst vechten kan

---

WHEN THE COMBAT on foot begins, it starts with the spear. They both stand to defend.

DIE VOR RED mitt dem text
Wer absumet vechten zu fussen beginnet der schick sin sper Zway sten an heben recht wer

---

NOTE THAT YOU should know that when two fight on foot in armor, they should have three weapons: a spear, a sword, and a dagger. First they should begin the fight with the spear. You should be prepared for the fight with two positions as will be explained.

MÖRCK DASS SOLT du also versten Wenn zwen zu fussen in harnasch mitt ain andern fechten wollen so soll yeder man haben dryerlay wer:ain sper ain schwert und ain degenn Und dass erste anheben soll geschechen mitt dem langen sper Domitt solt du dich rechter wer schicken indem anheben in zwayen stent alss du hernach horn wilst

---

THE TEXT OF THE TWO POSITIONS
The spear and the point thrust first. Thrust with strength, jump and wind, and set rightly on. If he defends, pull away and place it in his face.

DER TEXT VON ZWAIEN STEND
Sper und den ort vorstich Stich on forcht springe winde setz recht an Wert er zucke dass gesigt im an

THIS IS THE first position with the spear. When both have dismounted stand with the left foot forward and hold your spear ready to throw it, and step in this way closer with the left foot leading. Wait so that you can throw just before him and then follow through with the sword so that he can't get a safe throw against you. And take hold of the sword.

DASS IST DER erst stand mitt dem sper Wann ir bayde von den rossen abgetretten sind so stand mitt dem lincken fuss vor und halt din sper zu dem schuss und tritt also zu im dass allweg din lincker fuss vor blyb Und wart das du ee schusst den er Und volg bald dem schuss nach zu im mitt dem schwert so kan er kainen gewissen schuss uff dich haben Und gryff zu dem schwert

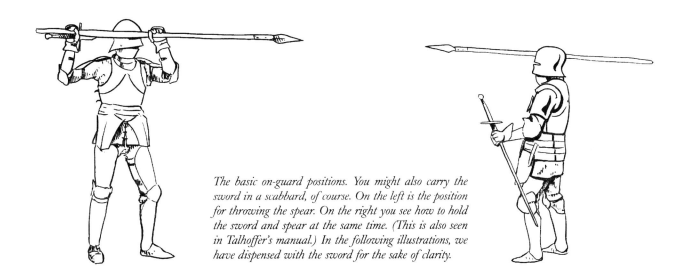

The basic on-guard positions. You might also carry the sword in a scabbard, of course. On the left is the position for throwing the spear. On the right you see how to hold the sword and spear at the same time. (This is also seen in Talhoffer's manual.) In the following illustrations, we have dispensed with the sword for the sake of clarity.

THE SECOND POSITION WITH THE SPEAR

Note that if you do not want to throw your spear, then hold it below on your right side in the lower guard and step close to him and thrust with skill from below at his face before he does it to you. If he thrusts or displaces at the same time, then go up into the high guard (his point will remain on your left arm) and hang the point over his arm and into his face. If he moves it aside and displaces with the left arm, then pull away and set the point under his left shoulder in the opening.

DAS ANDER STAND IM SPER

Mörck ob du din spcr nitt verschiessen wilt so halt es neben diner rechten sytten zu der undern hutt und gee also zu im unnd stich im kunlich von unden uff zu dem gesicht ee wann er dir Sticht er dann mitt dir glich ein oder versetzt so far uff mitt dem sper in die obern hut So blypt dir sin ort uff dinem lincken arm Und mitt dem so heng im den ort uber sinen arm in sin gesicht Fört er dann uff und versetzt mitt dem lincken arm so zuch und setz iim den ort under sin lincke uchsen in die blöss

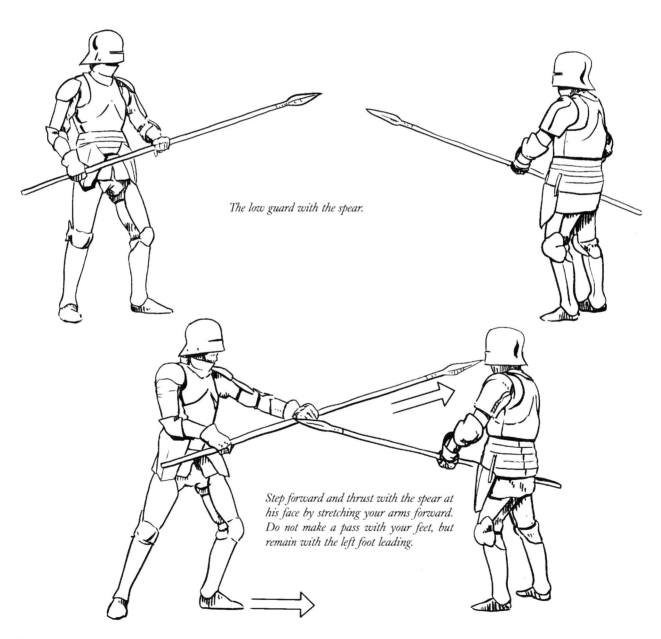

The low guard with the spear.

Step forward and thrust with the spear at his face by stretching your arms forward. Do not make a pass with your feet, but remain with the left foot leading.

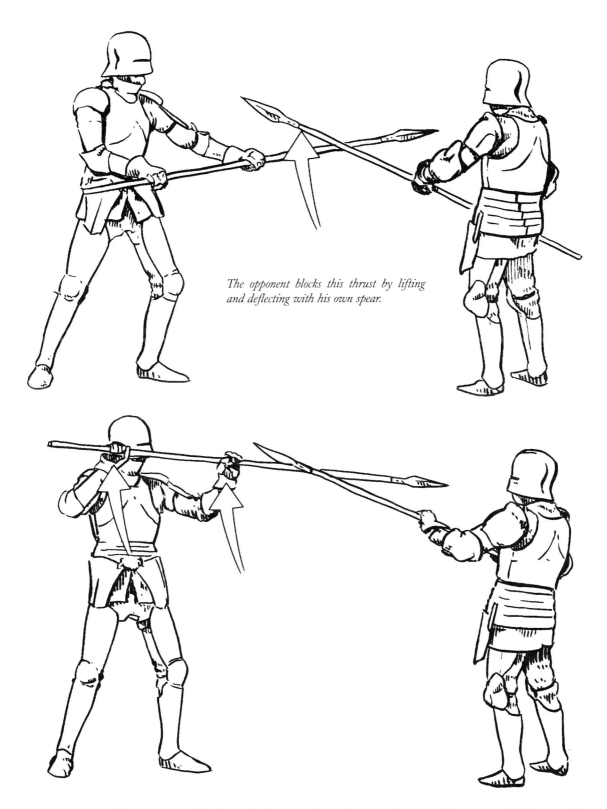

The opponent blocks this thrust by lifting and deflecting with his own spear.

You continue your attack by going into the high guard. If you are closer, the opponent's spear will rest on your left forearm; if you are farther apart, it will remain on your spear (shown here).

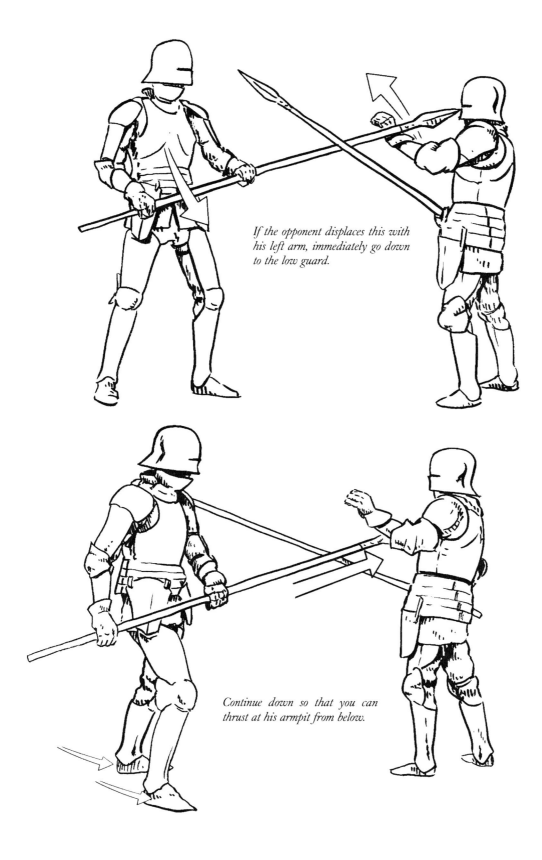

If the opponent displaces this with his left arm, immediately go down to the low guard.

Continue down so that you can thrust at his armpit from below.

THE TEXT ON HOW TO WITHDRAW

If you want to thrust while you withdraw, then learn to counter. Note that this means that you should learn to withdraw, and notice that as you thrust from the low guard and he displaces it with the spear and his point goes to the side and below yours, then withdraw. Go through and thrust at him on the other side. If he tries the other displacement with the point in front of the face, then do not withdraw but remain with your spear on his and work with winden (turning) to the nearest opening that you can create.

DER TEXT WIE MAN ZUCKEN SOLL

Wilt du mitt stechen mit zucken lern vor brechen

Mörck dass ist dass du wol lernen solt dass du also zuckest Unnd vernym dass also wann du im uss der undern hut zu stichst versetzt er mitt dem sper das sin ort besytz neben dir uss gat so zuck durch und stich im zu der anderen sytten Oder pleibt er dir mitt der andern versatung mitt dem ort vor dem gesicht so zucke nicht Und pleyb mitt dem sper an dem synen und arbait mitt dem winden zu der nechsten blöss die dir werden mag

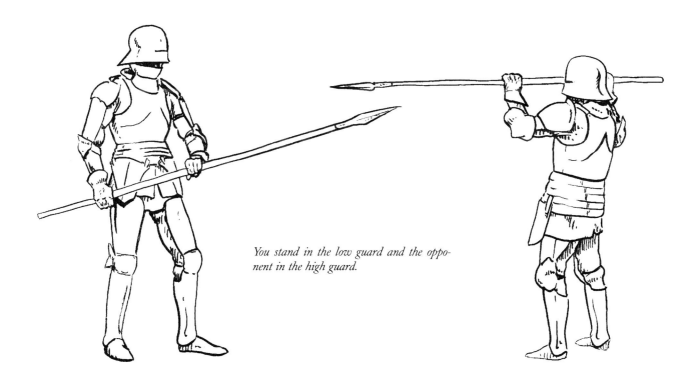

You stand in the low guard and the opponent in the high guard.

Step forward and thrust at his face from below. The opponent displaces this by turning his spear so the point is toward the ground, deflecting your thrust to the outside.

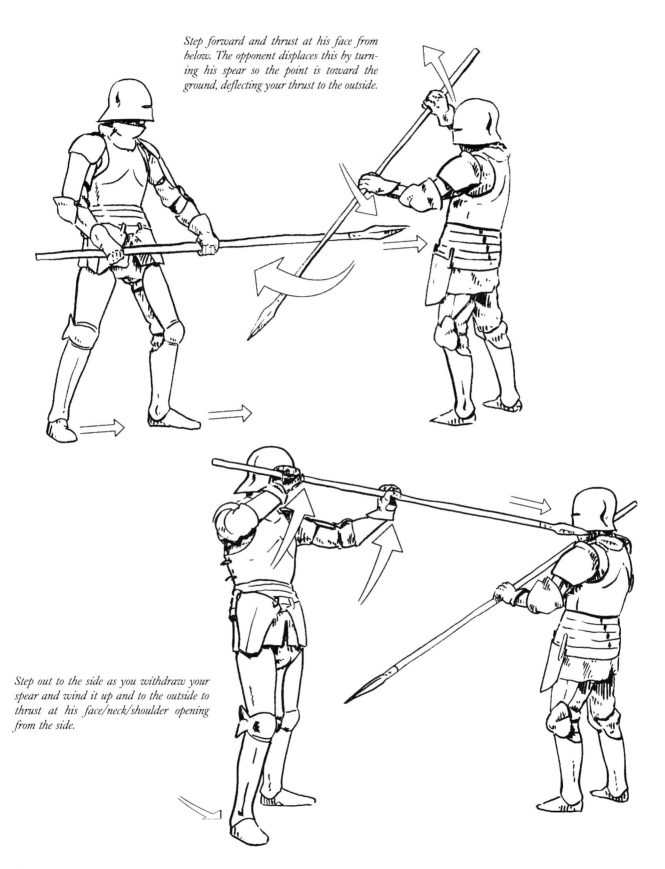

Step out to the side as you withdraw your spear and wind it up and to the outside to thrust at his face/neck/shoulder opening from the side.

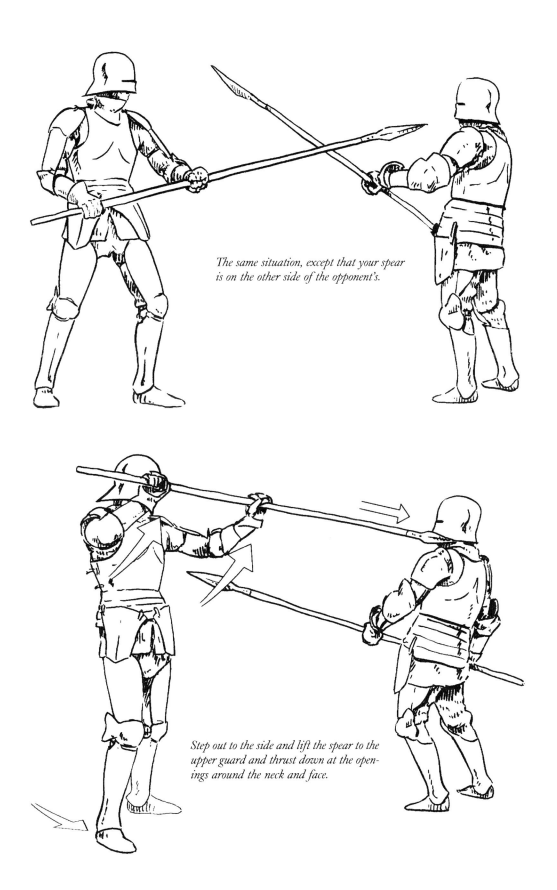

The same situation, except that your spear is on the other side of the opponent's.

Step out to the side and lift the spear to the upper guard and thrust down at the openings around the neck and face.

THE TEXT

Note that if he escapes from harm and flees, then you should go after him and stay on his trail.

Note that this is how you should travel after with the spear. Note that when you thrust at him first and he displaces you and tries to disengage, then follow him with the point. If you hit him with it, then push him back. If he tries to withdraw and turns one side to you, then run in to that side and take hold with wrestling and arm-breaking, as will be described hereafter.

DER TEXT

Mörck will er ziechen von schaid und will fliechenn so solt du im nachen Ja wysslich wart dess fahen

Merck dass ist wie du solt nachraissen mitt dem sper Mörck wann du vorkumst mitt dem stich versetzt er und will sich am sper abziechen (aus dem band lösen) so volg im nach mitt dem ort Triffest du in do mitt so dring in fur dich Will er dann uss dem ort hindersich fliechen und wendt dir zu ein sytten so wart das du im zu derselben sytten ein lauffest und in wysslich begryffest mitt ringen und mitt armbruchen lass du hernach geschriben fundest

Starting position in the lower and upper guard respectively.

Step out to the side and thrust at the opponent's openings around the shoulder and armpit. The opponent responds to the attack by turning the point down and deflecting. (If he is also in a lower guard, he can displace by simply deflecting to the outside with the point up.)

The opponent disengages and steps back with his lead foot and follows with the other.

Press forward, pushing your point at his face as he moves back; the earlier you can do this the better.

The opponent turns and tries to run away, turning his back to you as he goes.

Run after him at once and close the distance as fast as you can, getting one leg in front of him if at all possible. Then try to push him over that leg.

Combat Wrestling

HERE RINGECK OFFERS some advice on the fundamentals of wrestling in full armor, and later he expands on this with another section. Why these are separate I do not know, but we have decided to keep the sections in this order.

AS OPPOSED TO the very fluid wrestling Ringeck describes out of armor, wrestling while armored is described as mainly a pushing and pulling business. This makes good sense, since most of the wrestling moves done in clothing are simply not possible to do in a full suit of armor. Your tactile sensitivity is greatly reduced, as is your ability to swiftly make subtle changes in balance and weight distribution. This does not mean that wrestling in armor is a clumsy affair–far from it. But the added weight and the way it is distributed on your body will affect the way you move as well as the possible attacks and defenses.

THE TEXT OF WRESTLING IN COMBAT

If you wish to wrestle, learn to step in behind the right leg and place a bar with skill to close off the leg.

DER TEXT VON RINGEN ZU KAMPFFE

Ob du wilt ringen hinderpein recht lern springen rigel fur schiessen dass vorbain kunstlich beschliessen

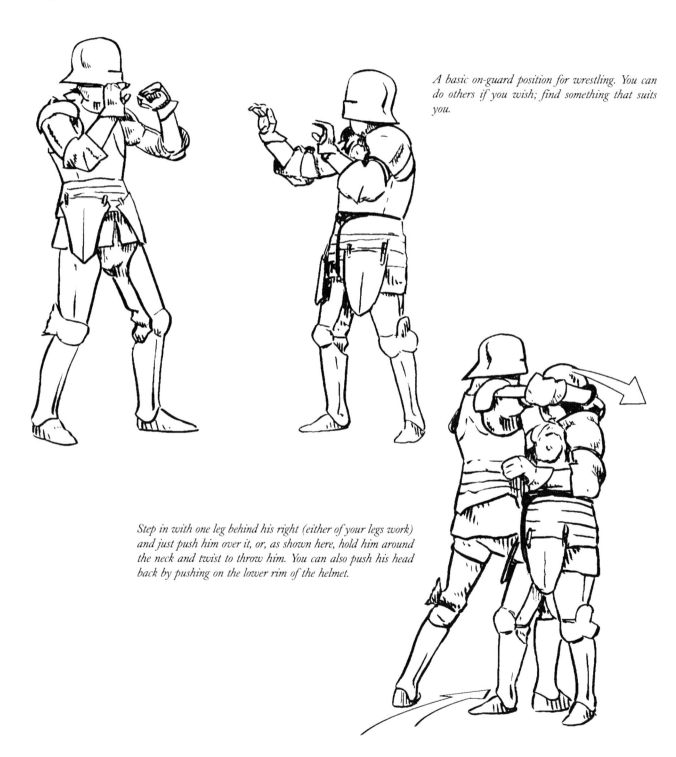

A basic on-guard position for wrestling. You can do others if you wish; find something that suits you.

Step in with one leg behind his right (either of your legs work) and just push him over it, or, as shown here, hold him around the neck and twist to throw him. You can also push his head back by pushing on the lower rim of the helmet.

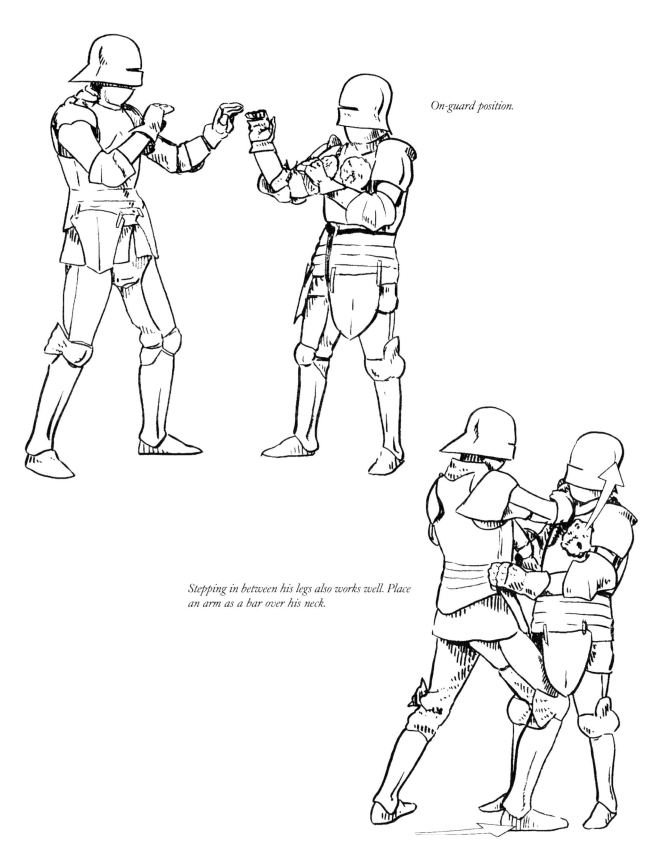

On-guard position.

Stepping in between his legs also works well. Place an arm as a bar over his neck.

Step in behind his leading leg with your right and push him back with your forearm.

Step in behind his lead leg with your right and catch hold of him around the neck to twist and throw him over your leg.

WHEN YOU CLOSE with someone and wish to wrestle, then you must understand whether you should step in front of or behind his leg. And you should only take one step to accomplish this.

When you attack with wrestling and he attacks you, note which foot he is leading with. If he leads with the left then strike his left hand away with your right. With the strike, leap with your right foot behind his left and press in with your right knee behind his left knee and push him with both hands over the knee.

Note another one when you leap in with the right foot behind his left, then follow with the left in between his legs and lock his left knee between both of your knees and hold him fast. Then strike him in the forehead with your left hand while seizing him to the rear on the side with your right hand.

DASS IST WENN du mitt im kumst zu ringen so solt di wissen wie du fornen oder hinden fur dass bain springen solt Und soll geschechen nicht mer dann mit ainem zu tritt

Item mörck den thu also wenn du angriffest mitt ringen und er dich wider welchen fuss vorsetz Hat er den lincken vor so schlach im sin lincke hand uss mitt diner rechten Unnd mitt dem ussschlagen so spring mitt dinem rechten fuss hinde sinen lincken und truck in mitt dem rechten kny hinden sin linck knyckel Und ruck in mitt baiden henden uber dass selbig kny

Item mörck ain anderss wenn du springst mitt dem rechten fuss hinder sinen lincken so schrytt mitt dem lincken hin nach zwischen sine baide bain Und fass sin linckes kny zwischen din bayde kny und halt es domitt föst unnd stoss in mitt der lincken hand vornen an die hawben und mitt der rechtz zeuch in hinden uff die sytten

From an on-guard position.

177

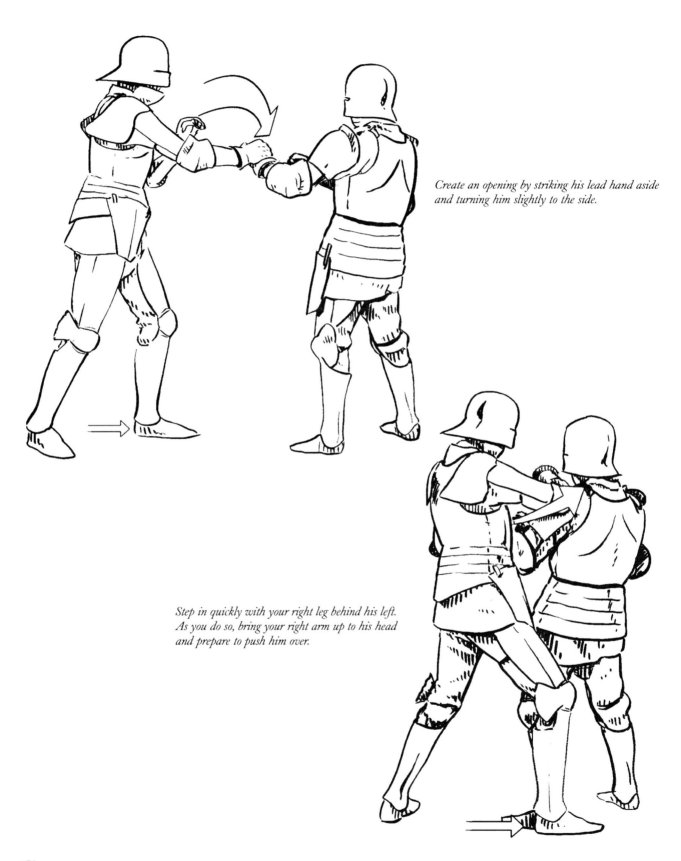

Create an opening by striking his lead hand aside and turning him slightly to the side.

Step in quickly with your right leg behind his left. As you do so, bring your right arm up to his head and prepare to push him over.

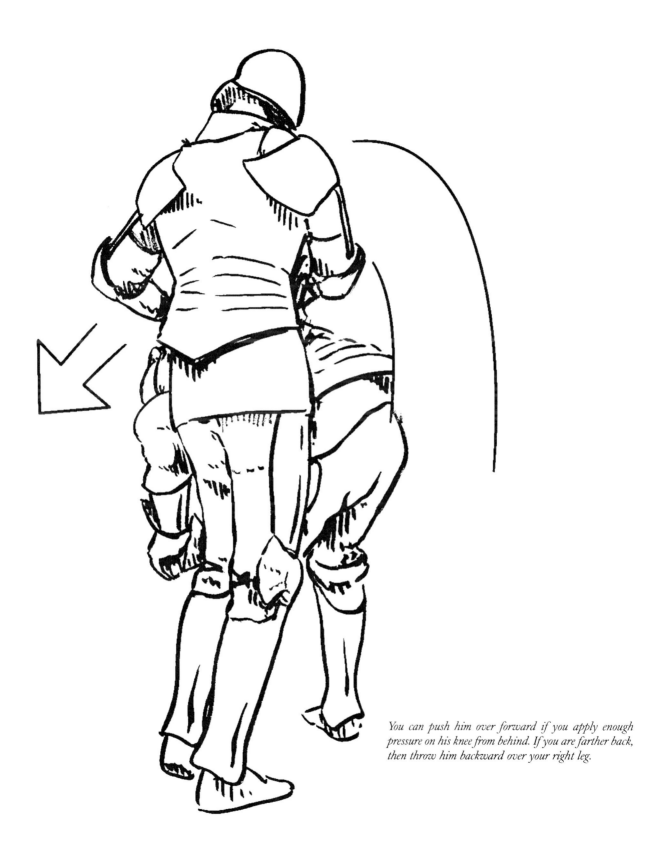

You can push him over forward if you apply enough pressure on his knee from behind. If you are farther back, then throw him backward over your right leg.

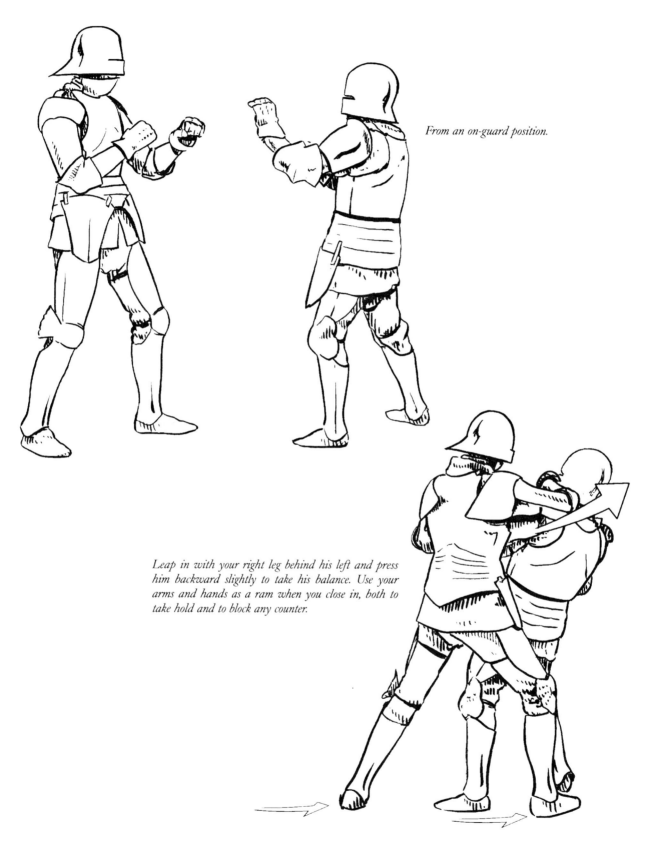

From an on-guard position.

Leap in with your right leg behind his left and press him backward slightly to take his balance. Use your arms and hands as a ram when you close in, both to take hold and to block any counter.

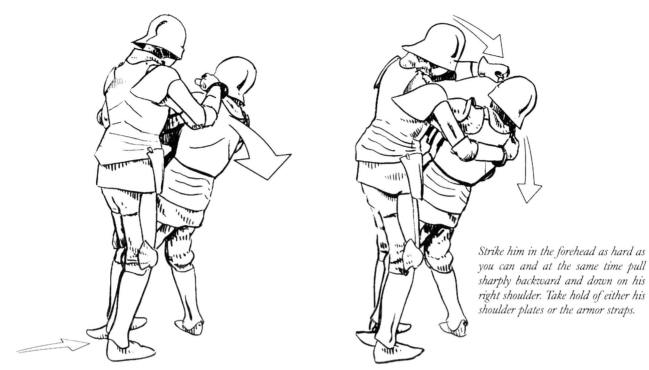

Strike him in the forehead as hard as you can and at the same time pull sharply backward and down on his right shoulder. Take hold of either his shoulder plates or the armor straps.

Step in with your left leg between the opponent's legs; control him by maintaining pressure from behind on his left knee with your right leg. Then use both your legs to pin his left leg.

Close-up of the hold and the strike.

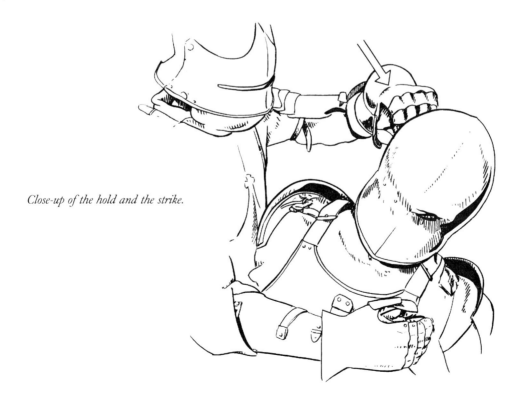

The text

From above with both hands, you will skillfully end it.

Der text

Von bayden henden ob du mitt kunst gerst zu enden

That means that you should know all wrestling moves from both sides so that you can finish it skillfully when you close with him. And do it like this: when you step in behind with the right foot behind his left, if he steps back with his left foot then follow him at once to the other side with your left foot behind his right and throw him over the knee. Or lock his knee using your legs as has been described.

Dass ist dass du alle ringen solt wissen zu tribenn von baiden sytten ist dass du mitt kunst enden wilt dar nach alss du an in kumst Und das vernym also Wann du mitt dem rechten fuss springst hinder sinen lincken tritt er dann im sprung mitt sinem lincken fuss zu rucke so volg im bald nach zu der andern sytten mitt dinem lincken fuss hinder sinen rechten und wirff in uber das kny Oder verschlaiss im sin kny mitt dinen bain alss vor geschriben stät

On-guard position.

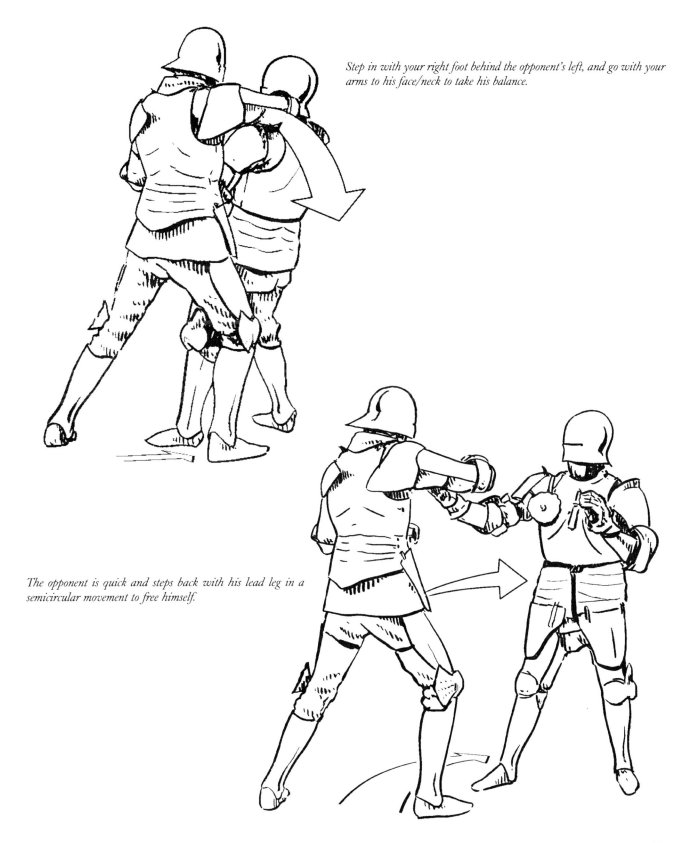

Step in with your right foot behind the opponent's left, and go with your arms to his face/neck to take his balance.

The opponent is quick and steps back with his lead leg in a semicircular movement to free himself.

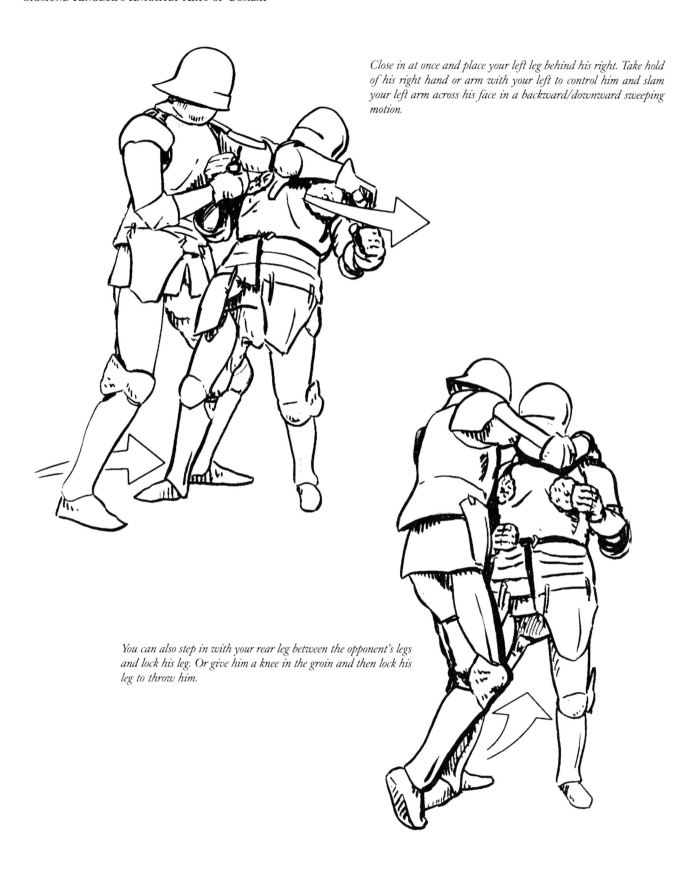

Close in at once and place your left leg behind his right. Take hold of his right hand or arm with your left to control him and slam your left arm across his face in a backward/downward sweeping motion.

You can also step in with your rear leg between the opponent's legs and lock his leg. Or give him a knee in the groin and then lock his leg to throw him.

Sword Against Spear

Fighting with the spear against the sword and vice versa was a certainty in the judicial duels in Germany in the 15th century. In the duels there were three weapons used: the spear, the longsword, and the dagger. Combat began with the spear, followed by sword and dagger.

This short section deals with how to counter the longer reach of the spear with the shorter longsword. It is also interesting to note the movements of the spear and how the fighter tries to utilize its greater reach without it getting caught. On the other hand, the swordfighter tries to overcome the sword's shorter reach by bypassing the dangerous point and stepping into a range where the length of the spear is a hindrance and liability.

THIS IS THE text of how to handle the sword against the spear.

DASS IST DER text wie man sich sol schicken mitt dem sper wider dass schwert Ob er sich verruckt dass schwert gegen sper wurd gezuckt Der stych war nym Spring, fahe ringens eyl zu im

---

NOTE THAT WHEN you have thrown your spear and your opponent retains his, then go against him with the sword. Take hold with the left hand in the middle of the blade and hold the sword in front of you with the middle in front of your left knee in the guard, or hold it below on your right side in the lower guard.

MÖRCK DASS IST wann du din gleffen verschossen hast und er behelt die sinen so schick dich also gegen im mitt dem schwert Griff mitt der lincken hand mitten in die clingen und leg das schwert fur dich mitten uff din linckes kny in die hut oder halt es neben diner rechten sytten in der undern hut.

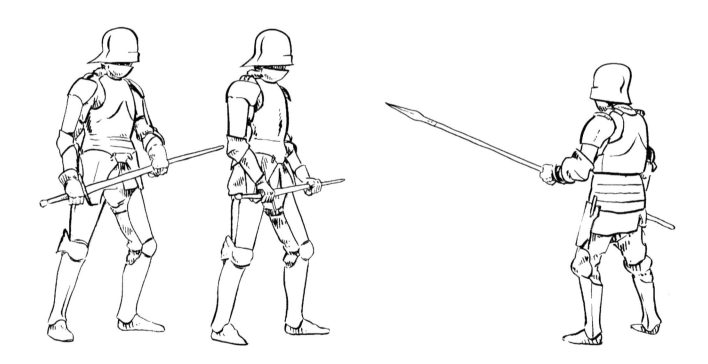

On-guard positions with sword and spear. Note that there are two options for the longsword: in front of the lead leg or more on the side. Both differ in their offensive and defensive capabilities. Try them yourself.

NOTE, IF HE thrusts high at you with his spear, go up and displace the thrust in front of your left hand with the sword on the left side and leap close to him and give the point. If you cannot come close to him, then let your sword fall and wait for the wrestling.

If he thrusts at you with his spear when you are in the lower guard, then displace the thrust with your sword in front of your left hand on your right side and give him the point or wrestle.

ITEM MÖRCK STICHT er dir dann mitt der gleffen oben eyn zu so far uff und setz im den stich ab vor diner lincken hand mitt dem schwert uff din lincke sytten und spring zu im und wart des ansetzens Magst du denn zu nicht komen so lauss din schwert fallen unnd wart der ringen

Item sticht er dir zu mitt der glefen wann du stäst in der undern hut so setz im den stich ab mitt der schwert vor diner lincken hand uff sin rechte sytten und wart dess ansetzens oder der ringen.

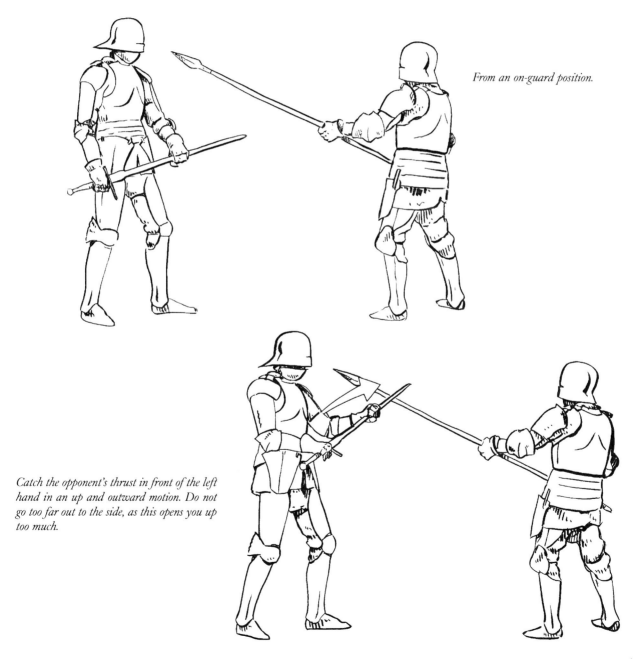

From an on-guard position.

Catch the opponent's thrust in front of the left hand in an up and outward motion. Do not go too far out to the side, as this opens you up too much.

187

Step forward with the rear foot and wind the sword out, turning the point in (pushing the pommel out to the side does this) and thrusting at the opponent in the opening around the shoulder.

You can also go up with the sword and thrust downward behind the bevor.

Or you can drop the sword and close in to wrestle with him, attacking from the side and taking advantage of the fact that the opponent is holding onto a long spear.

From an on-guard position.

The opponent steps forward and thrusts at your face from below (or at the armpit). Lift the sword and catch the thrust in front of the left hand, pushing the spear point to your right side.

Step forward and lift your rear hand up to turn your point down. Push the sword at the opponent, using the contact point with the spear as a swivel.

THE TEXT ABOUT displacing with the open hand.

Strike long with the left hand. Leap with intent [*closer to him, probably*] and take hold. If he wishes to pull away to escape, grasp and press in and place the sword point in the opening to attack.

DER TEXT VON absetzen mitt der lerer hand

Lincke lanck von hand schlache Spring wysslich und den fache Ob er will zucken von schaiden fach und truck in dass in die blöss mitt schwertes ort verdross

From an on-guard position.

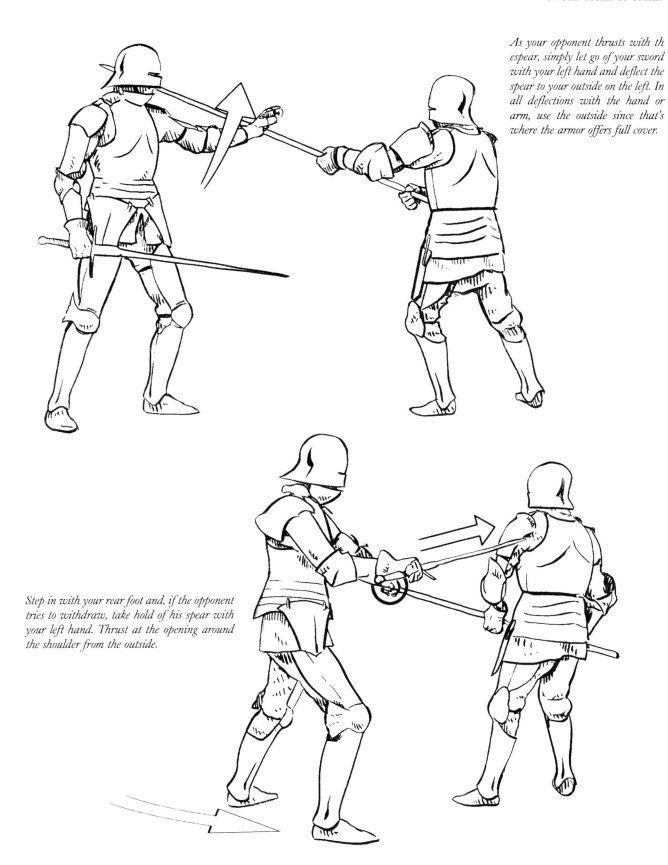

As your opponent thrusts with th espear, simply let go of your sword with your left hand and deflect the spear to your outside on the left. In all deflections with the hand or arm, use the outside since that's where the armor offers full cover.

Step in with your rear foot and, if the opponent tries to withdraw, take hold of his spear with your left hand. Thrust at the opening around the shoulder from the outside.

191

WHEN YOU STAND in the lower guard and he thrusts high at you with the spear and holds it so that the point is far in front of his hand, strike his spear down with your left hand and take hold of your sword at once with the left hand in the middle of the blade. Then leap forward and go at him.

WENN DU STAUST in der undern hut sticht er dir an oben zu mitt dcm spcr und hat das gcfasst dass im der ort lang fur die hand uss gat und sticht dir domitt oben zu so schlach in mitt der lincken hand sin sper beseytz abe und begryff din schwert bald wider mitt der lincken hand mitten in der clingen Und spring zu im und setz im an

From an on-guard position.

The opponent steps forward and thrusts at your face. Deflect the spear to your left outside using your left hand.

Step out with your right foot and take hold of your sword blade in the middle and thrust at the opening closest to you. The step and sword grasp should take place in one forward motion that ends in a thrust.

193

NOTE, IF HE thrusts below at your groin, seize his spear with your left hand and hold it fast and thrust at the same time down in his groin. If he then pulls his spear to him with force and tries to wrench it from your hand, let the spear go high up and above him from your hand, then he will show his openings. Then grab your sword at once with the left hand in the middle of the blade and follow him at once and set to him.

ITEM STICHT ER dir mitt dem sper unden zu dem gemächt so fahe sin sper in die lincken hand und halt es domitt vast Und stich im mitt der rechten unden zu dem gemacht Und ruckt er dann sin sper fast an sich und will dir dass uss der hand ryssen so lauss dass sper uber in uss der hand far So gibt er sich blöss So begriff din schwert bald mit der lincken hand wider mitten in der clingen und volg im bald nach und setz im an

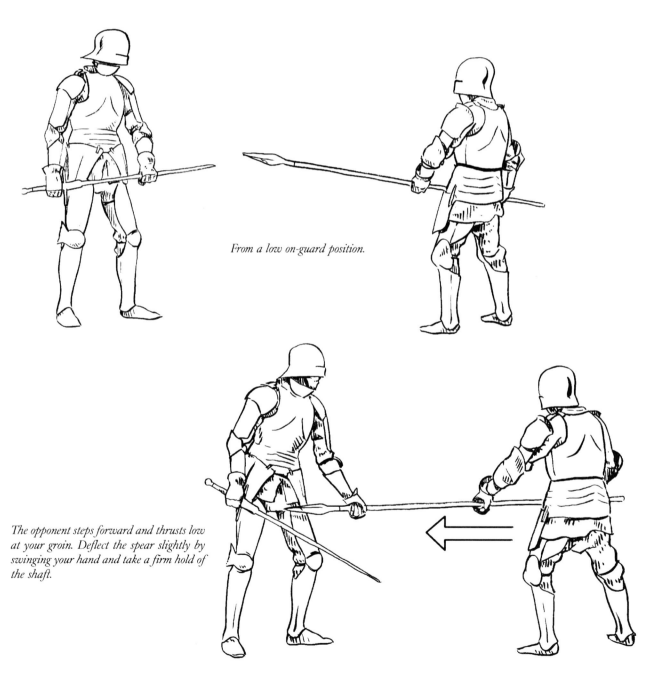

From a low on-guard position.

The opponent steps forward and thrusts low at your groin. Deflect the spear slightly by swinging your hand and take a firm hold of the shaft.

Step forward and thrust at the opponent's groin without letting go of his spear. Do this quickly, reaching out a bit with the sword as you thrust.

The opponent steps back and tries to yank the spear out of your hand. Now feel the direction of his force.

As the opponent pulls at the spear, let it go suddenly by shoving it up and toward the opponent; since he is pulling in the same direction, he will open up a lot. Step in at once and thrust with your sword. His armpit will be your most likely target.

The Openings
on a Man in Armor

RINGECK HERE OFFERS a short section on finding the possible openings on a fully armored man. This, it must be remembered, is only applicable on the mid- to late 15th-century armor, though Ringeck's text may offer ideas on where to look on other armor types.

IN ESSENCE, THE 15th-century full armor showed openings only at the joints, where mobility requirements made solid steel plating impossible. These gaps in the armor were frequently complemented with mail to give some protection.

WHEN FIGHTING IN armor, a major tactical idea was to force your opponent to move in such a way that it opened one or more of these weak points as he defended from the attack or tried to counter. The chinks created would then be attacked, primarily with the point of the sword—in effect using it as a short spear.

BUT IT IS worth noticing that a man in full armor standing in a lower guard does not have many significant openings that may be attacked at once. These must be gradually opened and exposed to attacks, and this is the basis for the plays in this section. Deflections are done not so much by absorbing hits on the armor itself but by deflecting attacks to the outside or inside using the sword as a scooping tool. Of course, if the opponent wore large sections of mail rather than plate, using the edge to cut would be an added option with good effect.

THE TEXT ABOUT THE OPENINGS
Leather and gauntlets and the eyes are openings to seek out.

DER TEXT VON DEN BLOSSEN
Leder unnd handschuch unnd den augen die blöss recht such

THIS IS WHEN you face an armored man and wish to attack him, you should always be aware of the openings. The first is in the face or below the shoulder or in the palm or the rear of the gauntlet, or behind the knee, or between the legs, or in all the openings and joints in the armor. When you face a man these are the best to attack. And the openings you should know and seek out so that you do not seek one farther away, but use these weaknesses that are close. Do this with all that belong to the fight.

DAS IST WANN du ainem gewapneten man ansetzen wilt so solt du der blöss eben war nemen Der ersten in dass gesicht oder under den uchsen oder in den tennern oder hindern in die handtschuch oder in die knyckeln oder zwischen den bainen oder in allen glidern da der harnesch sin gelenck innen hat Wann an den stetten ist der man am besten zegewinnen Und die blossen solt du recht wissen zu suchen das du nach ainer nicht wyt griffen solt wann dir ain nächere werden mag Dass tu mitt aller were die zu dem kanpff gehörent

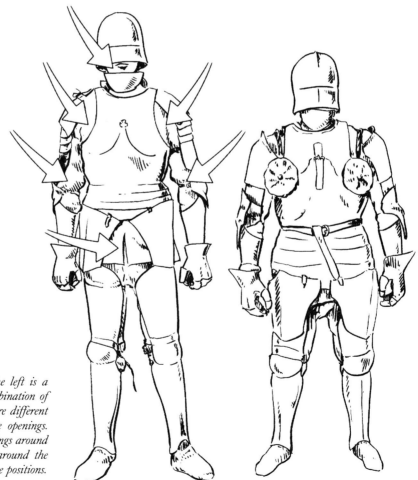

Look at these two sets of armor. The left is a German style and the right is a combination of Flemish/English and Italian. They are different in that the German set shows more openings. Notably, you see that both have openings around the armpit, inside the elbows, and around the groin, as well as the lower face in some positions.

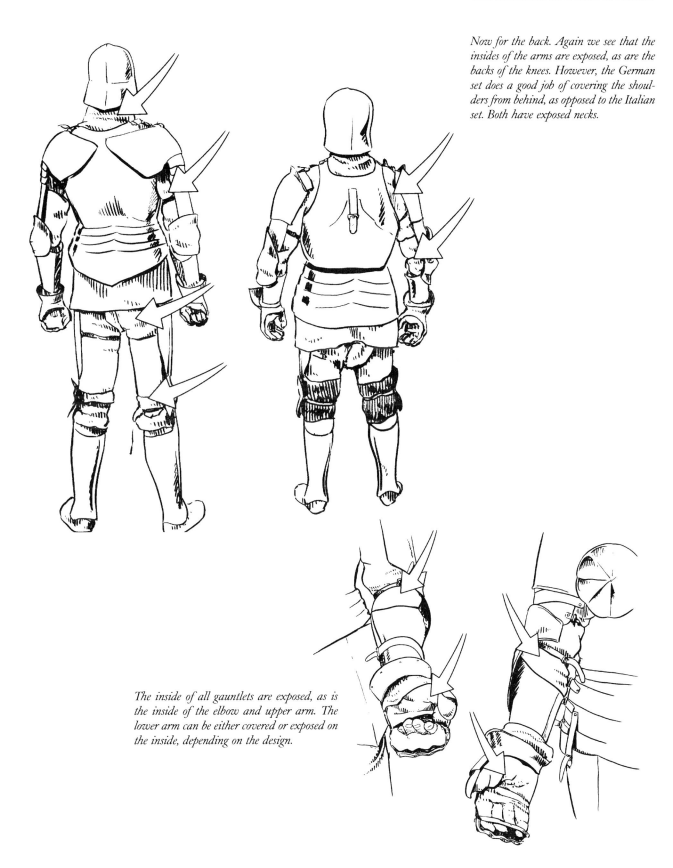

Now for the back. Again we see that the insides of the arms are exposed, as are the backs of the knees. However, the German set does a good job of covering the shoulders from behind, as opposed to the Italian set. Both have exposed necks.

The inside of all gauntlets are exposed, as is the inside of the elbow and upper arm. The lower arm can be either covered or exposed on the inside, depending on the design.

199

Wrestling in Armor

HERE WE HAVE the second section on wrestling in armor. The techniques are very efficient, with the primary goal being to get him on the ground, or prepare to get him there, so that you can pin him down and finish the job by stabbing him to death with your dagger.

MERELY DISABLING THE opponent is difficult since he is encased in steel. Perhaps the most important thing to understand when wrestling in armor is that the effects of joint locks are limited. This is because the armor itself will hinder several techniques, such as twisting or pressing the elbow joint in certain directions.

WHAT WORKS DEPENDS on the specific design of the armor your opponent happens to be wearing. It is therefore a good idea to test the techniques against different types of armor. And always practice in your armor: practicing without armor is next to useless since it will not be anywhere near the real thing.

THE TEXT OF THE SECRET WRESTLING
You should learn to use forbidden wrestling. Find out how to close in, and use strength to turn from above.

THAT IS WHEN someone closes with you. Then let your sword fall and carefully apply the wrestling that belongs to the fight. These are forbidden by all wise masters of the sword to disclose in public schools, since these are used for fighting with intent in combat fencing. These are the arm break, leg break, groin strikes, murder strike, knee strike, finger breaks, eye gouges, and others as well.

[Here we have just made some quick suggestions for what the above techniques may be.]

DER TEXT VON DEM VERBORGNEN RINGEN
Verbotten ringen wysslich zu lern bringen Zu schlissen finde die starcken domitt uber winde

DAS IST WANN ainer dem andern ein laufft so lausst din schwert fallen und wardt domitt wysslich der ringen die zu dem kampf gehören und verbotten sin von allen wysen maistern des schwerts dass man die uff offenbaren schulen nyemantz lernen noch sechen lasen sol darum dass sy zu dem kampff fechten gehörn Und dass sind die armbruch bainbruch hoden stoss mortschlag knystoss vinger läsunge augen griff und dar zu mer

A basic on-guard position. Others are possible.

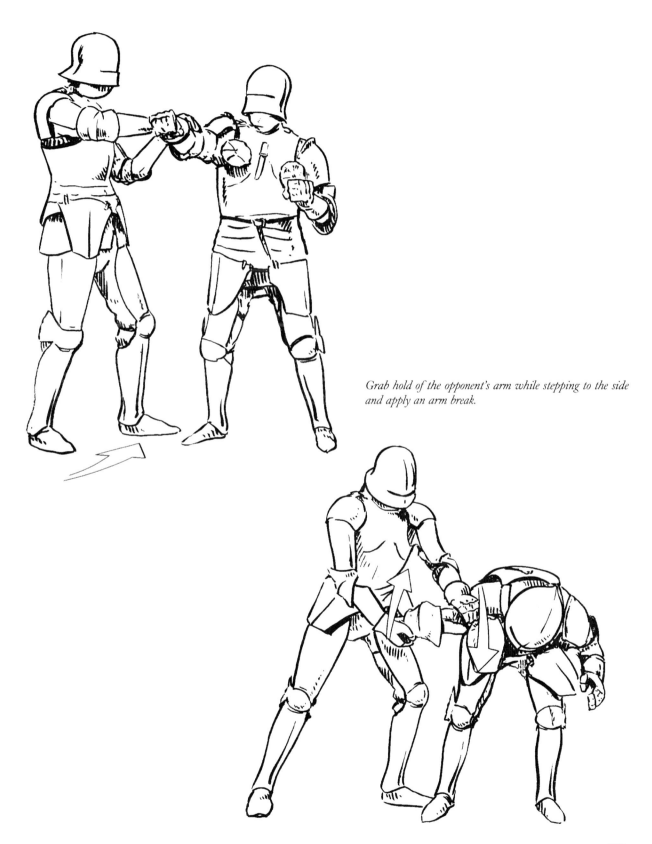

Grab hold of the opponent's arm while stepping to the side and apply an arm break.

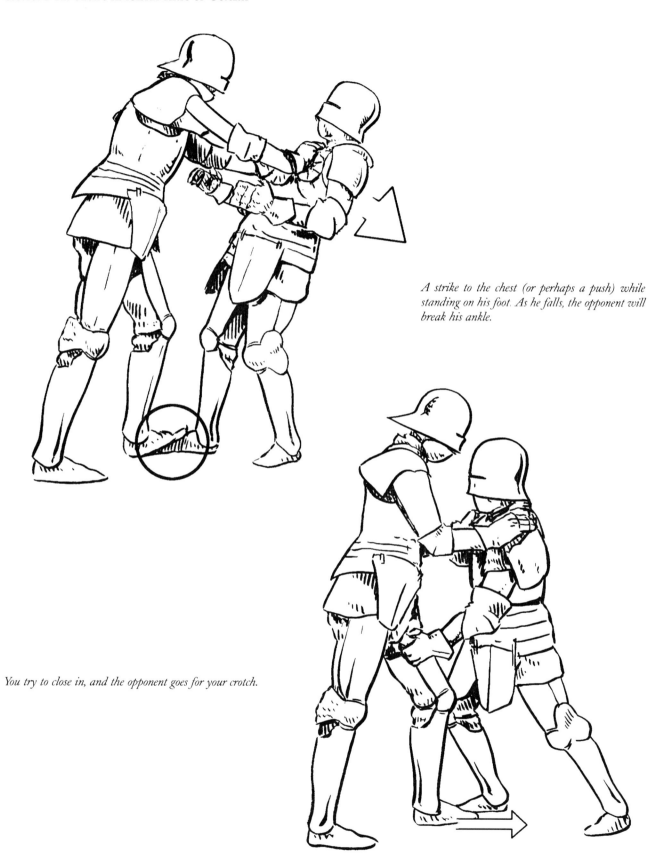

A strike to the chest (or perhaps a push) while standing on his foot. As he falls, the opponent will break his ankle.

You try to close in, and the opponent goes for your crotch.

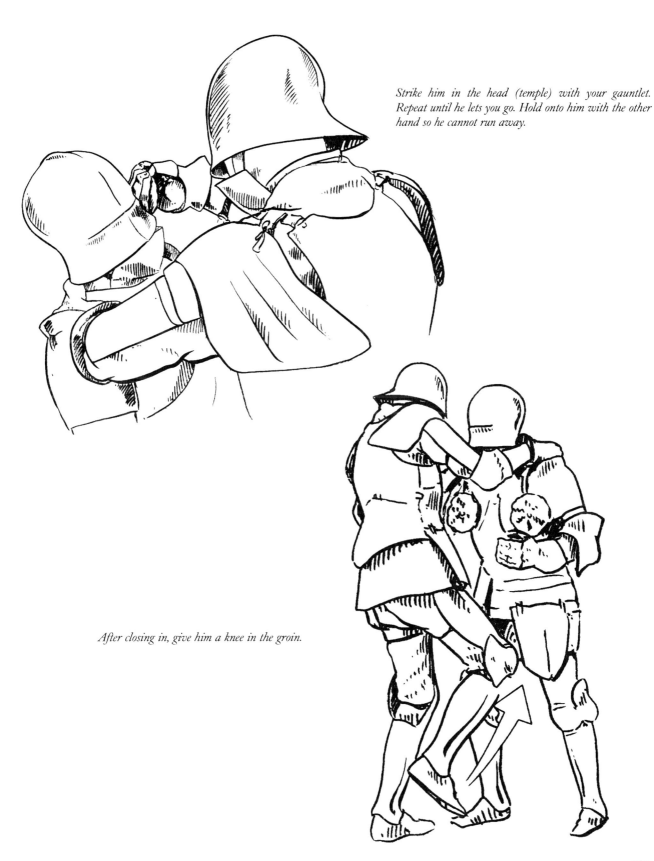

Strike him in the head (temple) with your gauntlet. Repeat until he lets you go. Hold onto him with the other hand so he cannot run away.

After closing in, give him a knee in the groin.

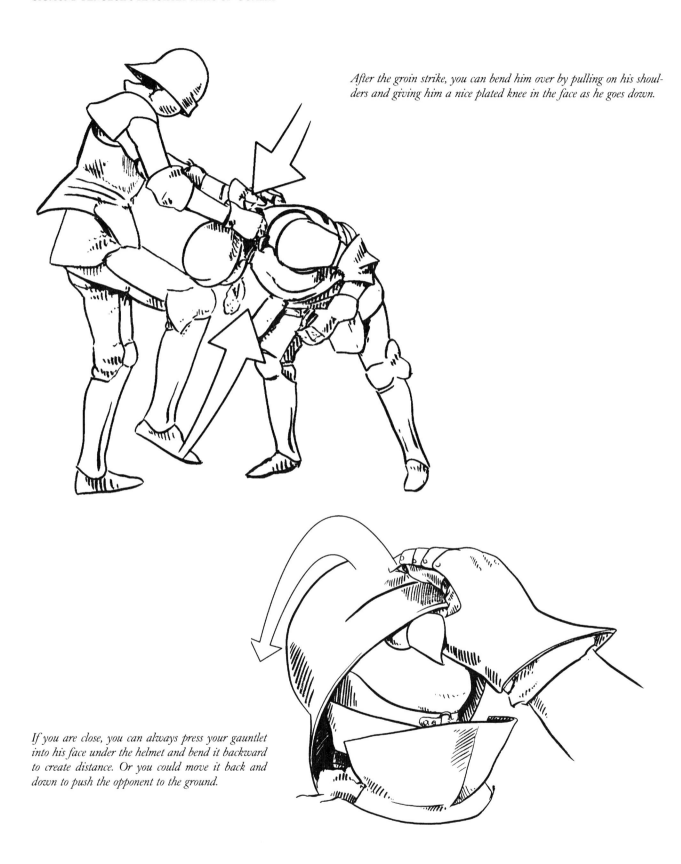

After the groin strike, you can bend him over by pulling on his shoulders and giving him a nice plated knee in the face as he goes down.

If you are close, you can always press your gauntlet into his face under the helmet and bend it backward to create distance. Or you could move it back and down to push the opponent to the ground.

HERE NOTE THE wrestling.

Note, if someone grabs hold of you high with a wrestling move and tries to pull you to him with force or thrust you away, then strike him with your right arm over his left above the hand and push with both hands on his chest as you step with the right foot behind his left and throw him over the knee by your feet.

HIE SOLT DU morcken die ringen

Item grifft dich an ainer oben mitt ringen und will dich mitt störck zu im rucken oder von im stossen so schlach den rechten arm ussen uber sin lincken vornen by siner hand Unnd truck den mitt baiden henden an din brust und spring mitt dim rechten fuss hinder sinen lincken Und wirff in uber das kny uss dem fuss

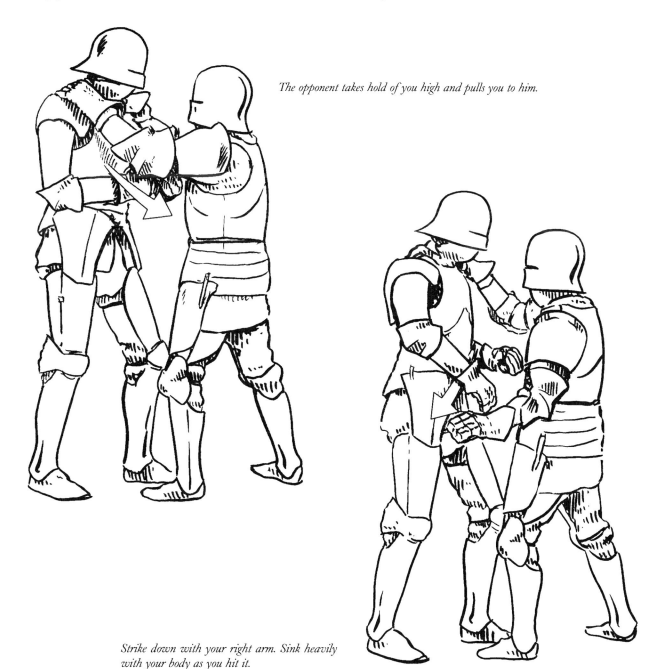

The opponent takes hold of you high and pulls you to him.

Strike down with your right arm. Sink heavily with your body as you hit it.

Step forward and place your right foot behind his left and strike or push him backward over your leg.

NOTE, IF SOMEONE grabs you with a wrestling move and does not hold you fast, then grab his right hand with your right and pull toward you. And with the left hand take hold of the elbow and step with the left foot in front of his right and pull him over it. Or fall down with your chest on his arm and break it.

ITEM GRIFFT ER dich an mitt ringen und halt er dich dann nitt vast so begryff sin rechte hand mitt diner rechten und ruck in zu dir mitt der lincken begryff im den elnbogen und schrytt mitt dem lincken fuss fur sinen rechten und ruck in also daru- ber Oder fall im mitt der brust uff den arm und brich im den also

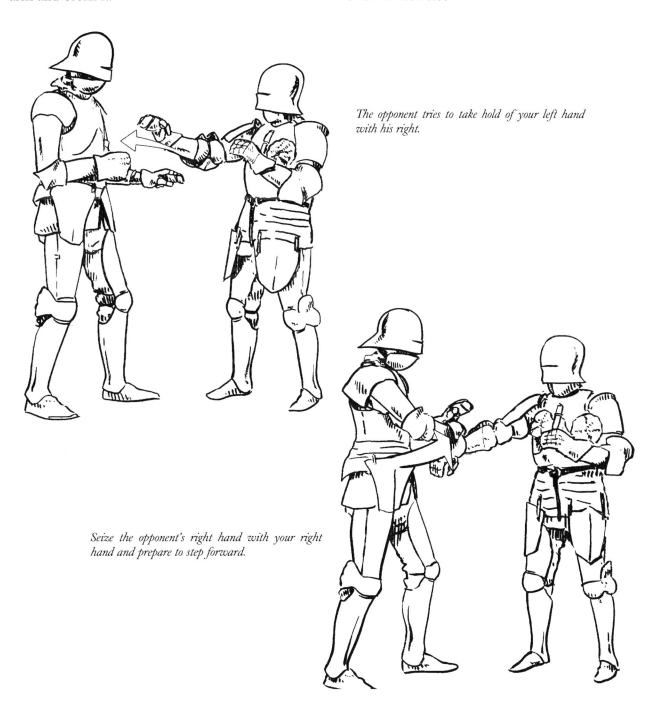

The opponent tries to take hold of your left hand with his right.

Seize the opponent's right hand with your right hand and prepare to step forward.

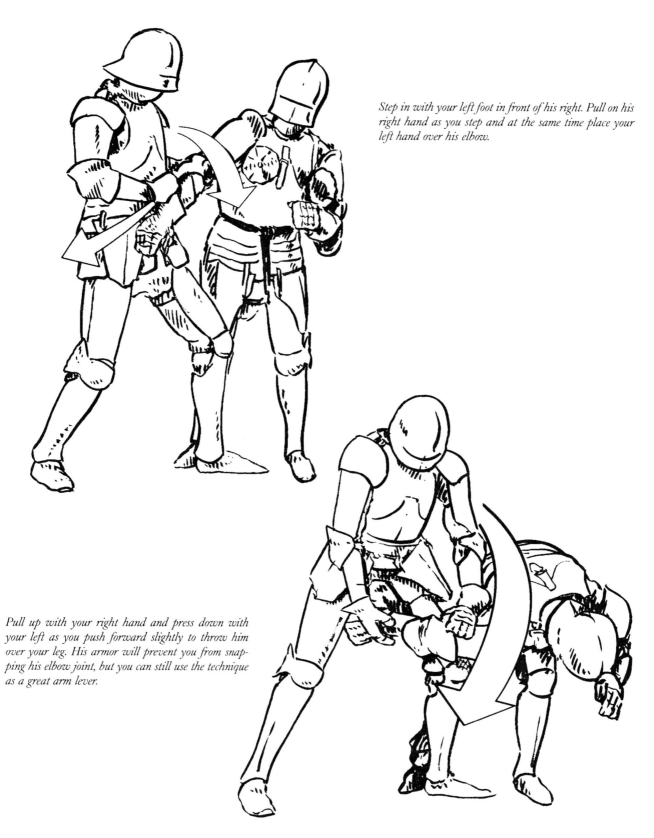

Step in with your left foot in front of his right. Pull on his right hand as you step and at the same time place your left hand over his elbow.

Pull up with your right hand and press down with your left as you push forward slightly to throw him over your leg. His armor will prevent you from snapping his elbow joint, but you can still use the technique as a great arm lever.

NOTE, USING YOUR left hand grab his left hand and pull him toward you. Strike your right arm over his left with force in/over/across the elbow joint and using your left hand break his left over your right. Leap with the right foot behind his right and throw him over it also.

ITEM, GRYFF MITT der lincken hand sin lincke vornen by der hand und ruck in zu dir und schlach din rechten arm mitt störck uber sin lincken in das glenck der armbuge und brich mitt der lincke hannd sin lincke uber din rechten Und spring mitt dem rechten fuss hinder sinen rechten und wirff in also daruber

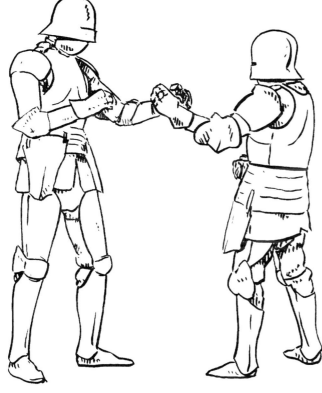

Grab hold of the opponent's left hand with your left without reaching too far out. Step closer instead if you need to.

Step in close behind his leg (shown here on the opponent's left rather than right, but it works on both sides) and place your right arm over his left and begin to break it backward and down.

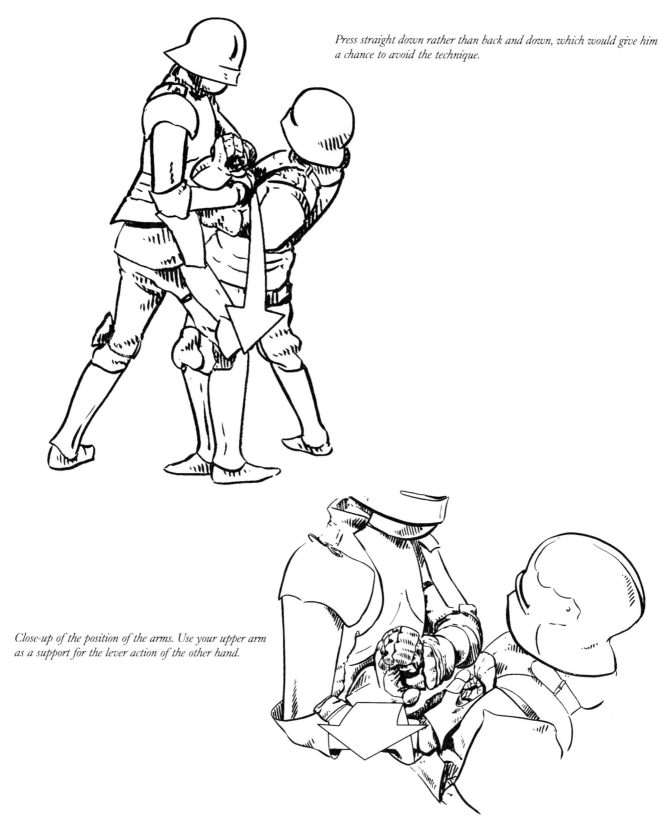

Press straight down rather than back and down, which would give him a chance to avoid the technique.

Close-up of the position of the arms. Use your upper arm as a support for the lever action of the other hand.

NOTE, IF HE moves in with his left arm under your right to seize you around the body, then strike him with your right arm from above with force on the outside of his left elbow joint and turn thereby away from him.

ITEM FÖRT ER dir mitt dem lincken arm under dinen rechten durch um din lybe so schlach in mitt dem rechten arm starck von oben nyder usswendig in dass glenck sins lincken elnbogens und wend dich do mitt von im

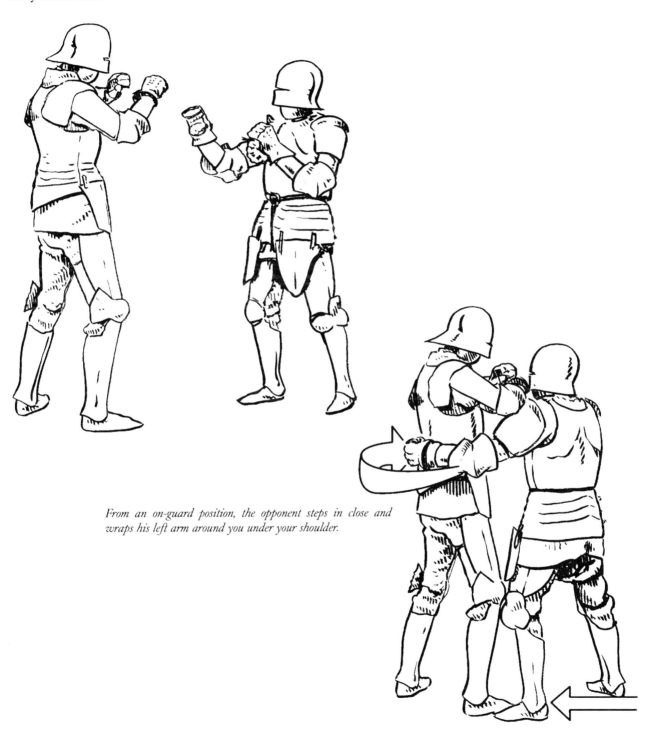

From an on-guard position, the opponent steps in close and wraps his left arm around you under your shoulder.

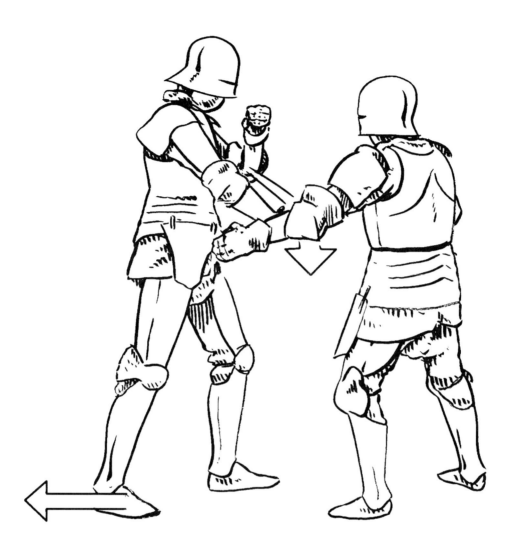

Step back and strike down in a circular motion from the inside or outside of his elbow joint. Striking on the outside goes against the joint, which is good, but armor is often in the way. Striking from above on the unprotected inside often works better.

NOTE, WHEN HE holds you by the arm with force and you hold him, and he has stretched his foot forward, then thrust at the same knee and then he will break his foot.

ITEM WANN ER dich fasst by den armen und du in wider stat er dann gestrackts mitt dem fuss so stoss in uff dass selbig kny so brichst im den fuss

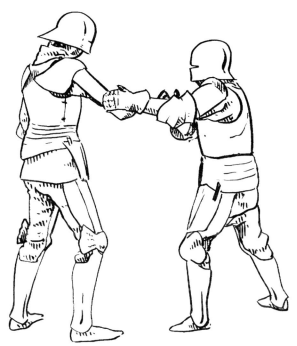

You both hold each other's arms, and you notice that your opponent has one leg (it does not matter which one) within your reach.

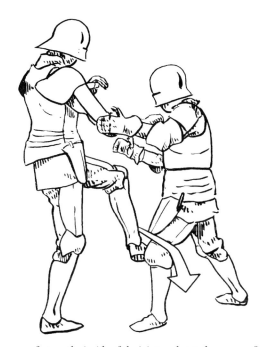

Place your foot on the inside of the joint and step down very firmly to break his knee. You can also kick there, but a good solid stomp is better. Hold onto the opponent to prevent him from going with the press to avoid injury.

It is possible to stamp from the front, but since the armor of the knee will lock in place well before the knee joint is snapped, this does not work as well.

215

NOTE, YOU CAN try to use the knee or the foot in the groin, but be careful that he does not catch you by the foot.

ITEM DU MAGST im och mitt dem kny oder mitt dem fuss zu dem gemächten stossen wenn es dir eben ist Aber du solt dich fur sechen dass er dich by dem fusse nitt begryffe

This can be avoided by blocking with the hands in a cross block.

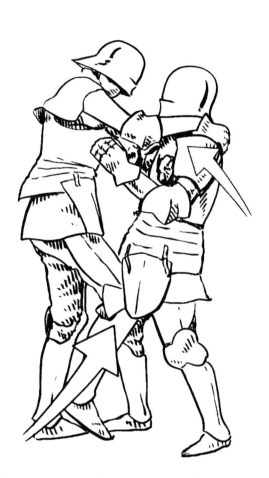

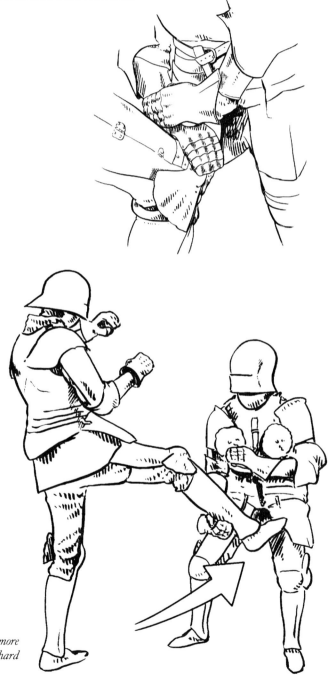

When you are close to the opponent you can always knee him in the groin.

You can also kick the opponent, but since you will move somewhat more slowly in armor due to the added weight on the legs, it is not that hard for your opponent to catch your foot.

NOTE THAT WHEN he grabs you with open hands or outstretched fingers, then wait and grab one of his fingers from above and break it upward and move him to the edge. You can also win over him by going to the side and gain even greater advantage.

ITEM WANN ER nach dir gryfft mitt offen henden oder mitt gerackten fingern so wart ob du im ainen finger begruffen mugst und bruch im den ubersich und fur in domitt zu dem krayss Auch gewinst du im do mitt die sytten an und sunst vill anderer grosser vortail

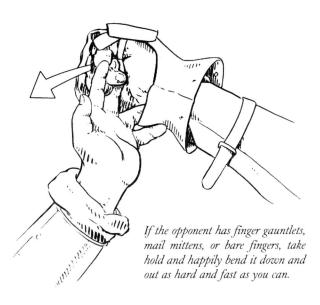

If the opponent has finger gauntlets, mail mittens, or bare fingers, take hold and happily bend it down and out as hard and fast as you can.

Always break straight down, not away from you and down.

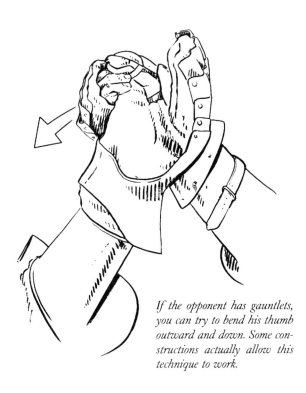

If the opponent has gauntlets, you can try to bend his thumb outward and down. Some constructions actually allow this technique to work.

Fighting in Armor with the Longsword

RINGECK'S TECHNIQUES FOR fighting with swords in armor differ from his unarmored techniques. The armored techniques are built on the foundation of fighting unarmored, but they are developed to suit the changed circumstances of the fight. (There is only one technique in that section where you half-sword and one more where you actually grasp the blade.) When fighting in armor, the edge strike is next to useless in the sense that it will not penetrate the armor or damage the body underneath it; the plate armor of the 15th century was much too strong to allow that. Test cutting has shown that it is simply not possible to penetrate at all, and severed arms and legs in armor depicted in period illustrations must be considered either the medieval equivalent of Hollywood movies or the result of the use of polearms or battleaxes.

THE MAJOR PROBLEM with half-swording is that you must grab a sharp blade and retain your hold without injuring your hand. This is difficult when you try to follow Ringeck's instructions. Trying to grasp a sharp blade would, therefore, run the risk of doing serious injury to the hand. (Possibly some detail in mail or plate gauntlets allowed for it with reduced danger.) The problem is, if the blade is sharp enough to hurt the opponent, then you could be hurt by it, too.

IN RINGECK IT is, however, worth noticing that most half-swording techniques start from that position and then continue to work from it, or require the release of the lead hand from the blade. Ringeck is very discrete with techniques where you have to switch your grip to take hold of the blade on the run, so to speak. But there were options on how to use the longsword while grabbing the blade. Half-swording makes use of the point and the pommel as the primary weapons. The pommel functions like a mace and inflicts blunt damage, while the point is like a short spear.

SINCE RINGECK'S HALF-SWORD is used exclusively in armored, one-on-one combat, it comes to mind that perhaps these are special occasions of the judicial duel. I believe that the swords used were not fully sharpened (there would have been no need for that, and it would have made half-swording impossible), and that half-sword is the key to fighting in armor with swords. These techniques make use of the sword as a very long dagger or short spear; the attacks are thrusts with the point or strikes with the pommel.

AN ALTERNATIVE WAS suggested by a student of Guy Windsor, who said that wet leather gloves actually allow you to both grab and work with a sharp blade without injury. The wet leather sticks to the steel like glue. I have not tried this with sharp blades, but it does make sense. (And I know that my gloves would be soaked with sweat if I were in a duel for life and death.) Another possibility is that only the outermost 15 centimeters of the sword were really sharp. This would allow for a grip further in while retaining both cutting and thrusting capacity.

THE TEACHING TEXT
Note, always seek the opening with the point.

DER TEXT VON AINER LERE
Item aller were den ort gegen der bloss köre

THAT IS THAT you in the wards belonging to the fight always try to thrust at the openings with your point if there is an opportunity and nothing else since it will bring you to harm.

[This is an interesting admonition to use the point alone and refrain from other techniques with the sword, indicating that the author knew that the sword simply would not penetrate. And a faulty attack would leave you open to a counter by the opponent.]

DASS IST DASS du mitt allen dry wörn die zu dem kampff gehörn allweg mitt dem ort zu den blossen stechen solt die dir vorgenant sind Und sunst nicht anders es bringt dir schaden

---

THE TEXT OF how to fight with sword against sword in combat
How you draw the sword from the scabbard using both, so shall you strengthen it, and always note the thrust.

[You draw the sword by pulling the blade out and at the same time pulling the scabbard back for a quicker draw.]

DER TEXT WIE man soll fechten im schwert gegen schwert zu kampff
Wo man von schaiden schwert zucken sicht von in baiden so soll man stercken Die schutten recht eben mörcken

---

THAT IS, IF both have thrown their spears and come to fighting with the swords, then before everything else you should note this: the four guards with the short sword, and then always thrust to the openings. If he thrusts at you at the same time or is weak at the sword, then when you see this use the strong against this as is described in the following.

[A general introduction, indicating the four guards, the importance of thrusting with the point, and remembering indes and strong against weak and vice versa knowing when to use what by understanding fuhlen.]

DASS IST ÖB sy baide die sper verschossen hettenn und solten vechten mitt den schwerten so salt du vor allen dingen mörcken und wissen dass:die vier huten mitt dem kurtzen schwert Und daruss stichh im allweg zu der obern blöss Sticht er dann mitt dir glich ein oder waich am schwert ist Und wenn du enpfunnden haust so tryb die störck gegen im die du hernach geschriben wirst sehen

The first guard of the half-sword

Note, hold your sword with the right hand on the grip and with the left grab hold of the middle of the blade. Hold it on your right side over your head and let the point hang down toward his face.

Die ersten hut in dem halben schwert

Item halt din schwert mitt der rechten hand by der handhäbe und mitt der lincken gryff mitten in die clingen Und halt es neben diner rechten sytten uber din haupt und lass den ort undersich hangen dem man gegen dem gesicht

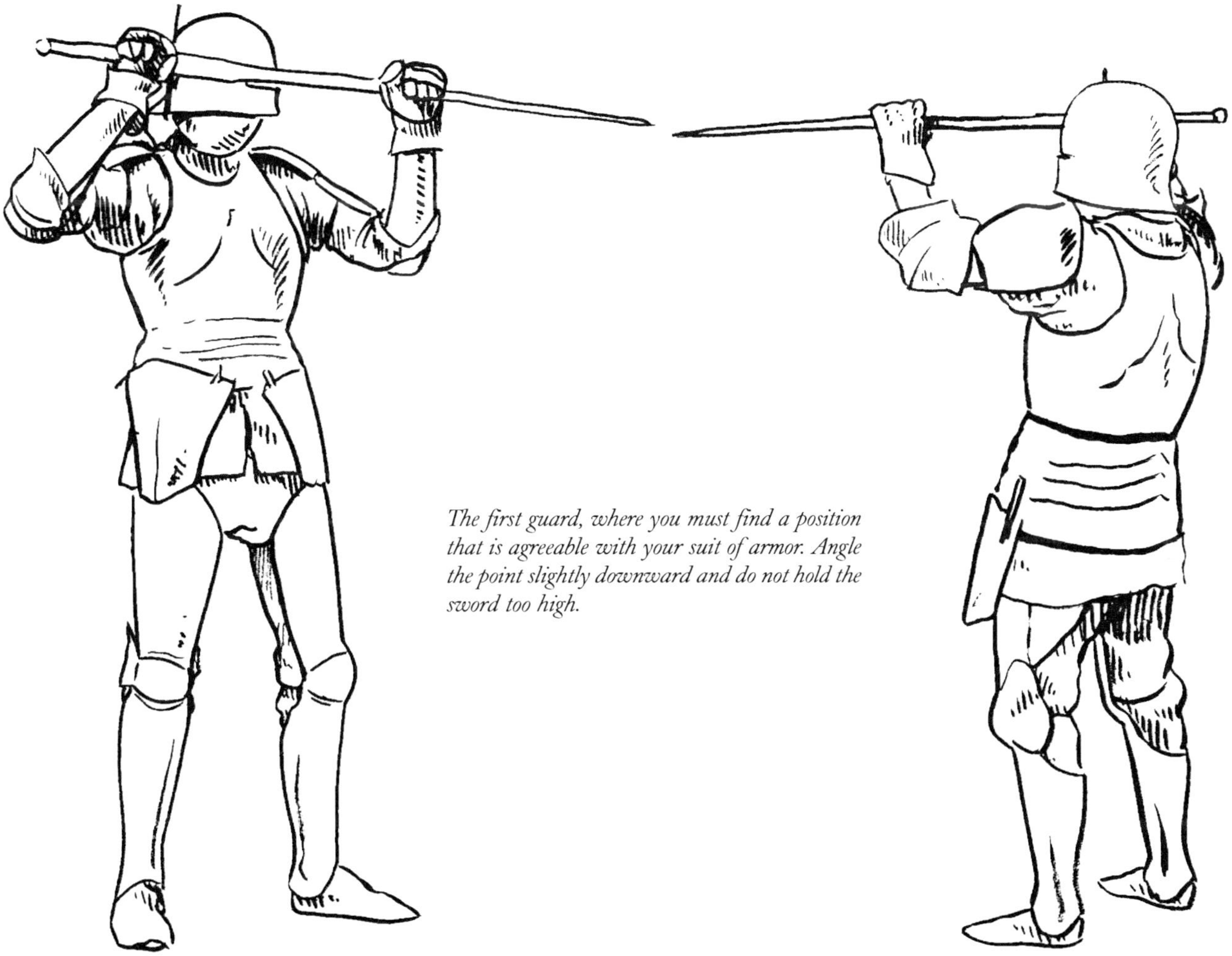

The first guard, where you must find a position that is agreeable with your suit of armor. Angle the point slightly downward and do not hold the sword too high.

NOTE, IF HE stands against you in the lower guard and tries to thrust at you from below, then thrust through from above downward between his sword and his foremost hand and push the pommel down and wind the point at the sword down and through to your right side and set at him.

ITEM STÄTT ER dann gegen dir in der undern hut und will dir unden zu stechen so stich durch von oben nider zwischen dem schwert und siner vorgesätzner hand und truck den knopff undersich und wind im den ort am schwert unden durch gegen siner rechten sytten und setz im an

The opponent stands in a lower guard; you stand in the upper guard.

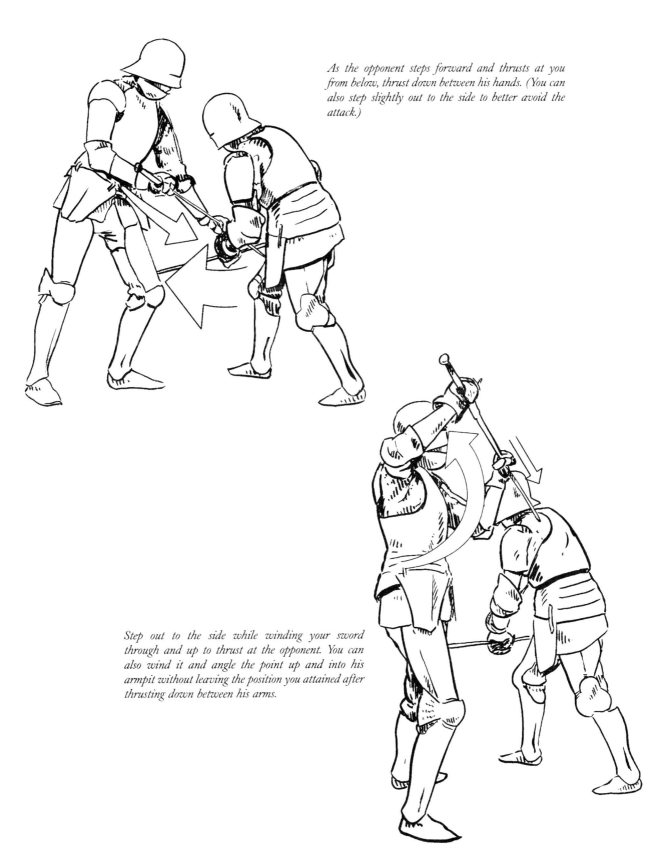

As the opponent steps forward and thrusts at you from below, thrust down between his hands. (You can also step slightly out to the side to better avoid the attack.)

Step out to the side while winding your sword through and up to thrust at the opponent. You can also wind it and angle the point up and into his armpit without leaving the position you attained after thrusting down between his arms.

Note, thrust at his face from the first guard. If he displaces this then pull away or go through with the thrust on the opposite side. Or when you have attacked him then strike your sword under your right shoulder with the hilt on your chest and push him away from you.

Item stich im uss der ersten hut zu dem gesicht Wert ers so zuck oder ge durch mitt dem stich -alss vor- zu der anderen sytten Und wenn du im haust angesetzt so schlach din schwert under din rechte uchsen mitt dem gehultz an die brust und dring in also von dir hin

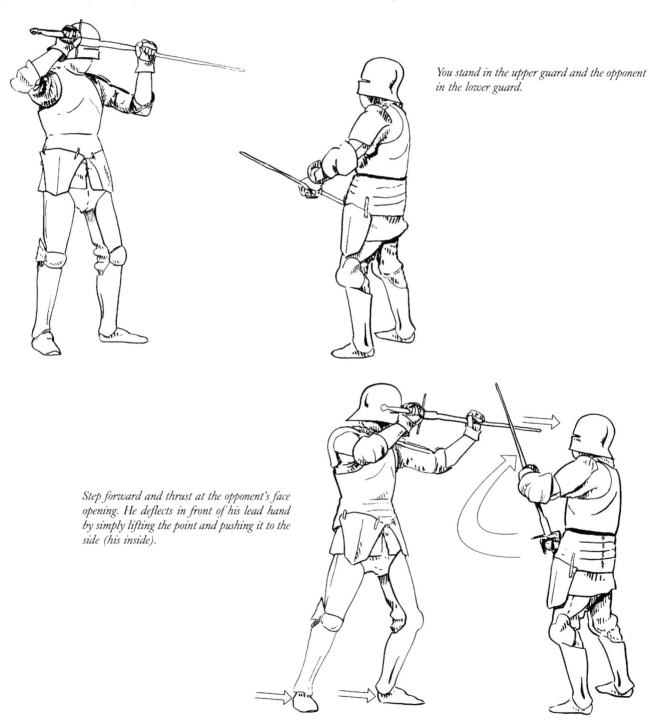

You stand in the upper guard and the opponent in the lower guard.

Step forward and thrust at the opponent's face opening. He deflects in front of his lead hand by simply lifting the point and pushing it to the side (his inside).

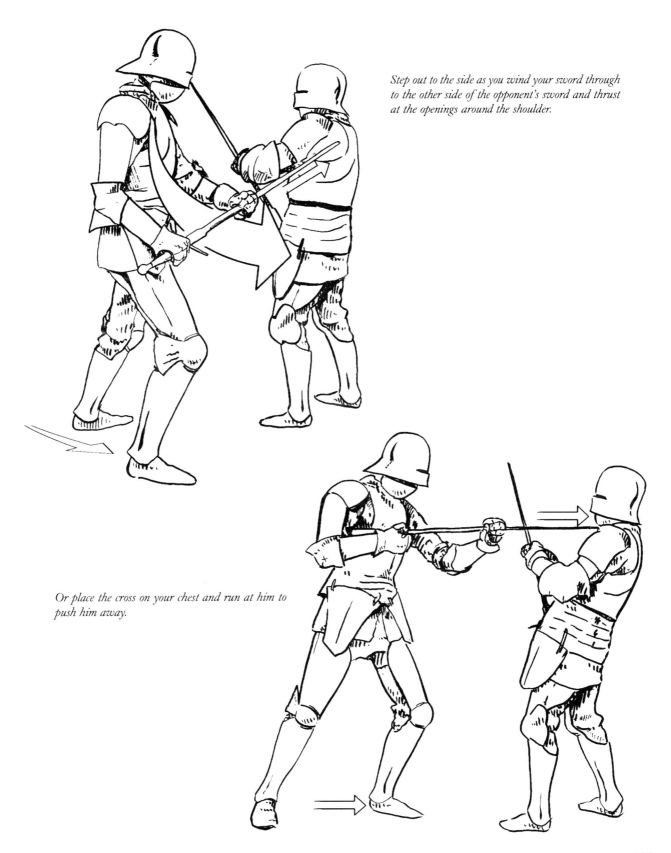

Step out to the side as you wind your sword through to the other side of the opponent's sword and thrust at the openings around the shoulder.

Or place the cross on your chest and run at him to push him away.

225

NOTE, ANOTHER THRUST against him as before. If he displaces this with his sword in front of his left hand and keeps his point in your face and tries to attack you, then take hold of his sword point with your left hand and hold it fast. Then thrust him forcefully in the groin with the right hand. If he pulls away his sword to free it from your hand, suddenly let the sword go, which will create an opening, then grab hold of your sword with the left hand in the middle of the blade and follow him.

ITEM MÖRCK AIN anders stich im zu alss vor Versetzt er vor siner lincken hannd mitt dem schwert und blipt dir mitt dem ort vor dem gesicht und will dir ansetzen so begryff mitt der lincken hand syn schwert by dem ort und halt dass föst und mitt der kerechten hand stich im kröffticlichen zu dem gemächten Zuckt er dann syn schwert vast an sich und will dir dass uss der hand rissen so lass im das schwert urbringe faren so gibt er sich bloss So begriff din schwert bald mitt der lincken hand wider mitten in der clingen und folg im nach

You thrust at the opponent from the high guard and he displaces in front of his left hand.

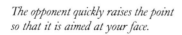

The opponent quickly raises the point so that it is aimed at your face.

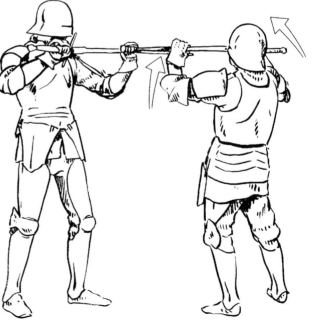

226

Grab the opponent's sword point with your left hand, pulling it down and out to the left in a firm motion. Drop your own sword and thrust him in the groin single-hand.

If he pulls strongly on his sword, let him have it immediately.

Step in and take hold of your sword with your left hand to steady the point and thrust at the opening closest to you.

NOTE ANOTHER. If you take hold of his sword and he yours then throw his sword from the left hand and at once grab hold in the middle of yours and wind the point on the outside of his left hand and then go at him

Note, or throw your sword down in front of you and try his left hand with your left and try an arm break or other wrestling moves.

ITEM AN ANDERS Begryffstu sin schwert und er das din so wirff sin schwert uss der lincken hand und do mitt begryff dass din wider mitten inder clingen und wind im den ort ausen uber sin lincke hand und setz im an

Item oder wirff im din schwert fur die fuss und begriff sin lincke hand mit diner lincken und tryb den arm bruch oder sunst ander ringen

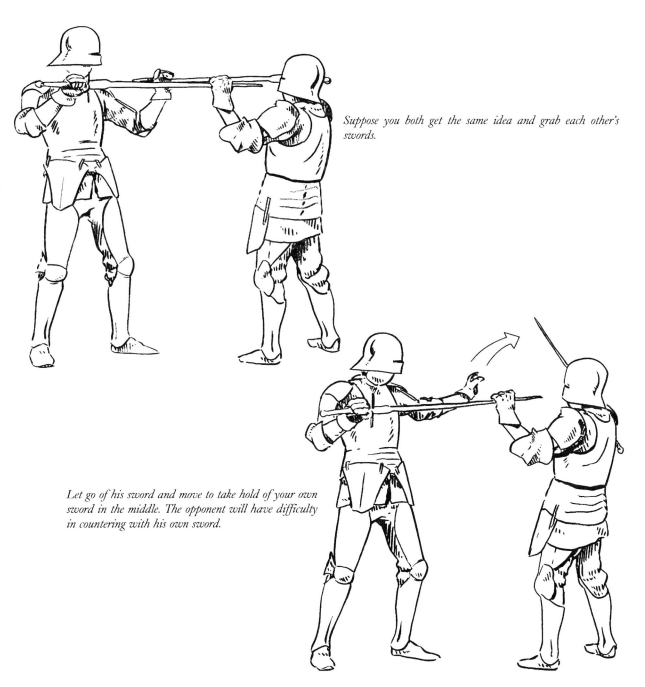

Suppose you both get the same idea and grab each other's swords.

Let go of his sword and move to take hold of your own sword in the middle. The opponent will have difficulty in countering with his own sword.

Wind the point either over or under his hand to create an opening.

If the opponent keeps holding on for dear life, swivel the sword around and strike him in the opening with the pommel as hard as you can and either wrestle or work your sword loose and thrust at the nearest opening.

Or simply drop your sword and his, leaving the opponent standing there quite immobilized for a second or so.

Step in to either side and wrestle.

In this case, apply an arm break, pushing the opponent backward over your leg.

Note that if you thrust from the upper guard and he takes hold of your sword with his left hand between your hands, then go on the outside or on the inside of his left hand and go to your right side and then go at him. You can also strike at him from the upper guard using the pommel if you get a chance.

Item wann du im uss der obern hut zu stichst fölt er dir dann mitt der lincken hannd in din schwert zwischen dinen baiden henden so far im mitt dem knopff usswendig oder inwendig uber sin lincke hannd und reyss uff din rechte sytten und setz im an Auch magst du uss der obern hut mitt dem knopff wol schlachen wann es dir eben ist

You thrust down at the opponent from the upper guard.

As you thrust, the opponent sidesteps and grabs your sword between his hands.

Wind the point over the opponent's arm, forcing him to release his hold.

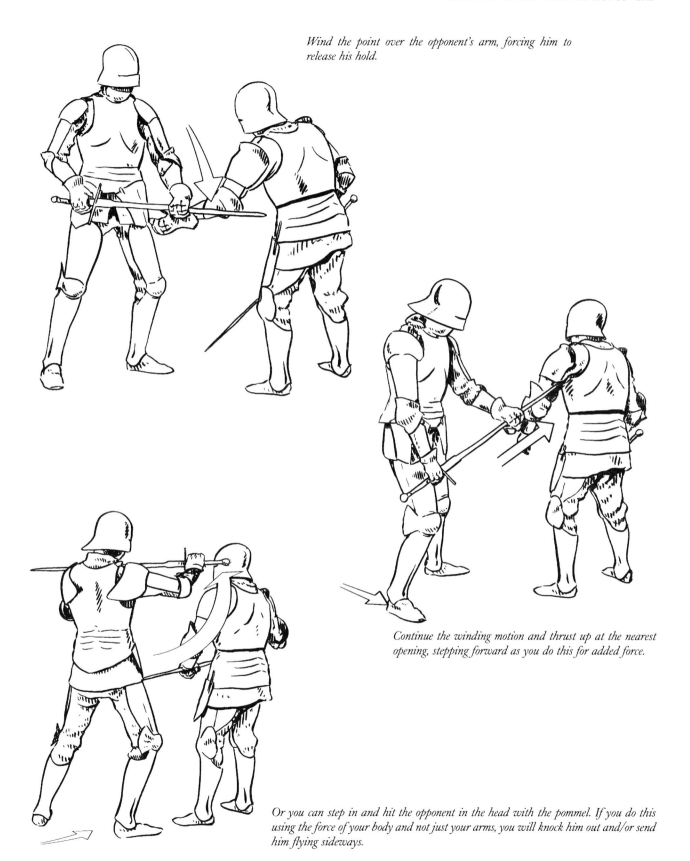

Continue the winding motion and thrust up at the nearest opening, stepping forward as you do this for added force.

Or you can step in and hit the opponent in the head with the pommel. If you do this using the force of your body and not just your arms, you will knock him out and/or send him flying sideways.

THE SECOND GUARD WITH THE SHORT SWORD IN COMBAT

Note, hold your sword with both hands and hold it below on your right side with the grip below your right knee and lead with your left foot and keep your point in his face.

DIE ANDERN HUT MITT DEM KURTZEN SCHWERT ZU KAMPFF

Merck halt din schwert mitt baiden henden und halt dass undersich zu diner rechten sytten mitt der handhäben neben dinem rechten kny und das din lincker fuss vor stee und din ort dem man gegen sin gesicht

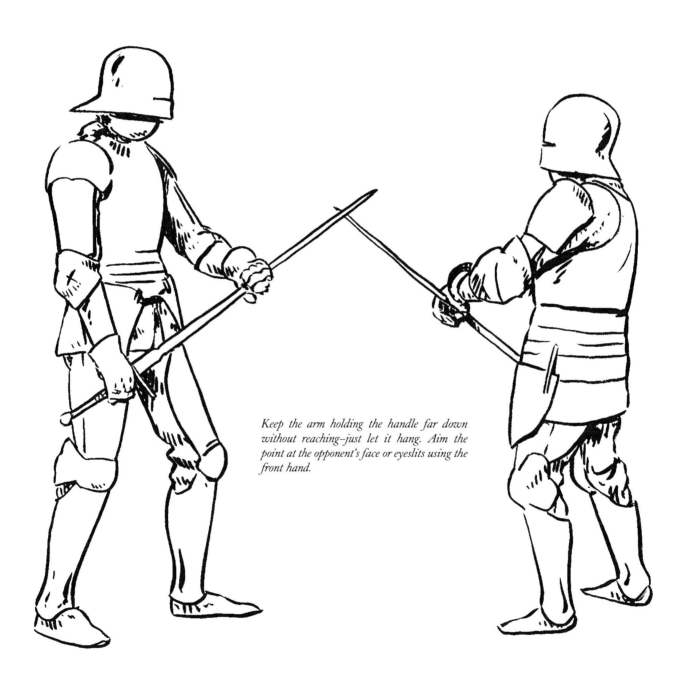

Keep the arm holding the handle far down without reaching–just let it hang. Aim the point at the opponent's face or eyeslits using the front hand.

NOTE, IF YOU are also on guard and he is in the upper guard and tries to attack you above, then thrust foreward and place the point in front of his foremost hand in the opening of the gauntlet. Or thrust at him over his foremost hand with your sword and then press your pommel to the ground and go at his other opening.

ITEM WENN DU also steest in der hut stet er dann gegen dir in der obern hut und will dir oben ansetzen so stich du vor und setz im den ort fur sin furgesetzte hand zu der bloss des teners Oder stich im uber sin vorgesetzten hand durch (mitt) din schwert Und truck dinen knopff gegen der erden und setz im an zu der andern sytten

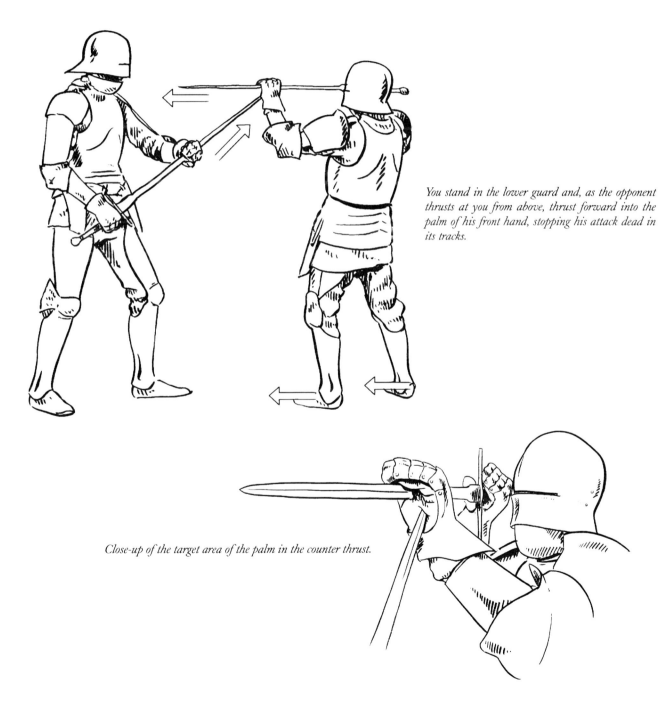

You stand in the lower guard and, as the opponent thrusts at you from above, thrust forward into the palm of his front hand, stopping his attack dead in its tracks.

Close-up of the target area of the palm in the counter thrust.

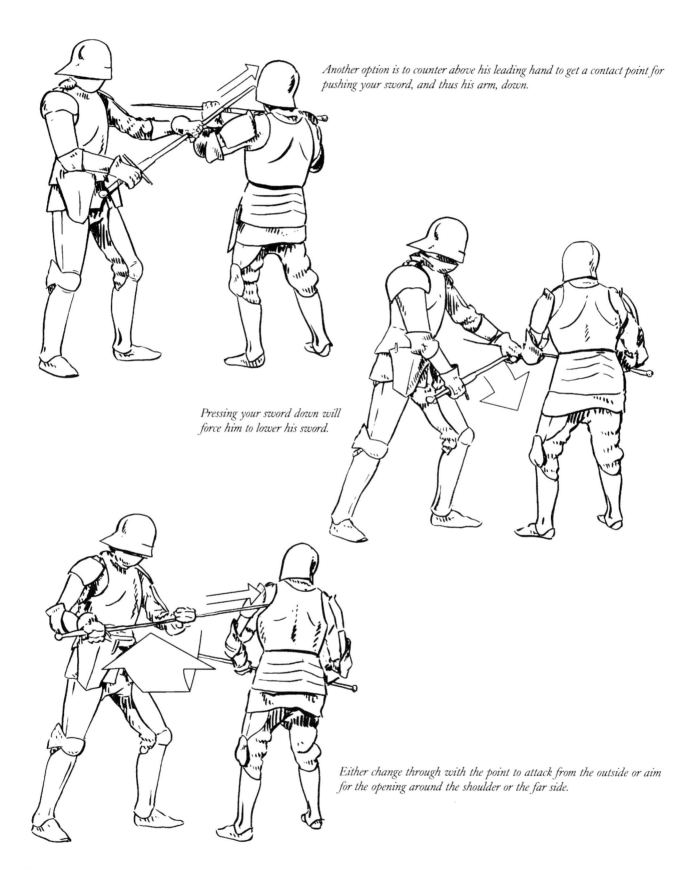

Another option is to counter above his leading hand to get a contact point for pushing your sword, and thus his arm, down.

Pressing your sword down will force him to lower his sword.

Either change through with the point to attack from the outside or aim for the opening around the shoulder or the far side.

NOTE, WHEN HE thrusts at you from above, then with your left hand take hold of his sword in front of his left hand and, with the right, set your sword with the hilt on your chest and go at him.

ITEM WANN ER dir oben zu sticht so gryffe mitt der lincken hand sin schwert vor siner lincken Und mitt der rechten setz din schwert mitt dem gehultz an din brust unnd setz im an

As the opponent thrusts at you, let go with your front hand and take hold of his sword. Pull it a bit to the outside to open him up.

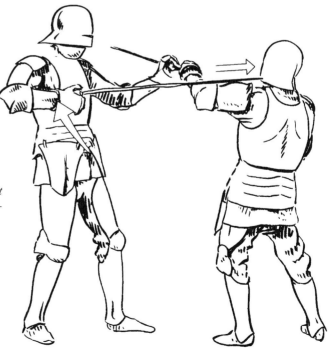

Raise the crossguard so that you can place it in front of your chest for support, still keeping his sword out to the side, and step forward to thrust.

A technique against getting through

Note, when you thrust at him from the lower guard and he thrusts at you from the upper guard between your outstretched hands and the sword then note: and he tries to push the pommel down, then go up into the upper guard and go at him.

Ain bruch wider dass durchsetzen

Item wann du im uss der under hut zu stichst sticht er dir uss der obern hut durch zwischen diner vorgesätzen hand und dem schwert so mörck: Die wil er den knopff nider truckt so far uff zu der obern hut und setz im an

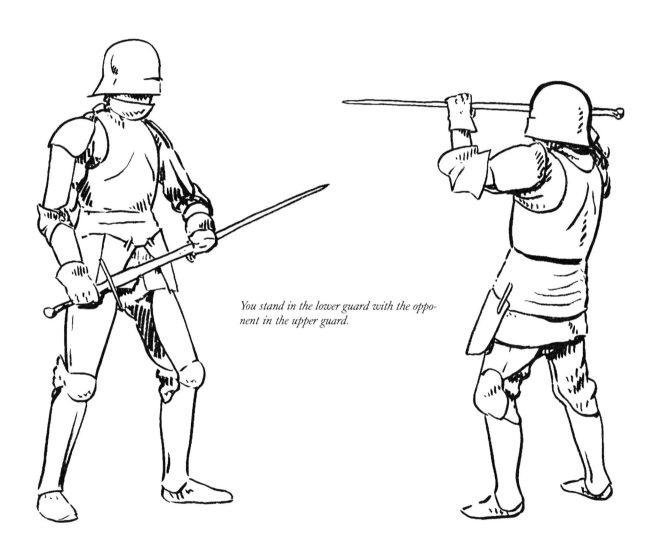

You stand in the lower guard with the opponent in the upper guard.

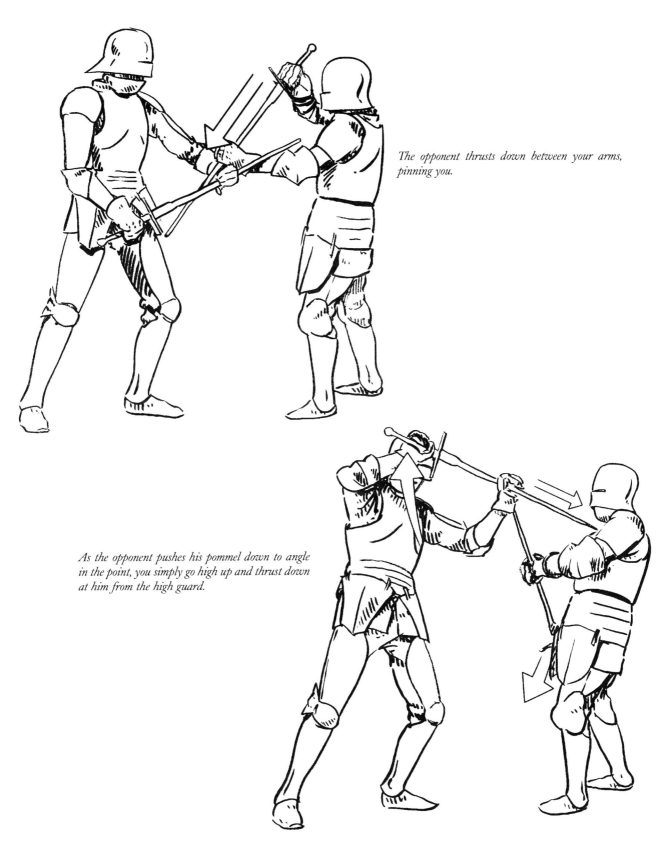

The opponent thrusts down between your arms, pinning you.

As the opponent pushes his pommel down to angle in the point, you simply go high up and thrust down at him from the high guard.

NOTE, THRUST AT him from the lower guard, if he then moves through with the pommel under your sword to displace, then remain with the point steadily in front of his face and push his right hand down and go at him. You can also change through below with the pommel and set aside his thrust.

ITEM STICH IM zu uss der undern hut Fert er dann durch mitt dem knopff under sin schwert und will domitt absetzen so blyb im mitt dem ort starck vor dem gesicht und truck im sin gerechte hand also undersich und und setz im an Auch magst du unden durchwechseln mitt dem knopff und im dem stich absetzen

As you thrust at the opponent, he will displace the attack in front of his lead hand.

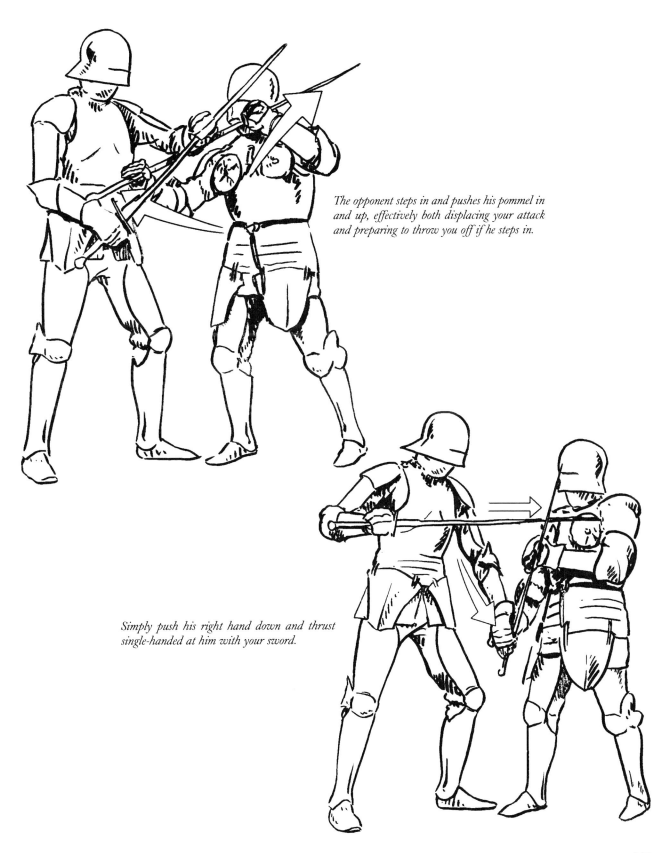

The opponent steps in and pushes his pommel in and up, effectively both displacing your attack and preparing to throw you off if he steps in.

Simply push his right hand down and thrust single-handed at him with your sword.

NOTE, YOU WIND and hereafter is described how you should do the third guard and how to strike your opponent with the pommel.

ITEM DU WINDEST och hernach geschriben wie du uss der drytten hut dic schläg dic man schlächt mitt dem knopff versetzen soll

---

THE FOURTH GUARD WITH THE SHORT SWORD IN COMBAT

Note, hold the sword with both hands as described before and hold it with the grip under your right shoulder and set the crossguard in front of your chest on the right side with the point against him. And you should come into this guard from all three aforementioned guards. And when you thrust at him and the point gets stuck in the armor, then wind your hilt at your chest and push him back in front of you, and do not let him escape from the point, since he will be able to thrust, cut, and strike

DIE VIERD HUTT MITT DEM KURTZEN SCHWERT ZU KAMPFF

Item halt das schwert mitt baiden henden alss vor geschriben stät und halt es mitt der handhäbe under din rechte uchsen und setz dass gehultz vornen an die rechte brust dass der ort gegen dem man stee Und in die hut solt du uff allen dryen vorgenampten hutten kumen Also wenn du im stichst zu der blöss und das der ort hafft in dem harnasch so winde allwegen din gehultz an din brust und dring in also von dir hinweg Und lauss in nitt von dem ort abkomen so maag er weder stechen noch hawen noch schlachen

Hold the sword with the point forward and rest the inside of the crossguard on your breastplate. Aim with the front hand, not by maneuvering the rear hand.

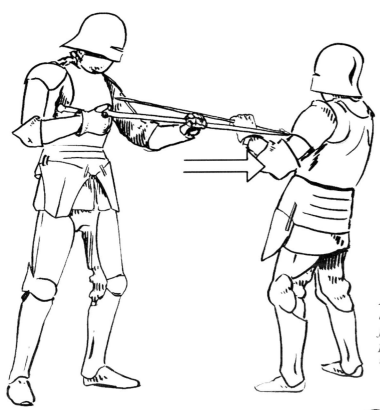

As you thrust at the opponent's armor chinks around the armpit, if the point gets stuck (from another position or from this one) simply rest the crossguard on the breast-plate and push him backward using your whole body, not just the arms. Press forward with the legs.

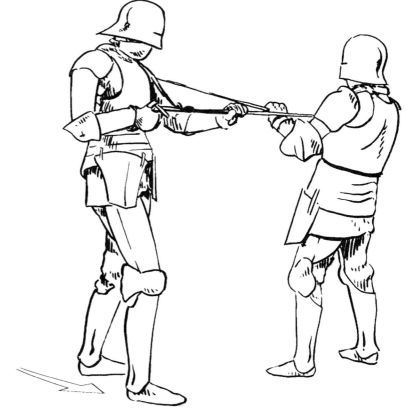

Note when you have attacked him, if he is taller then push him away from you with the point high and go at the small, round plates that cover the front of the armpits. But if he is shorter than you are, then go to the right with your pommel at your right side by the right hip and your point aimed upward and go well at the rings as before. And thus you will push him before you and not let him escape the sword.

Item wann du im hast angesetzt ist er dann lenger wann du bist so dring in also von dir dass din ort ubersich uff gee und im wol in die ringe gesetzt sylst er aber kurtzer dann du bist so lauss din schwert mitt dem knopff zu diner rechten sytten under sich ab sincken biss uff die rechten huffe und dass din ort ubersich stande und im in die ring wol gesetzt sy alss vor Und dring in also fur dich und lauss in von dem schwert nicht abkomen

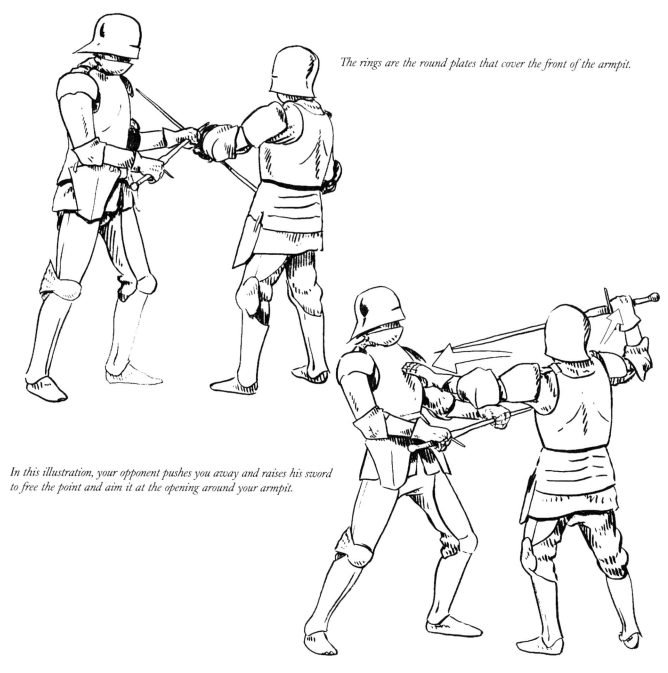

The rings are the round plates that cover the front of the armpit.

In this illustration, your opponent pushes you away and raises his sword to free the point and aim it at the opening around your armpit.

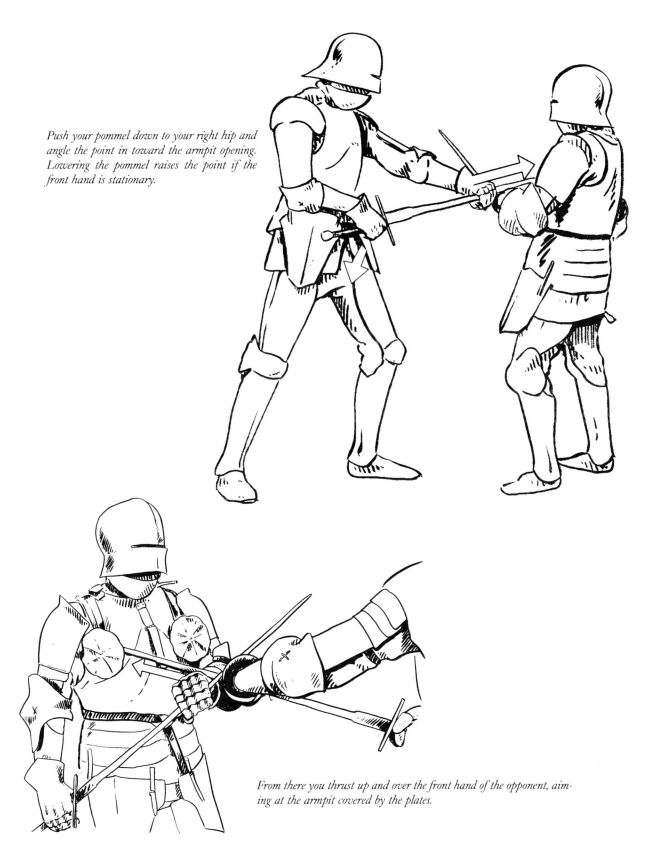

Push your pommel down to your right hip and angle the point in toward the armpit opening. Lowering the pommel raises the point if the front hand is stationary.

From there you thrust up and over the front hand of the opponent, aiming at the armpit covered by the plates.

245

THE TEXT ON the vor and the nach.

Understand these two things. Learn to leap away.

You should in all things always know the vor or the nach because from these two things stem all fighting arts. That is, you should always move before the opponent with a strike or with a thrust, since he will then be forced to be displaced. And as soon as he is displaced and binds the sword try this technique. Thus his techniques will not come before your work, and this is the vor.

Note here the nach. These are all the techniques he will try against you, and you will have to displace them by watching his hand [at once] in the displacement and seek the next opening with the point. Thus you will win with your displacement, and this is the nach.

DER TEXT VON den vor und nach

Vor und nach die zway ding bricffe wysslicher Lere mitt ab spring

Das ist das du vor allen sachen solt wissen dass vor und dass nach wann uss den zwayen dingen gett alle kunst zu kampffe Doch so gedenck dass du allweg vor komest ee dann er es sy mitt ainem schlag oder mitt ainem stich

so muss er dir versetzen Und alss balde alss er mitt der versatzung an dass schwert bindt so trybe din stuck behentlich So mag er sinen stucken vor diner arbayt nicht komen Und dass haisst dass Vor

Item hie mörck dass Nach Dass sind die bruch wider alle stuck die er uff dich trypt Und dass vernym also Kumpt er vor das du im versetzen must so such zu hand mitt dcr versätzung mitt dem ort die nechsten blöss So gewinst du mitt diner versätzung die arbait Unnd das haisst dass Nach

[Vor is about taking the initiative when it is appropriate, not attacking indiscriminately. That is really bad swordsmanship and nothing else. The attack should come when you have the opponent flatfooted, insecure, or just indecisive. When you move in he will be forced to react rather than act. Then be sure to follow up. The attacks should flow like water one after the other without any interruption. Remember that from every position of the weapon there is a natural continuation; find that movement and you will win.

Nach is when he moves first. Then you must retake the initiative by nullifying the opponent's movement. Again, your attack must flow forward in a natural way. If you must exert pressure or force, you are doing something wrong. Keep in mind that you must in a sense always be moving forward even if you do not step forward.]

From an on-guard position. A low guard is shown here.

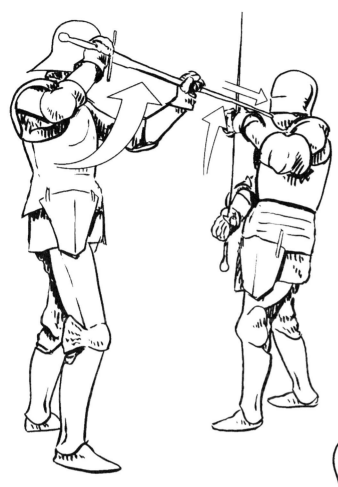

You step in to attack first with a thrust to the opponent's armpit opening. He must then displace and will thus remain in nach; he will be forced to respond to your actions rather than acting himself.

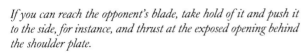

If you can reach the opponent's blade, take hold of it and push it to the side, for instance, and thrust at the exposed opening behind the shoulder plate.

247

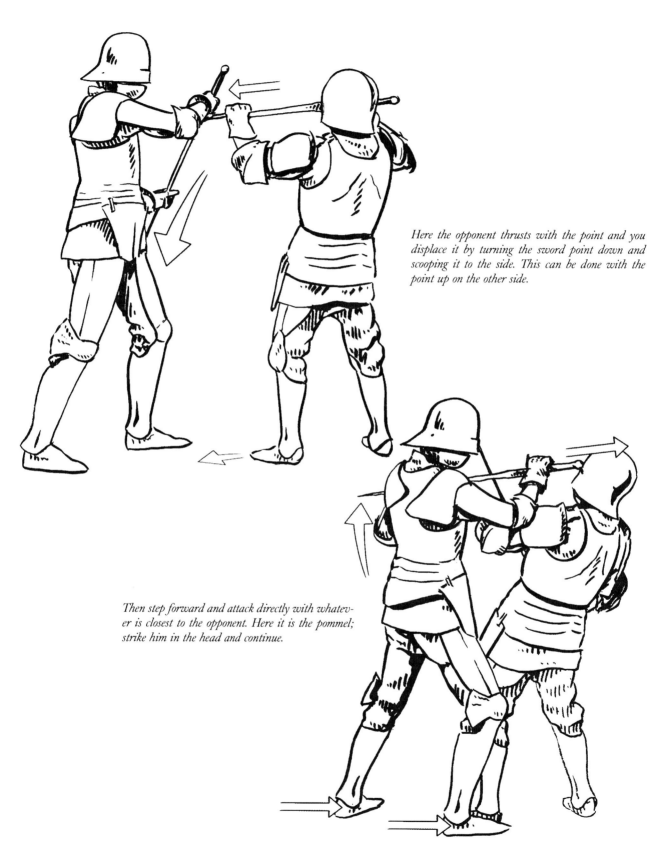

Here the opponent thrusts with the point and you displace it by turning the sword point down and scooping it to the side. This can be done with the point up on the other side.

Then step forward and attack directly with whatever is closest to the opponent. Here it is the pommel; strike him in the head and continue.

NOTE THIS: YOU should know that in combat fencing you should never take more than a single step toward or away from him. This means that if he overwhelms you so that you cannot shift, then you should take only a single step back with the left foot. And be sure that you still can close with him by a single step with the left foot to attack or to wrestle.

[Stepping and distance are crucial when fighting in armor. You carry a lot more weight, which hampers your movements, and the helmet limits your vision. All this makes it important to avoid wide and possible unbalanced movements. Furthermore, your grip on your weapon decreases its reach, dictating a closer range, so there is a fundamental difference in the space between the swordsmen when fighting in armor as compared to without. Try it yourself.]

ITEM HIE SOLT du mörcken dass in dem kampff fechten nicht mer soll sin wann ain abtritt und ain zutritt Und dass vernym also Uberylt er dich dass du zu kainer versatzung komen magst so solt du nur ain tritt zu ruck thon mitt lincken fuss Und wart wysslich dass du im mitt ainem zu tritt dess lincken fuss wider an setzest oder mitt ringen begryffest

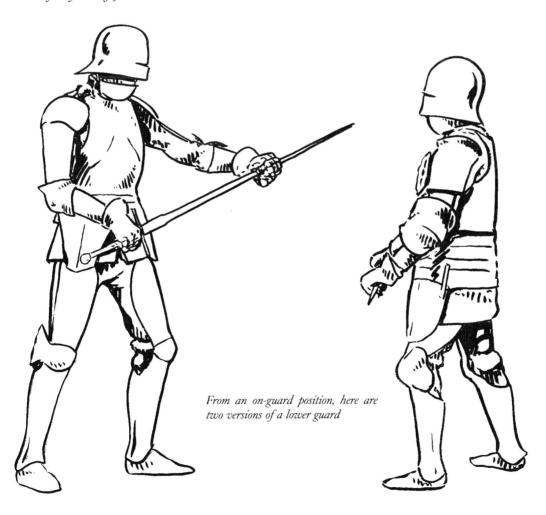

From an on-guard position, here are two versions of a lower guard

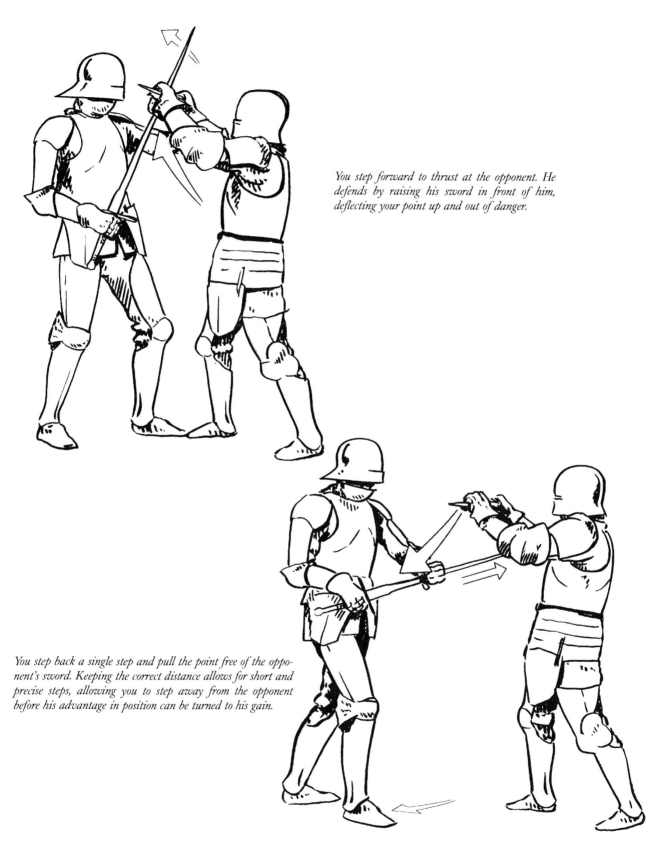

You step forward to thrust at the opponent. He defends by raising his sword in front of him, deflecting your point up and out of danger.

You step back a single step and pull the point free of the opponent's sword. Keeping the correct distance allows for short and precise steps, allowing you to step away from the opponent before his advantage in position can be turned to his gain.

THE TEXT ON traveling after in combat with the sword.

Follow all hits that the strong wish to make; if he defends then withdraw, if he thrusts then go to him. If he seems extended, then direct your thrust artfully.

["Traveling after" can mean that you move after the opponent when he or his weapon withdraws. It can also mean that when he attacks, you should follow his attack and counter at the place where he is extended and vulnerable. Nachrayssen (traveling after) may mean many things: try it out with a sword.]

DER TEXT VON nachraysen mitt dem schwert zu kampff

Volge allen treffen den starcken wilt du sy treffen Wört er so zucke Stich wert er zu im rucke Öb er langk sicht so byss du kunstlich bericht

From an on-guard position, step forward and thrust at one of the openings. The opponent deflects the attack to the side.

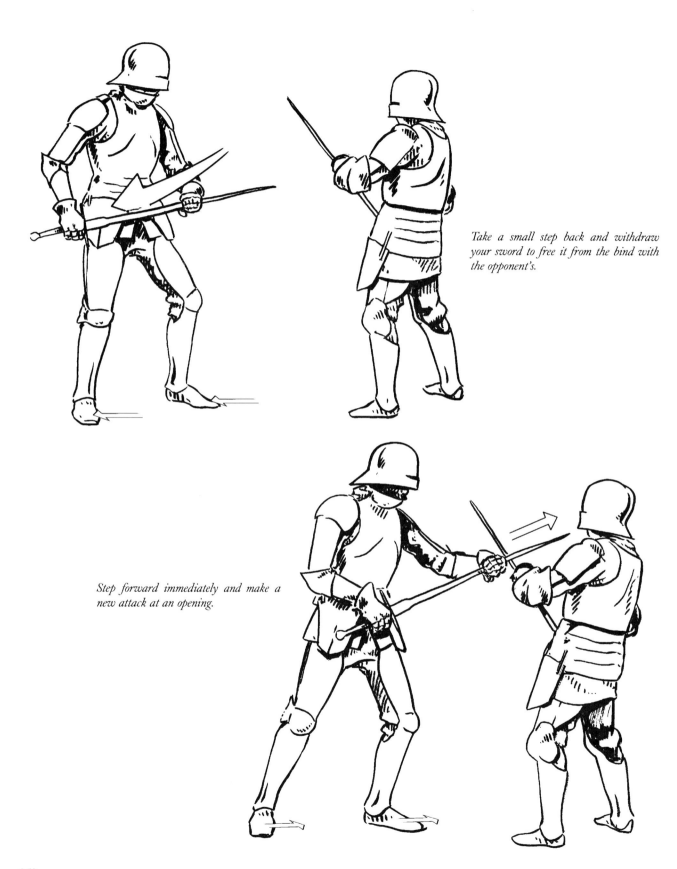

Take a small step back and withdraw your sword to free it from the bind with the opponent's.

Step forward immediately and make a new attack at an opening.

If the opponent is extended he will expose several openings and also be in a position to act slower. Here you thrust at the opening on the inside of his gauntlet.

THIS IS THE traveling after, which you should use against an opponent who fences forcefully and lies long. [*This refers to a fighter who uses long or overextended movements.*] He does not know the true art.

NOTE, AGAINST IT do this. Stand against him in a guard if he also assumes one, then note always when his sword is pulled back. If he wishes to thrust or pulls up in order to strike, then follow at once with the point to the next opening that is exposed before he can complete the thrust or strike. But if he is aware of your attack and displaces it immediately with the sword and searches for an opening on you, then at once withdraw (zucken), and at all times do this when he shifts his sword alone. With it you come to the arm breaks and other techniques. And that is the art for use against all who forget how to fence and lie long and strike at the sword rather than the man.

DASS IST DIE nachraysen solt du tryben gegen den starcken die do lang und wyt fechten und wöllend sunst von rechter kunst nicht halten

ITEM GEGEN DEN schick dich also Leg dich gegen im in ain hut Legt er sich dann och in aine so mörck eben wann er sin schwert an sich zucht Will (er) stechen oder uff hept und will schlachen so folg im bald nach mitt dem ort zu der nechsten blösse ee wenn er den stich oder den schlag verbringt Wirt er dann des ansetzens gewar und versetzt aber wyt mitt dem schwert und sucht an dir kain bloss mitt dem ort so zuck aber durch Und dass zuchen tryb allwegen lass offt er dir mitt versätzung nach dem schwert fert Do mittso kompst du och zu den arm bruchen und zu andern bruchen Unnd dass ist die kunst wider alle die die do lang und wyt fechten zu dem schwert und nicht zu dem man

From an on-guard position where the opponent lifts the sword to strike with the pommel, step forward at once and thrust at the opening around the shoulder and armpit.

If the attack fails, wind the sword up and thrust down at the openings around the gauntlets or any other chink available.

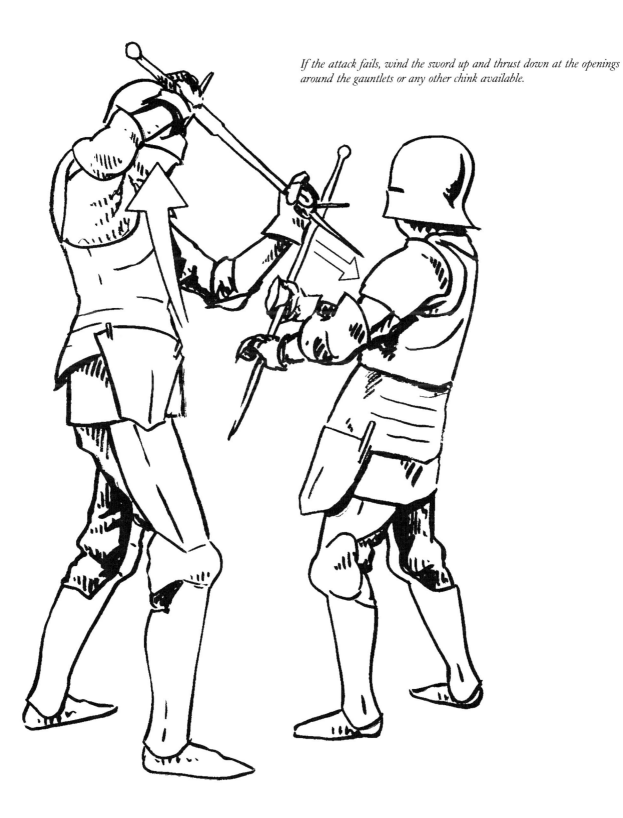

TEXT ON ATTACKING.

If he grabs, take hold with force, then use the shooting attack against him.

This is when someone goes at you and pushes you backward: then thrust at the palm of his hand that holds the sword at the middle. Or if he has his hand turned around then thrust down from above from the same guard.

Or thrust at his arm from behind in the gauntlet, and when the thrust catches step in front of you, thus winning the side and a large advantage. Or thrust through at him over his foremost hand and push your sword down from above and set your crossguard on your chest and go at him.

DER TEXT VON ansetzen

Gryfft er och starcke an dass schiessen sigt im an

Das ist wenn dir ainer hat angesetzt und dich dringet so stich in in den tener der hand do er dass schwert in der mitti by helt Oder hat er die hand umb gewändt so stich von oben nyder aber in die selbigen hut

Oder stich im uff sinen arm hinden in den händschuch Und wann der stich hafft so lauff fur dich so gewinst du im die sytten an und sunst ain gross vortel Oder stich im durch uber sin vorgesatzen hand und (druck) din schwert von oben nider und setz din gehultz an din brust und setz im an

---

NOTE IF HE makes an attack aimed at your left shoulder then step back with the left foot so that his point goes off and keep your locked; or you may increase the reach of your sword by putting the pommel on your chest.

ITEM HAT ER dir dann angesetzet an din lincke achsel so tritt zu rucke mitt dem lincken fuss so gat sin ort abe und der din haffte Auch magst du din schwert erlengen wann du mitt dem ringen dine knopff fur dich zuckest an din brust

From a low on-guard position, step back with the left foot. You can then either keep the sword on the right side as you deflect or move it over to the left side as you step back, depending on what you intend to do next.

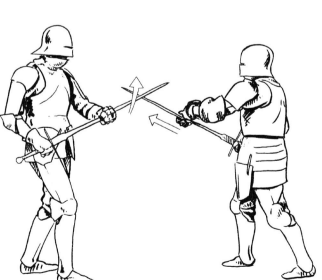

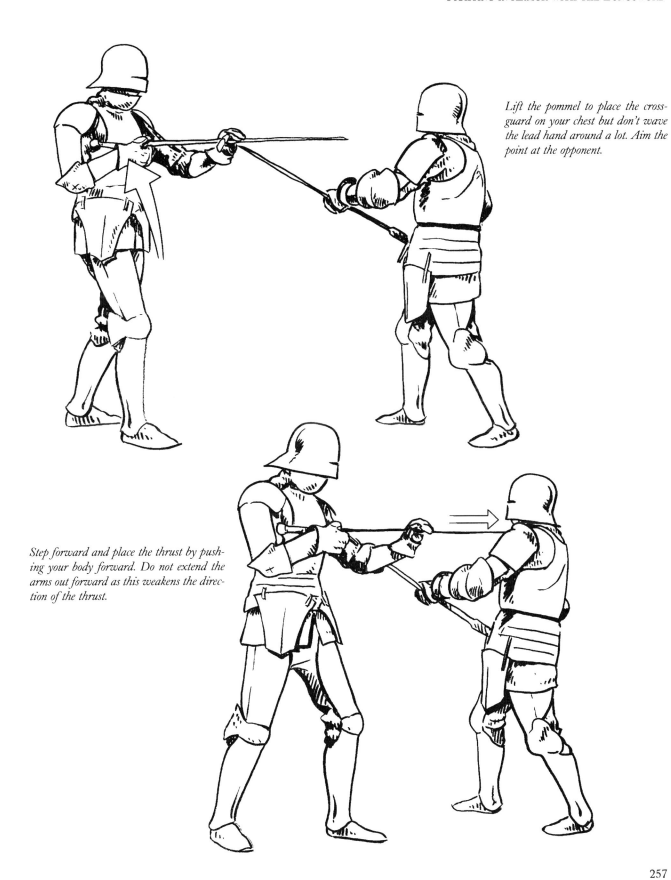

Lift the pommel to place the cross-guard on your chest but don't wave the lead hand around a lot. Aim the point at the opponent.

Step forward and place the thrust by pushing your body forward. Do not extend the arms out forward as this weakens the direction of the thrust.

257

THE TEXT ON how to displace the strikes.

With your striking point shoot out from you, hit one with both hands. The point you should learn to turn to the eyes.

DER TEXT WIE man die schlege versetzen soll

Mitt sinem schlachenden ort schutzt er sich Trifft one forcht mitt baiden henden Den ort zu den augen lere wenden

From an on-guard position holding the handle with both hands.

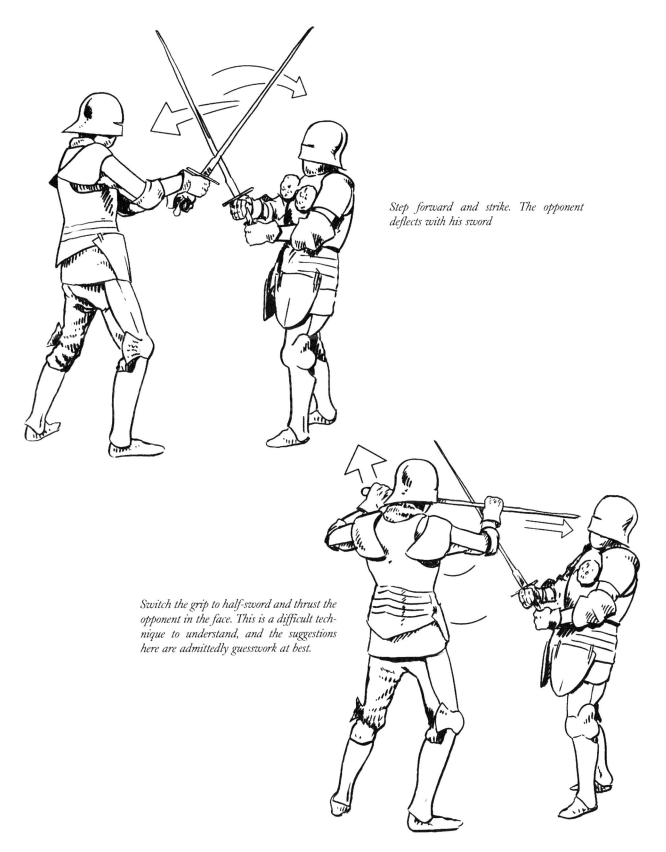

Step forward and strike. The opponent deflects with his sword

Switch the grip to half-sword and thrust the opponent in the face. This is a difficult technique to understand, and the suggestions here are admittedly guesswork at best.

NOTE, THE POMMEL is the striking point. If he then wishes to run over you with strong strikes, then hold your sword over your left knee below in the guard. If he strikes at the head—and is a strong man—then knock the strike away with the sword in front of your left hand toward your right side and go up with the sword to the upper guard. Or if he is weaker than you, then step briskly in and catch the strike between your hands on the sword and set the point in his face

MÖRCK DER KNOPFF ist der schlahent ort Will er dich domitt uberlauffen mitt starckcn schlcgcn so halt din schwert uber din lincke kny und (unten) in der hut Schlecht er dir dann zu dem haupt—und ist ain starcker manne—so streych im den schlag ab mitt dem schwert vor diner lincken hand gegen siner rechten sytten Und far uff am schwert in die obern hut Oder ist er schwecher dann du bist so tritt im frischlich ein und fach den schlach zwischen bayden henden in din schwert und setz im den ort inn dass gesicht

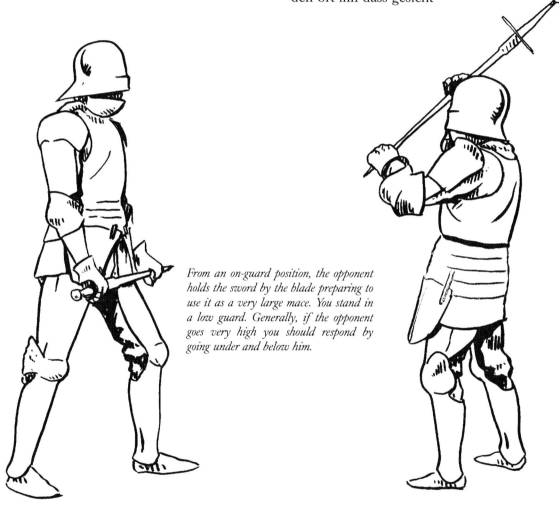

From an on-guard position, the opponent holds the sword by the blade preparing to use it as a very large mace. You stand in a low guard. Generally, if the opponent goes very high you should respond by going under and below him.

[The reason for using the sword as a mace is that, while plate armor is very resistant to damage, a well-placed strike with either the pommel or the sharpened point of the crossguard will do serious damage. How far out you hold the sword depends on the stiffness of the blade (a stiffer blade can be held farther out and will yield a harder strike). However, that is a sharp portion of the blade so maybe it is better for you to position your foremost hand further in. Try different configurations since they will yield very different results.]

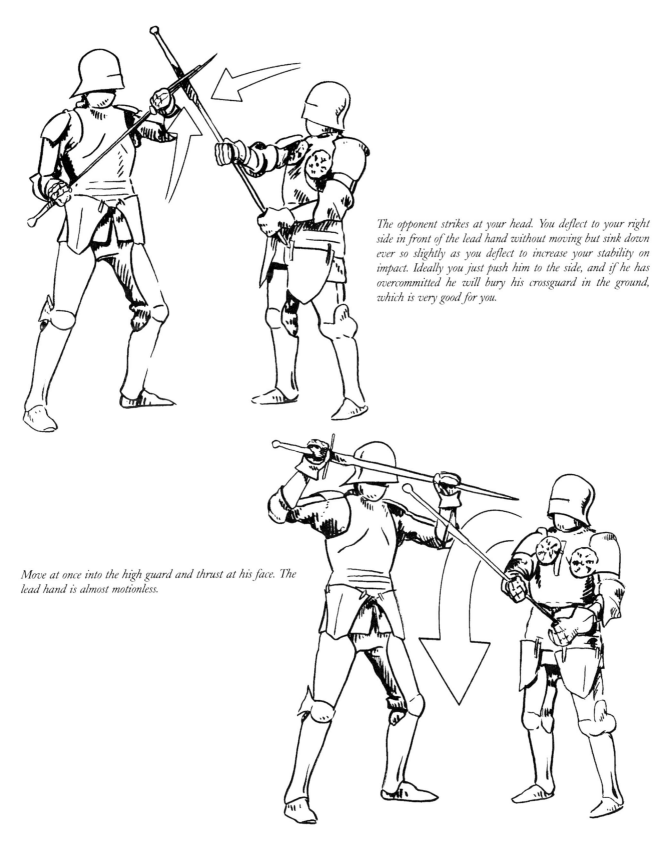

The opponent strikes at your head. You deflect to your right side in front of the lead hand without moving but sink down ever so slightly as you deflect to increase your stability on impact. Ideally you just push him to the side, and if he has overcommitted he will bury his crossguard in the ground, which is very good for you.

Move at once into the high guard and thrust at his face. The lead hand is almost motionless.

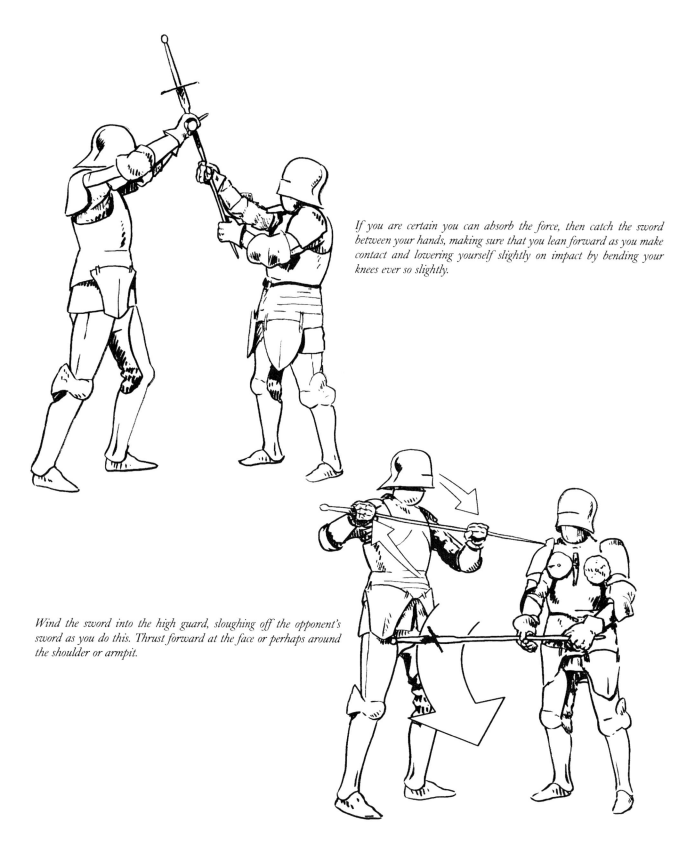

If you are certain you can absorb the force, then catch the sword between your hands, making sure that you lean forward as you make contact and lowering yourself slightly on impact by bending your knees ever so slightly.

Wind the sword into the high guard, sloughing off the opponent's sword as you do this. Thrust forward at the face or perhaps around the shoulder or armpit.

WHEN YOU CATCH the strike with the pommel in the middle of the sword, then go with the pommel over his sword in front of the crossguard and pull it up and to your right side. Then you will take his sword.

ITEM WENN DU den schlag mitt dem knopff fächst mitten in din schwert so far mitt dem knopff uber sin schwert vornen by dem gehultz und ruck domit ubersich uff din rechte sytten som nymst du im sin schwert

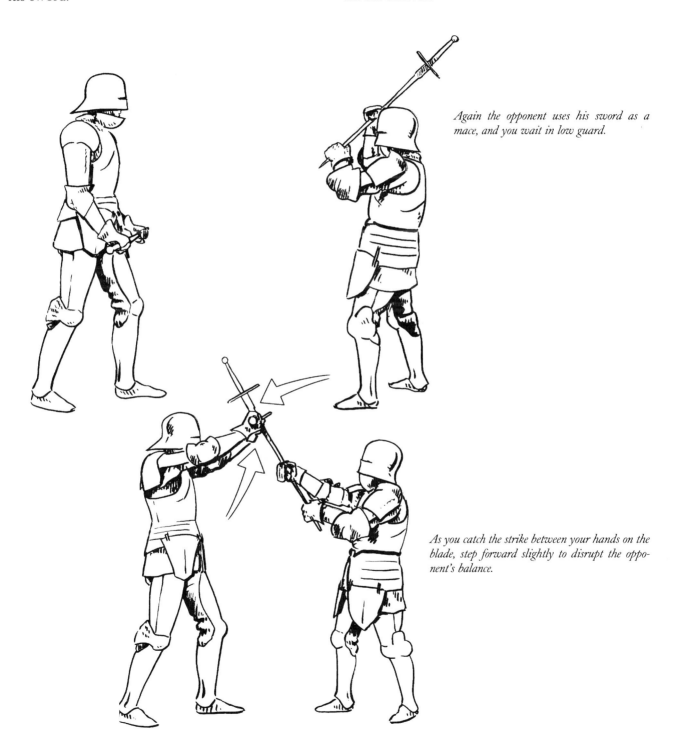

Again the opponent uses his sword as a mace, and you wait in low guard.

As you catch the strike between your hands on the blade, step forward slightly to disrupt the opponent's balance.

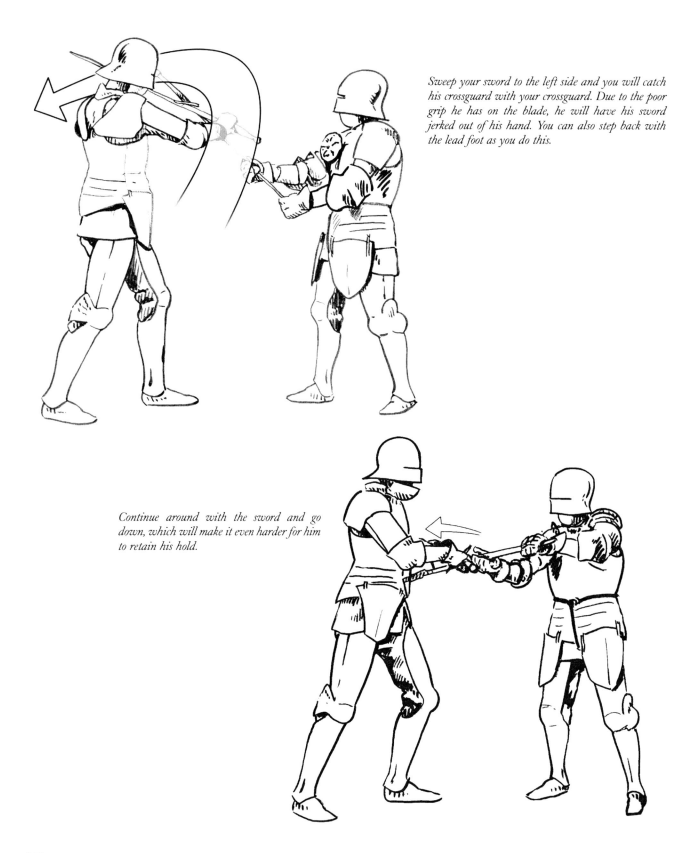

Sweep your sword to the left side and you will catch his crossguard with your crossguard. Due to the poor grip he has on the blade, he will have his sword jerked out of his hand. You can also step back with the lead foot as you do this.

Continue around with the sword and go down, which will make it even harder for him to retain his hold.

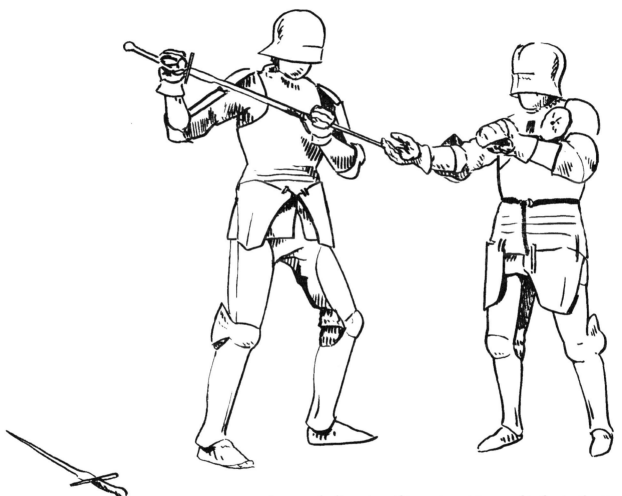

As soon as the disarm is complete, go at once into a guard to threaten the opponent with your point and prevent him from rushing in. You can also step back as you do this, but stay between him and his sword on the ground.

Note, if he strikes at your left knee, then catch the strike between your hands and let the pommel of your sword hang to the ground. Go with the pommel through below his sword in front of the hilt and pull up on your right side and you will tear his sword out of his hands.

Item schlecht er dir zu dem lincken kny so fach den schlag zwischen dinen henden in dass schwert dass der knopff zu der erden hang Und far mitt dem knopff unden durch sin schwert vornen by dem gehultz und ruck ubersich uff din rechten sytten so ruckst im sin schwert uss den henden

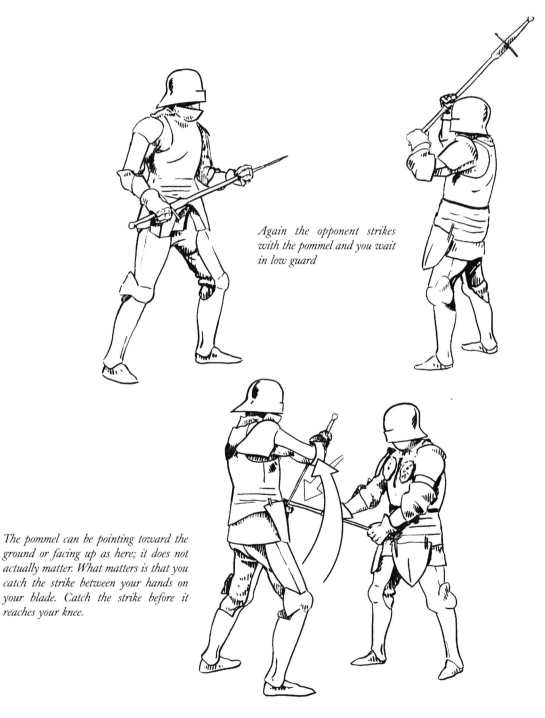

Again the opponent strikes with the pommel and you wait in low guard

The pommel can be pointing toward the ground or facing up as here; it does not actually matter. What matters is that you catch the strike between your hands on your blade. Catch the strike before it reaches your knee.

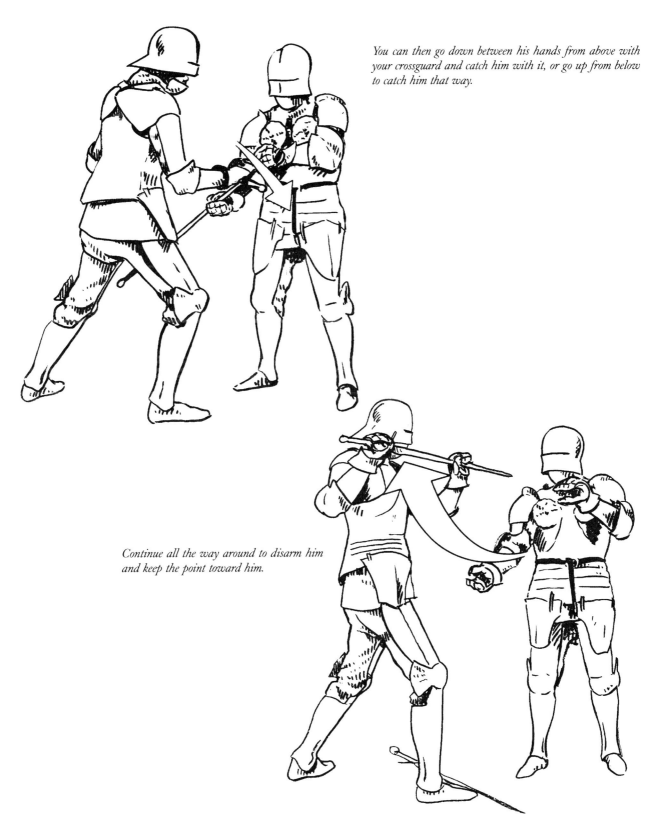

You can then go down between his hands from above with your crossguard and catch him with it, or go up from below to catch him that way.

Continue all the way around to disarm him and keep the point toward him.

Note, or if he strikes you with the pommel aiming at your foot, then throw your sword with the pommel to your left side to the ground against his strike and leap at the same time close to him and begin to wrestle.

[Generally, when the opponent strikes using his pommel it provides an excellent opportunity to step in and gain a serious advantage as you start to wrestle. You must not hesitate when closing in to wrestle.]

Item oder schlecht er dir mitt dem knopff nach dem fuss wirff din schwert mitt dem knopff zu diner lincken sytten in die erden gegen sinen schlag und spring do mitt zu im unnd wart der ringen

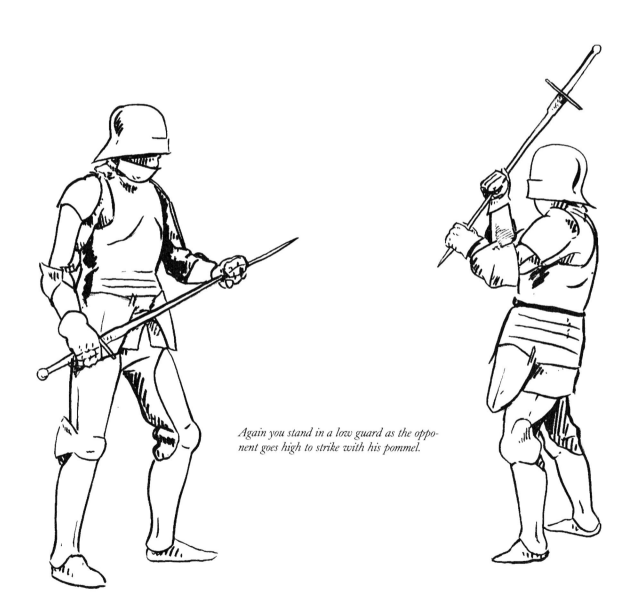

Again you stand in a low guard as the opponent goes high to strike with his pommel.

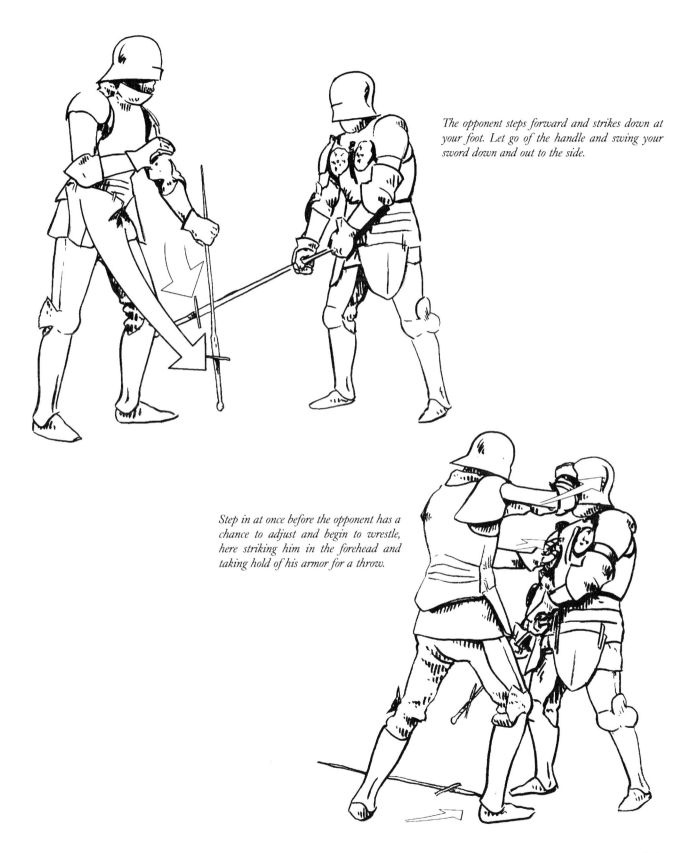

The opponent steps forward and strikes down at your foot. Let go of the handle and swing your sword down and out to the side.

Step in at once before the opponent has a chance to adjust and begin to wrestle, here striking him in the forehead and taking hold of his armor for a throw.

NOTE, WHEN YOU have your sword below on your right side in the lower guard, if he then strikes at you with the pommel at the point of your sword and at the same time steps in, then leap at him and strike him with your pommel over you–this is not bad for you–and go at him.

Note, and you can travel after and attack where you please when he withdraws the pommel to him.

ITEM WANN DU häst din schwert neben diner rechten sytten in der undern hut schlecht er dir dann mitt dem knopff nach dem ort und lausst in wyt umb dich lauffen so spring die wil kunlich zu im so schlecht er mitt dem knopff uberdich–dass ist dir nicht schädlich–und setz im an

Item och magst du im nach raysen und an setzen wo du wilt die will er den knopff also wyt lasst umb sich lauffen

From an on-guard position, the opponent steps in and strikes your point down. Do not resist but go with the force and use it for your next movement.

Go with the turning motion that is created when your point is forced down and step in with it to strike with your pommel or crossguard. Strike from above in a downward motion and lower your body into the strike for the best effect. Aim the pommel at the side of his helmet; with the pointed crossguard aim at the opening around the shoulder and side of the neck.

The text of striking with the pommel.
The foremost foot you must hit with the strike.

Der text von den schlegen mitt dem knopff
Dess fordern fuss mitt schlegen du hietten must

You stand in high guard holding the sword by the blade to strike with the pommel or cross-guard. Here it is important that you are aware of your vulnerability should you fail to hit. You must not overextend yourself.

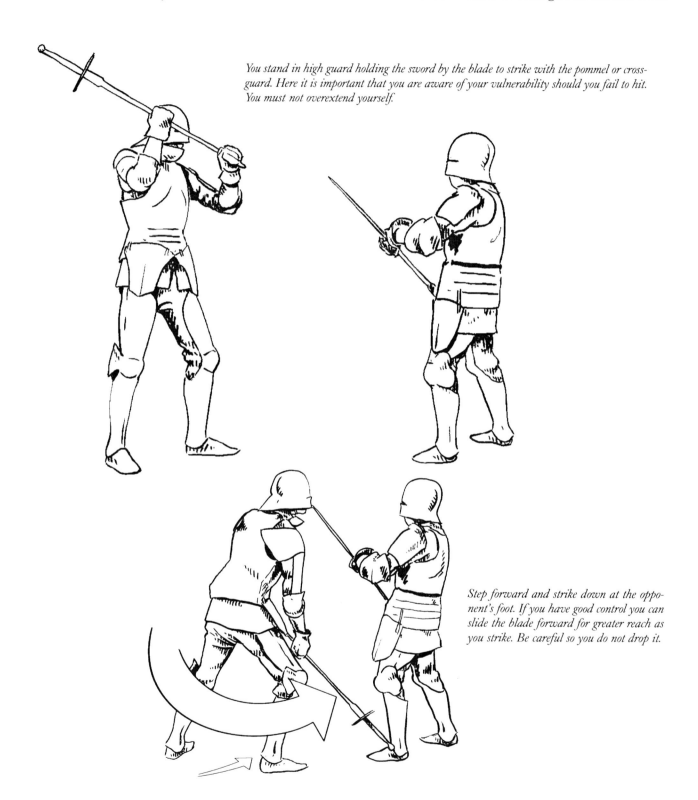

Step forward and strike down at the opponent's foot. If you have good control you can slide the blade forward for greater reach as you strike. Be careful so you do not drop it.

WHEN YOU WISH to strike with the pommel aim always at his outstretched parts, and do it thus: When you want to strike then hold your sword in the guard over your head and do as if you wanted to hit his face, and let your sword go from the right hand and go with it to help the left in the middle of the blade and strike with the pommel at his foremost foot or his foremost hand if he is holding the sword in the middle. You can also strike from the lower guard on the right side.

WENN DU MITT dem knopff schlachen wilt so solt du do mitt gar eben remen siner vorgesätzen glider Und dass vernym also Wann du schlachen wilt so halt din schwert in der hut uber din haupt und thu alss du im in dass gesicht an wöllest setzen Unnd lauss din schwert farn uss der rechten hannd und ko do mitt der lincken zu hilff mitten in die clingen und schlach in mitt dem knopff zu dem furgesetzten fuss oder zu siner furgesetzer hand do er das schwert in der mitte da mitt helt Also magst du uss der undere hut von der rechten sytten auch schlachen

Again you hold your sword ready to strike with the pommel or crossguard.

SIGMUND RINGECK'S KNIGHTLY ARTS OF COMBAT

Strike down at the opponent's foremost hand as you step forward. You can also strike up from below if you hold the sword low on either side. This can be very effective, especially against someone who goes high up.

When you stand in a low guard on the right side, prepare for the strike by adjusting your hands.

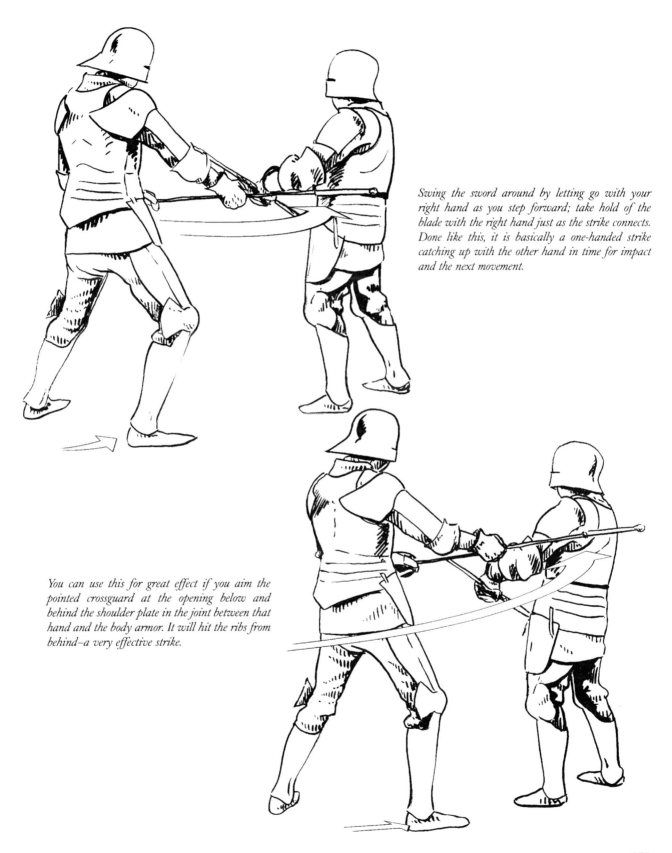

Swing the sword around by letting go with your right hand as you step forward; take hold of the blade with the right hand just as the strike connects. Done like this, it is basically a one-handed strike catching up with the other hand in time for impact and the next movement.

You can use this for great effect if you aim the pointed crossguard at the opening below and behind the shoulder plate in the joint between that hand and the body armor. It will hit the ribs from behind—a very effective strike.

Note, you should always note if he is about to strike at your foremost knee or hand, so that you can disrupt the strike with the aforementioned counter so that he cannot harm you.

Item du solt och gar eben fursechen wann er dir mitt dem knopff zu dinem vorgesetzen kny oder zu diner furgesätzter hand schlecht dass du im den schlag also versetzest mitt den vor geschribnen bruchen dass er dir nitt schaden muge

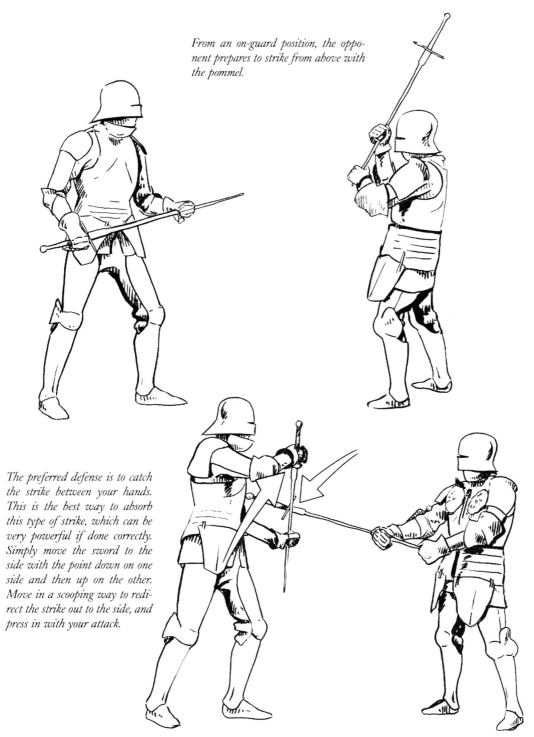

From an on-guard position, the opponent prepares to strike from above with the pommel.

The preferred defense is to catch the strike between your hands. This is the best way to absorb this type of strike, which can be very powerful if done correctly. Simply move the sword to the side with the point down on one side and then up on the other. Move in a scooping way to redirect the strike out to the side, and press in with your attack.

Appendix A:
Albion Swords
and Peter Johnsson

IN MAKING THE illustrations and working through the techniques to create this book, we had the pleasure and great fortune to work with two swords from Albion Swords' Museum Line.

PETER JOHNSSON AND Albion started collaborating with the aim of, among other things, recreating historical swords such as those we have used and creating new swords for the modern practitioner based on the old models. The great difference between these blades and those of other modern makers is the exactitude of the recreation of the historical originals. Handling the two Albion blades has really helped us in working with the techniques in Ringeck's manual. I have handled several original swords in various states of preservation, and I feel that these recreations are closest to their medieval ancestors.

INCLUDED HERE IS some information and pictures of these swords for the interested reader. Visit Albion Swords at http://www.albion-swords.com to look at their complete line of swords.

THE BRESCIA SPADONA

THE BRESCIA SPADONA is a faithful recreation of a historical sword named after the city where it now resides, in the Museo Civico L. Mazzoli in Brescia, Italy. This longsword is referred to as "spadona da una mano e mezza," or "longsword of one hand and a half," and dates from the mid-1400s. The original sword was born from a meeting between great sword-manufacturing areas—forged by one of the master swordsmiths in the renowned workshops of

The Brescia Spadona blends German and Italian design.

Passau, in southern Germany, then exported to a northern Italian cutler who mounted the blade according to his and his customers' ideals. The beautifully proportioned hilt is of Italian manufacture in a style that was popular during the first half of the 15th century. The well-forged cross combines graceful shape with sturdy construction, and the pommel is octagonal, with its upper faces hollowground for an elegant appearance and deadly effect in close quarter combat. The sword could be described as an Oakeshott type XVIIIa or possibly a XVIa as described in *The Sword in the Age of Chivalry*.

THE SOLINGEN SWORD

THE ORIGINAL SWORD now resides in the Deutsches Klingenmusem, in Solingen, Germany. It has a close sibling in the Royal Armories in Leeds with the same pommel, cross, and general blade shape. The blade has a form that places it somewhere between type XII and type XIV according to the Oakeshott typology. The pronounced point is good for slashing attacks as well as thrusts. The careful distribution of mass in the blade makes the sword very quick and precise in handling while allowing it to cut with authority. Profile and distal taper helps achieve sweet handling characteristics, while at the same time keeping the thin cutting section of the blade stiff.

THIS IS A very good example of a sword where overall shape and aesthetic design are intrinsic parts of the functional aspects of the weapon. The master craftsman (or craftsmen) who made this sword sometime in the 13th century shaped the blade and hilt components with subtlety and a deep understanding of volumes and mass distribution. A sword of this type would be perfect for sword and buckler fighting and shares many characteristics with the swords depicted in *I:33*. As opposed to the more massive swords of war of the time, this responsive weapon excels in performance when put to use with the advanced fencing styles of the period.

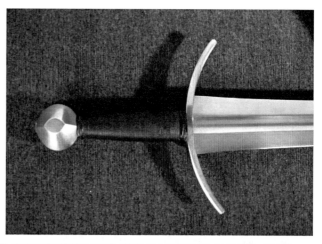

Albion Swords' Solingen Sword, from their Museum Line.

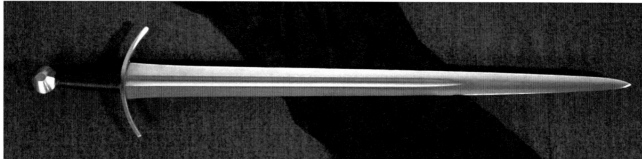

Appendix B:
Via Armorari
and Albert Collins

ALBERT COLLINS IS a modern-day armorer, carrying on a European craft that once was central to success in warfare as well as survival in tournments and duels.

BORN IN 1975, Collins has worked professionally in reconstructing medieval armor for the past 10 years. His work is on display in several museums, including Götlands Fornsal, Kalmar Länsmuseum, and Uppsala Länsmuseum, and he has served as a consultant and craftsman on projects for the Swedish Board of Antiquities.

Albert Collins.

COLLINS HAS ALSO made some of the armor worn by members of discerning and renowned reenactment and Western martial arts groups in Europe. Collins says that historical accuracy, along with full functionality, is what must guide a modern-day armorer in the process of recreating historical armor for a client. The goal is that the client, when wearing his armor, will actually experience the same degree of mobility and protection that the originals once offered. This is very important for the reconstruction of the medieval combat techniques that are described in this book, for example. The functionality and efficiency of the techniques are to a large extent determined by the functionality and utility of the armor worn. In order to achieve this, it is of prime importance to research existing original armor pieces and historical artwork to understand shape, material, and functionality of the armor itself. Another important source of information is the feedback from individuals who have used this armor in reenacting or recreating medieval martial techniques. This is a sort of experimental archaeology through the use of the armor itself.

VIA ARMORARI IN HISTORY

VIA ARMORARI IS an actual street in Milan, which during the latter part of the Middle Ages was a major center for armor manufacture in Europe.

279

This was the place where masters such as Tomasso Missagglia, Antonio Seroni, Pier Innocenzo da Faerno, and others worked. Here, everything from the most regal armor to the simplest soldier armor was manufactured and exported all over Europe. There were many different workshops in the area, and it was said that they could provide a full army with armor in a single a day. Export was extensive and it was not uncommon for enemies to meet in the field both wearing armor from Via Armorari.

VIA ARMORARI TODAY

VIA ARMORARI IS a company that manufactures armor of varying levels of historical accuracy for different uses, as per the customer's needs. The production is focused on creating as authentic an end product as possible, providing the customer with armor or armor detail that meets his or her desire for realism, both with regard to fit and comfort as well as to appearance and idiom. Visit Via Armorari at http://www.viaarmorari.com.

Henrik is wearing Italian armor for the English/Flemish market with some details from those areas. Late 15th century.

Mattias is wearing German armor with a coat over it and a German halberd to match. Late 15th century.

Biblography

Amberger, Christoph, J. *The Secret History of the Sword.* Unique Publications, 1999.

Angelo, Sydney. *The Martial Arts of Renaissance Europe.* Yale University Press, 2000.

Brown, Terry. *English Martial Arts.* Anglo-Saxon Books, 1997.

Clements, John. *Renaissance Swordsmanship.* Paladin Press, 1997.

Clements, John. *Medieval Swordsmanship.* Paladin Press, 1998.

Fiorato, Veronica, Anthea Boylston, Christopher Knusel (eds). *Blood Red Roses: The Archaeology of a Mass Grave from the Battle of Towton AD 1461.* Oxbow Books, 2000.

Hils, Hans-Peter. *Meister Johann Liechtenauer's Kunst des Langen Schwertes.* P. Lang, 1985.

Lindholm, David. *Fighting with the European Quarterstaff.* Chivalry Bookshelf, 2006.

Muhlberger, Steven. *Deeds of Arms.* Chivalry Bookshelf, 2005

Oakeshott. R. Ewart. *The Archaeology of Weapons: Arms and Armour from Prehistory to the Age of Chivalry.* Dover Publications, 1996

Oakeshott. R. Ewart. *The Sword in the Age of Chivalry.* Boydell Press, 1998.

Studer, Charles (ed.). *Das Solothurner Fechtbuch.* Zentralbiblithek Solothurn. No date.

Talhoffer, Hans, Mark Rector, John Clements. *Medieval Combat: A Fifteenth Century Illustrated manual of Swordfighting and Close-Quarter Combat.* Greenhill Books, 2000.

Tobler, Christian. *Secrets of Medieval German Swordsmanship: Sigmund Ringeck's Commentaries on Liechtenauer.* Chivalry Bookshelf, 2002.

Tobler, Christian. *Fighting with the German Longsword.* Chivalry Bookshelf, 2004.

Tobler, Christian. *In Service of the Duke.* Chivalry Bookshelf, 2006.

Vadi, Filippo (Luca Porzio and Gregory Mele, eds.). *Arte Gladiatora: 15th Century Swordsmanship of Master Filippo Vadi.* Chivalry Bookshelf, 2003.

Wierschin, Martin. *Meister Johann Liechtenauer's Kunst des Fechtens.* Munich, 1965.

Windsor, Guy. *The Swordsman's Companion: A Modern Training Manual for Medieval Longsword.* Chivalry Bookshelf, 2005.

Zabinski, Grzegorz and Bartlomiej Walczak. *Codex Wallerstein: A Medieval Fighting Book from the Fifteenth Century on the Longsword, Falchion, Dagger, and Wrestling.* Paladin Press, 2002.

MANUSCRIPTS OF INTEREST

Döbringer, Hanko. Codex MS 3227a
Germanisches Nationalmuseum, Nürnberg.
Lindholm, David. *Döbringer's fechtbuch (MS 3227a).*
    English translation at www.mhfs.se.
Ringeck, Sigmund. *Fechtbuch.* MS Dresd.C. 487.
    State Library of Saxony, Dresden.

Resources

SWORDS AND OTHER WEAPONS

Purpleheart Armoury
This company has longsword and shortsword wasters, singlesticks, staffs, polearms, and bucklers as well as books, videos, and accessories such as gloves and neck guards. They also offer Asian martial arts implements.

http://www.woodenswords.com

Albion Swords
This company manufactures fine swords designed with the help of swordsmith Peter Johnsson. They offer a complete line of swords in all classes–from exact replicas of historical originals to designs by Johnsson based on surviving historical weapons. Swords can be ordered sharp or blunted for practice.

http://www.albion-swords.com

ARMOR

Via Armorari
Armorer Albert Collins and Via Armorari offer the best armor you can buy today. It can be made according to any desired technique and using a wide variety of materials. Collins' specialty is hand-forging armor after historical originals and designs.

http://www.viaarmorari.com/

BOOKS

Chivalry Bookshelf
Chivalry Bookshelf offers titles dealing with historical European martial arts, chivalry, and weapons and armor.

http://www.chivalrybookshelf.com/

Paladin Press
Paladin Press has books and videos dealing with historical European martial arts, as well as a comprehensive library on physical training and other aspects of martial arts–Eastern and Western, historical and modern.

http://www.paladin-press.com/

FINDING FRIENDS ONLINE

We won't list groups here because URLs change and there are too many different groups for us to list them all. Instead, search the Internet and you are bound to find groups near you.

A good starting point is Sword Forum International, found at http://swordforum.com/ The forum is dedicated to historical European martial arts, and there are some very friendly and helpful people there who will point you in the right direction. If you have any questions you can e-mail the author at: 040.120617@telia.com, or contact him through Paladin Press.

About the Authors

David Lindholm in a suit of armor by Albert Collins. German, late 15th century.

DAVID LINDHOLM HAS an MA in Medieval Archaeology and History from the University of Lund in Sweden. He has also studied philosophy, ethnology, and prehistoric archaeology. He works as a writer and teaches history and philosophy in high school. He has been studying swordsmanship since 1986, including iaido, kendo, classical fencing, and koryu bujutsu. Historical Western martial arts have been David's field of study since 1996. David wrote the text of this book and made the translations. David's favorite sword is the Brescia Spadona from Albion–light, agile, and with a lot of punch.

PETER SVÄRD IS the art director and illustrator of the Swedish communication agency First Flight. He has been active in various reenactment societies since the late 1980s, training with swords on and off since the early 1990s. His spare time is spent with his family and new projects such as constructing and illustrating card and boardgames as a part of the Swedish game company Gigantoskop. His favorite sword is The Regent from Albion/Peter Johnsson. He illustrated this book.